Teaching for Spiritual Growth

Teaching for Spiritual Growth

An Introduction to Christian Education

Perry G. Downs

ZondervanPublishingHouse
Academic and Professional Books
Grand Rapids, Michigan

A Division of HarperCollinsPublishers

In honor of my parents

Elmer H. Downs (1914–1964)
and
Violet M. Downs

Fairfield, Connecticut

Teaching for Spiritual Growth
Copyright © 1994 by Perry G. Downs

Requests for information should be addressed to:
Zondervan Publishing House
Academic and Professional Books
Grand Rapids, Michigan 49530

Library of Congress Cataloging-in-Publication Data

Downs, Perry G.
  Teaching for spiritual growth / by Perry G. Downs.
    p.   cm.
  Includes bibliographical references and indexes.
  ISBN 0-310-59370-0 (alk. paper)
    1. Christian education—Philosophy.   I. Title.
  BV1464.D675   1994
  268'.01—dc20   93-41143
                                                              CIP

Cover design by Jerry Fahselt
Edited by Gerard H. Terpstra

Printed in the United States of America

94 95 96 97 98 99 /❖DC / 10 9 8 7 6 5 4 3 2 1

Contents

Preface

The discipline of Christian education has been wandering in recent years, as if in search of a mission. Interest in a variety of issues has caused a rather broad sprawl of topics covered under the rubric "Christian education." Topics such as specialized age group ministries, singles ministry, dysfunctional family ministry, management, and media have occupied the minds of many Christian educators. The positive outcome of this broadening of the field has been the establishment of some very fruitful ministries to various segments of society. The Church has become responsive to the special needs of an increasingly wounded society, and ministry has, at times, been brought more directly into the mainstream of modern culture.

But this diversity in interest has not been without cost. While the breadth of concern has increased, the depth and focus of the central issues have been compromised. The focus of the discipline, which is teaching for spiritual growth, has at times been marginalized. Psychology has become the primary foundation at the price of theological soundness. Responding to the felt needs of people is sometimes perceived as more important than responding to the real need of being reconciled to God. Helping people feel good has taken over helping people *be* good and *do* good. That is a price I am not willing to pay.

I have attempted in this book to offer a modest corrective. I have chosen to use the spiritual growth of God's people as my focus, and the Bible and theology as my primary foundation. I use psychology and learning theories as important sources of information, but always in conversation with theology. I do not want either the social sciences or theology to stand alone—both must be valued, but the Bible must remain as the final arbiter. Special revelation must always take precedence over general revelation.

The logic of the book is evident. In part one, "Teaching in Biblical Perspective," I begin to lay the groundwork for the nature of spiritual maturity. In part two, developmental psychology and learning theories provide the social science base, seeking to describe the nature of human development and how people learn. The book ends with an exploration of how we should teach for spiritual growth. Hence, the progression is from theology to psychology to education.

My own theological stance is Reformed, but I have tried to avoid polemics. There is enough common ground between the Augustinian and non-Augustinian traditions that these issues need not always divide us. They do matter, and matter greatly, but many of the points of difference come after the foundational questions are in place. The reader will decide if I have been successful in avoiding bringing division on these points.

In a sense, this book is a step backwards, but not in the sense of regression. Rather, it is a step back for the purpose of correction. I stress the importance of the Bible as essential for spiritual growth, and I offer nothing in terms of innovative programs. My reason is that I believe the answers we need for effective Christian education are in the historic understandings of the Church. I am not convinced that many of the contemporary programs have produced more holiness, piety, and love for God and neighbor. The reason for this is that we have lost our focus. My hope and prayer is that the present volume may help move us back to our central concern.

I have presented a philosophy of Christian education which helps the reader learn how to think about educational issues in the church. I have tried to model what conversation between the social sciences and theology sounds like. If the reader gains a better understanding of how to think about teaching for spiritual growth I shall be grateful.

Anyone who knows the field of Christian education will recognize Ted Ward's influence on my thinking. I have adapted his ideas in several instances, but his imprint is unmistakable. I am thankful to have such a stimulating and gracious colleague, who so freely shares his ideas with those around him. In addition, Warren Benson, Linda Cannell, Charles Sell, and my personal great encourager Mark Senter have all been wonderful partners in our Christian education department.

Preface

Trinity Evangelical Divinity School's remarkable sabbatical program allowed the time for research and writing. I wish to thank President Meyer and the Board of Regents for the sabbaticals necessary to complete this project.

The editors at Zondervan have been an absolute delight. Stan Gundry's initial belief in the project and James Ruark's gentle and insightful guidance have served me well. My friend Kiersten Crocker (soon to be Kiersten Seeman) developed the indexes with speed, accuracy, and her usual helpful spirit.

My wife Sandra is helpful beyond words. She makes it possible for me to work at home by providing an environment of peace and beauty. She supports me emotionally, cognitively, and spiritually. I have no idea where she ends and I begin. I think that is how it should be.

Finally, thank you to the many students who have helped refine my thoughts through endless classroom presentations. Dialogue in the classroom has served to enrich my understanding of these issues and correct me where I have been in error. Sometimes I think my students are my best teachers.

May Jesus Christ be praised.

Teaching in Biblical Perspective

1

Foundational Questions

Educational ministries require a great deal of energy and consume a large proportion of the resources of the church. Most of the church's building space is used for teaching, and the largest amount of volunteer help is involved in this aspect of the church ministry. Clearly church leaders see education as important, yet there is often a great deal of frustration on the part of teachers, leaders, and students.

Some teachers find that curriculum materials either are irrelevant to the lives of their students or make demands on teachers that cannot be met. Some leaders wonder why there are not better results from the expenditure of energy and money, for often the teaching does not result in changed lives. And students may find classes boring and uninspiring—sometimes interesting, but usually not speaking to the issues of the day in powerful ways.

Many people have tried to proclaim Sunday school outdated and unnecessary in today's world. But it is "as American as crabgrass," enduring and changing with the

13

times. It needs, however, to be improved and strengthened, as do almost all of the educational ministries of the church. As we prepare to move into the twenty-first century in a post-Christian United States, we need educational ministry that helps people "reach unity in the faith and in the knowledge of the Son of God and become mature, attaining to the whole measure of the fullness of Christ" (Eph. 4:13).

The purpose of this book is to develop a philosophy of Christian education that is sound, guided by those insights from both theology and the social sciences that are relevant to the task of educating people for spiritual growth. There are no easy solutions. In the long run easy answers do not last. Rather, there must be a thoughtful approach to Christian education that respects both social science and theology, leading to a unified philosophy of Christian education that enables the church to teach for spiritual maturity.

SOCIAL SCIENCES AND THEOLOGY

Some Christians disagree with using the social sciences to inform the process of Christian education, fearing that "secular" approaches will supersede the proper "biblical" approach. This concern, however, is rooted in a worldview that fails to understand the unity of truth. A Christian worldview sees validity in both science and theology, recognizing that both are necessary. When properly understood, these are not contradictory in nature but present a more complete picture of reality than can be achieved by viewing either the social sciences or theology exclusively. Figure 1 shows how social science and theology are best understood from a Christian perspective.

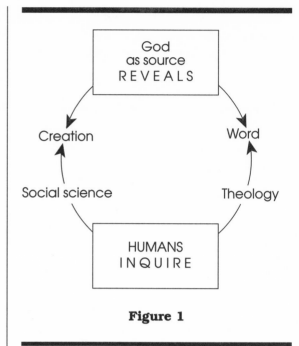

Figure 1

God Reveals

As creator of all that is, God is the source of all reality. God *reveals* truth in two modes: creation (general revelation) and the Word (special revelation). Both creation and Scripture are to be respected as sources of revelation by God and are to be studied to apprehend the wonders of God's wisdom and expression.

The top half of figure 1 is concerned with the metaphysical—that which is real. This reality is based on the truth that God is a creator and has created all things. God has called his creation into being by his words, and all that is has been created by him. Because God is the source of all that is, there is a unity of truth in creation. Christian perspective recognizes that truth, wherever it is found, has its source in God and therefore should be valued.

14

Humans Inquire

The lower half of figure 1 is concerned with epistemology—humankind's quest after knowledge, attempting to know what is true. While the metaphysical components are objective, standing independent of human experience, the epistemological aspects are mediated by the person. Epistemological inquiry is more subjective, prone to error or influence by the individual. There can be mistakes in both the social sciences and theology, because these are human efforts to understand God's revelation.

Theology is the systematic inquiry into Scripture. Theology is a human attempt to make sense of and draw conclusions from God's special revelation. The rules that control this inquiry are the rules of hermeneutics and logic. To do good theology one must attempt rigorous objectivity as he seeks to determine truth, but always with a degree of humility that acknowledges that only Scripture is absolute truth. Theology can be corrupted by human sinfulness and made unclear by lack of spiritual insight.

Science is the systematic inquiry into creation. Good science follows the rules of scientific inquiry, generally limiting itself to that which can be empirically observed. Properly understood, science is an investigation of God's created order and can aid in our understanding of general revelation. As such, scientific inquiry should be respected by the Christian.

Christian education can be informed by the findings of social science in its inquiry into God's sixth-day creation—humanity. Psychology, sociology, anthropology, and education (known collectively as the social sciences) are all human attempts to understand God's ultimate creation, humanity. Just as theology is prone to error, so also science can be distorted by sin and human limitations. But good science provides critical insights into how people learn and mature, providing important guidelines for the Christian educator.

Christian education must be guided by a worldview that values both general and special revelation. Clearly theological issues, such as the nature of spiritual maturity, must be considered from a theological base. But issues regarding normal human functions, such as how people learn, should be addressed from a scientific base. Naturally, none of these issues is purely theological or purely scientific; therefore an integrative approach must be maintained. But because all truth comes from God, ideally there should be no conflict between good science and good theology, and no distinction between "sacred" and "secular" truth.

The implication is that Christians must value both science and theology. Beyond asking, "Is it *biblical*?" we must ask "Is it *true*?" All of Scripture is true, but not all truth is contained in Scripture. Responsible educators study both general and special revelation to understand God's creation and to design ministry in accordance with how God has designed his world.

Framing the Questions

How the questions are framed is critical. Two priests, it is often told, were debating whether or not it is permissible to pray and smoke at the same time. Their dispute became so contentious that they decided to ask the pope to mediate. Each wrote to the Holy Father, asking his opinion, but they were astonished upon comparing the replies to their question. The pope agreed with both of them! "How did you pose the question?" the first asked. The other replied, "I asked if it is permissible to smoke while praying. His Holiness stated that it is not, because praying is very serious business. How did you phrase the question?"

The first explained, "I asked if it is permissible to pray while smoking, and His Holiness affirmed that it is, since it is always acceptable to pray."

How the question is stated will determine the answer we get. Questions about Christian education can be framed so that they are all theological or all scientific. The key is to maintain a balance that allows for *both* sources of information to inform our philosophy of education. Broadening the questions beyond "What is the biblical way to teach?" allows us to ask, "How do people learn and grow?" and enables us to use both the social sciences and theology to build our philosophy of education.

THE PURPOSE OF CHRISTIAN EDUCATION

Christian education, simply defined, is the ministry of bringing the believer to maturity in Jesus Christ. The operative question of the discipline is "How can we best enable Christians to grow toward maturity?" This definition suggests three key concepts: ministry, believers, and purpose.

Ministry

Christian education is a ministry, a means of service to others. The focus of educational ministry is to serve the body of Christ by teaching. There are ethical constraints on what we can do in educational programs. Methods must never be manipulative or demanding; rather, they are to serve others by enabling them to learn. When Jesus saw the multitude, as

> *Christian education, simply defined, is the ministry of bringing the believer to maturity in Jesus Christ.*

related in Mark 6:34, he had compassion on them because he saw them as sheep without a shepherd. He expressed his compassion by teaching them. The heart of the Christian educator must be motivated by love. While no one has absolutely pure motivation, still it must be the growing desire of our hearts to see people growing in their faith. Our educational ministry must not be self-serving but rather an act of service to others. Teaching should be presented as a gift of love to others. Only this motivation is worthy of the adjective *Christian*.

Believers

The definition suggests that Christian education is to be oriented toward believers. In its pure form, Christian education begins where evangelism ends, helping believers grow in their faith. The focus and design of educational ministries should be toward believers.

There is a rather long history of evangelizing through Christian education. Inviting nonbelievers into the church educational programs to hear the Gospel has brought about some significant results. However, the church must not forget that she functions first for the sake of the believers so that they may be built up in the faith.

An integral part of building believers in the faith is enabling them to be evangelists. Evangelism is close to God's heart and a key purpose of the church. But unbelievers do not flock into our churches to hear the Gospel. The church meets together to worship God and build up believers so that they may be sent out to testify and work in God's name. Therefore the focus of Christian education is educating Christians. That is to be our primary aim and concern.

Purpose

The definition also suggests that the purpose of educational ministry is to lead believers to spiritual maturity. Perhaps most people agree with this in theory, but it seems that there are as many definitions of spiritual maturity as there are Christian groups.

For some, spiritual maturity means knowing the Bible. The more a person knows the Bible, the more spiritual he or she is. For others, spiritual maturity means the ability to praise and worship. If people are worshipful and love to praise God, they can be considered mature. For still others, maturity is piety. The "deeper" one walks with God, the more mature that person is. For others, maturity means social action. Spiritual maturity is being involved with the poor and oppressed, alleviating their problems. For yet others, maturity means soul-winning. The truly spiritual person will be a personal evangelist. And for others, maturity means experiencing the fullness of the Spirit and exercising the gifts of the Holy Spirit in increasingly spectacular ways.

Admittedly, then, believers disagree on what it means to be Christian and what it means to be spiritually mature. But how purposes are defined will govern how educational ministries are designed.

Most distressing is that some Christian educators have never considered the matter of carefully defining spiritual maturity. Besides hindering one's own walk with God, this omission will also limit one's ability to lead others to maturity. It is critical for Christian educators to consider how they will define spiritual maturity.

The Bible uses a variety of terms and metaphors to describe spiritual maturity. Such terms as *proved* (2 Cor. 9:13), *mature* (Eph. 4:13), *holy* (1 Thess. 4:3), and *complete* (James 1:4) all refer to the concept of spiritual maturity. Metaphors such as Christ's dwelling in believers (Eph. 3:17), abiding or remaining in Christ (John 15:5), and believers walking as Jesus did (1 John 2:6) also describe the concept of maturity. But no single, simple definition is offered. Therefore a theological definition must be established to bring the breadth of biblical data together in any sort of a meaningful way.

For the purposes of Christian education, the concept of *faith* or *belief* can be used to determine the nature of spiritual maturity. It is clear from the gospels that our Lord valued faith and wanted his followers to have faith. He commended faith wherever he found it, and he rebuked lack of faith. The Bible declares that we are saved by faith (Eph. 2:8), the just shall live by faith (Rom. 1:17), and without faith it is impossible to please God (Heb. 11:6). The term *faith* is used in a variety of ways to describe what God desires in his people and is useful in describing what spiritual maturity is.

THE NATURE OF FAITH

Educating for maturity means educating for faith. But what is the nature and substance of faith? What does the Bible mean by the term *faith*?

Scripture speaks of faith in three different but interacting ways. A proper theological understanding of spiritual maturity includes each of these aspects of faith: the cognitive, the affective, and the volitional.

Cognitive

Faith has an intellectual (*notitia*) or cognitive aspect. There is an element of knowledge or content to faith. Scripture affirms that faith means believing certain things are true. There is a content to be believed, and that content has specifics. For example, in 1 Thessalonians 4:14 Paul says, "We believe that Jesus died and rose again," and John 20:31 declares that the purpose of the Gospel is "that you may believe that Jesus is the Christ, the Son of God. . . ."

Faith is more than a frothy hope that has no substance. The popular notion that "you gotta believe" is far removed from the biblical teaching that true faith has as its object the living God and his word revealed in Scripture. It is not enough that people have faith. *What* they believe is every bit as critical as the fact *that* they believe.

For some Christians, content is replaced with form. The experience of faith is more critical than the content of faith. People are deemed to be Christian simply because they can say, "I believe." There seems to be little concern over what the content of that belief happens to be. But the Bible stresses that *what* a person believes does matter. For example, both Romans and Galatians were written to inform or correct the *content* of the belief of the readers. Theology does matter, and what a person believes is important.

If educational ministries are to help people grow in faith, we must be concerned to communicate the content of the faith. Part of spiritual maturity is knowledge of God and knowledge of his Word. It is impossible to be spiritually mature and

yet be ignorant of the truths of God's Word. Spiritual maturity is contingent upon knowing what God has said.

Orthodox belief holds to correct content of faith, beliefs that have been identified and described by the various church councils down through history. Heresy is holding to beliefs that are not orthodox. Evangelicals must continue to be concerned for orthodoxy. We must be equally concerned for both the fact of faith and the content of faith.

A rediscovery of theology will help guard against Christian education that is not concerned with content and may therefore inadvertently introduce heresy into the church. A Christian education ministry that helps people grow in faith will be concerned with teaching the content of the faith accurately.

Relational

The Bible also speaks of faith as emotional (*assensus*) or relational. The epistle of James warns against the dangers of having a faith that is only content and tells us that orthodoxy alone is not sufficient. The content being believed must also capture the believer's heart and will.

True faith causes us to assent to the truthfulness of the object of faith and to have our hearts controlled. The Bible describes this as *believing in* God or *in* Jesus. This linguistic construction (*pisteuo eis*) is unique to the New Testament, implying a different kind of belief from the traditional Hellenistic notion that separated belief from commitment.

John 1:12 refers to "those who believed in his name." In Galatians 2:16 Paul says, "We, too, have put our faith in Christ Jesus." Thus "belief in" goes beyond the intellectual aspects of belief and calls for a belief that carries an emotional commitment to the object of one's faith.

The greatest commandment is that we love the Lord our God with all our heart and with all our soul and with all our strength (Deut. 6:5). This requires a faith that is relational and alive toward God, not a dispassionate intellectualism. What a person believes is important, but heart commitment is equally important. The mature believer will have a heart that loves God, delights in knowing him, and desires to please him in every way. It is not possible to speak of Christian maturity apart from these qualities of the heart.

Educational ministries that help people grow in faith must help people turn their hearts toward God. They must not only *understand* the truth but also *be captured by* the truth. Faith means a commitment to the truth of God and a heart that delights in the truth. The distinction between content and emotion in faith is the distinction between passive and active belief. The church must teach so that people actively embrace the Gospel as true and meaningful to their lives.

Volitional

The Bible also speaks of faith as volitional (*fiducia*). This final, crowning element of faith translates into lifestyle. True faith causes people to act on what they believe, engaging not only heart and mind, but also the will. Our Lord taught, "If you love me, you will obey what I command" (John 14:15). The outcome of saving faith is obedience to God. The ultimate test that one's faith is real is its being expressed by good works.

In an effort to protect the doctrine of justification by faith alone, some people have misunderstood the nature of faith, removing from it any understanding of or inclusion of works. But no one is ever justified by a faith that stands alone, apart from good works. Ephesians 2:8–9 teach-

es that salvation is by grace alone. But verse 10 stresses that "we are God's workmanship, created in Christ Jesus to do good works, which God prepared in advance for us to do." Our Lord warned that if our faith is not being expressed in obedience, it is not true faith at all (Matt. 7:21–23).

People cannot truthfully say they believe in Jesus unless they have a commitment to him that translates into active obedience. Part of loving God is a desire to please him by obedience. Paul described his ministry as calling people "to the obedience that comes from faith" (Rom. 1:5). True biblical faith ultimately affects the will, causing a person to desire to obey God. The process of sanctification is learning to become increasingly obedient to the Lord. Faith that justifies must have an aspect of this desire for obedience resident within it. James tells us emphatically that "as the body without the spirit is dead, so faith without deeds is dead" (James 2:26).

Proclaiming the Gospel

A complete understanding of faith has profound implications for how the Gospel is proclaimed. When people are invited to accept the gift of salvation, it must be with an understanding that faith in Christ connects belief with behavior. To receive Christ means more than receiving the benefits of the atonement; it means receiving *him*. It means believing that he died for the sins of humanity, loving him, and determining to strive to obey his commands.

Some churches are weak partly because they have failed to proclaim the Gospel properly. They have invited people to believe that Jesus died for them (*notitia*) without inviting them to receive him. There are people who think they are

Christians because their belief system is orthodox. But the demons have orthodox belief and are not saved (James 2:19)! Failure to teach that faith is not only intellectual but also affective and volitional has produced some weak churches.

Christian educators must teach what it means to have faith in Christ. We must understand that there may be people in the church who know the content of Christian belief, but do not truly know Christ. They do not have hearts that delight in him nor wills that are submissive to him. They believe that obedience is for a special class of Christians who want to go farther with Christ. They have reduced faith to a creedal statement, removing from it the transformational power it rightfully holds. As a result, their lives have not been changed, and they fail to experience the power of God.

Education worthy of the adjective *Christian* must be faithful to the Bible, proclaiming the fullness of its message. For too long the church has settled for teaching popular theology that tickles the ears but does not transform lives. The church must teach what it means to be Christian, to follow after Christ and be salt and light in a hungry world. This will happen only when the full biblical concept of faith is taught.

EDUCATING FOR SPIRITUAL MATURITY

Christian education, as I have defined it (p. 16) assumes that education is an effective means to help people grow to spiritual maturity. However, this assumption is made with the understanding that faith is first a gift from God. "No one can say 'Jesus is Lord,' except by the Holy Spirit" (1 Cor. 12:3). We are totally dependent on the Father to draw people to himself and give them the gift of faith.

Yet the church is mandated by her Lord to teach (Matt. 28:19–20). Our task is to discover the most effective ways to fulfill the Great Commission by learning to educate effectively.

Christian educators assume that it is possible to help people mature in their faith. But what does the process look like?

From all appearances, people must believe that the experience of sitting in rows listening to speakers is vital to spiritual growth. Why else would we spend so much time doing it? I am not content with that. There are other things we can do educationally to help people grow in their faith. I believe we can design other kinds of experiences to help people mature as believers.

Curriculum is a plan to design strategies for education. Figure 2 shows a sample curriculum model. Even though this model tends to look like a factory and fails to take into account the complexities of

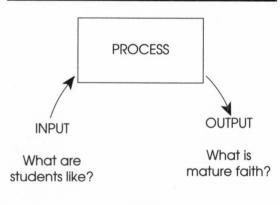

Figure 2

working with people, it does serve to open up certain critical issues.

It is best to "enter" the model from the right, thinking first about purpose or output. I have suggested that the purpose of Christian education is a well-developed faith that has cognitive, affective, and volitional components to it.

At the left side of the model we consider people, asking what they are like. Here, both developmental psychology and theology help us understand our students. We must draw on both sources to understand properly how God has created people to learn.

The top of the model focuses on educational process, asking what people must experience in order to grow in the ways we want. Most people involved in educational ministries become consumed with process issues, always trying to find the best way to teach.

Educational strategies are best determined when we have identified both the purpose of education and student characteristics. As we examine more of the theology of spiritual growth and consider how God has designed people to learn, issues of educational process will become clearer. There is no best way to teach, but we can draw important conclusions as to how we can carry out the educational ministry of the church so that people are enabled to grow in their faith.

2 Teaching in Biblical Perspective

Mᵧ seminary colleague Ted Ward has a disarming slogan: "Christian education is neither." His point is obvious. Christian education in many of its contemporary forms is neither "Christian" nor particularly educative. Christian education as a discipline has become so trivialized that many Christian schools have dropped it from their curriculum. In addition, what was once an important aspect of church life is now seen by many to be irrelevant and innocuous.

But rather than simply bemoaning the current state of Christian education, we are more responsible if we ask what the Bible teaches about teaching. If Scripture values the teaching ministry, the church must value it also. If teaching is critical in a biblical perspective, it must also be critical in our perspective for the twenty-first century.

Before we can develop an adequate approach to educational ministry, we must make an overview of the biblical perspective. Rather than attempting an exhaustive study, in this chapter I provide a sampling of key biblical texts and a summary of a biblical theology of teaching. My purpose is to establish the centrality of teaching as a means of enabling people to grow in their faith as Christians.

TEACHING IN THE OLD TESTAMENT

In the Old Testament the purpose of teaching was that Israel might learn to obey God's law so that their distinctive position as the people of God would be evident and God would be glorified. The book of Deuteronomy repeatedly makes this point.

> See, I have taught you decrees and laws as the LORD my God commanded me, so that you may follow them in the land you are entering to take possession of it. Observe them carefully, for this will show your wisdom and understanding to the nations, who will hear about all these decrees and say, "Surely this great nation is a wise and understanding people." What other nation is so great as to have their gods near them the way the LORD our God is near us whenever we pray to him? And what other nation is so great as to have such righteous decrees and laws as this body of laws I am setting before you today? (Deut. 4:5–8)

Obedience to the law is a constant theme in the Old Testament, illustrating the Hebrew concept of learning. Teaching and learning in the Old Testament did not involve only the communication of information but also instruction in the will of God and understanding how to live. The teacher was to teach people to *obey* the commandments of God, not simply to know them. In fact, knowledge was so linked to action in the Hebrew mind that the people could not claim to *know* what they did not do.

The purpose of Israel's obedience was that God might be honored and glorified.

Secondarily, obedience was to bring Israel peace and comfort. Both were to be outcomes of teaching, but the primary concern was that God might be praised.

To this theme Deuteronomy 6 adds the principle that the context for instruction is the home. The *Shema* (vv. 4–9) suggests a pattern of instruction that focuses on the responsibility of the parents to impress God's commands upon their children. It would be wrong to suggest that this passage prescribes a rigid pattern; rather, it emphasizes the natural communication between parent and child. But the parent is to teach *diligently* (NASB) the commands of God to the child, so that the child will live in obedience to God.

The Old Testament continually emphasizes the father's responsibility to provide religious training for his sons (Ex. 10:2; 12:26; 13:8; Deut. 6:20ff.). Given the clearly defined sex roles and restricted responsibilities for women in that culture, the mother was to teach the girls. But it was the mother who provided the primary moral education for the children and began the rudiments of their formal education (Prov. 1:8; 6:20). In this sense there was a true partnership between the parents, as both had responsibility for educating the children in the home.

Deuteronomy 31 provides guidance for public instruction in the Word of God, offering further insight into the concept of learning from a Hebrew perspective.

> Then Moses commanded them: "At the end of every seven years, in the year for canceling debts, during the Feast of Tabernacles, when all Israel comes to appear before the LORD your God at the place he will choose, you shall read this law before them in their hearing. Assemble the people—men, women and children, and the aliens living in your towns—so they can listen and learn to fear the LORD your God and follow care-

fully all the words of this law. Their children, who do not know this law, must hear it and learn to fear the LORD your God as long as you live in the land you are crossing the Jordan to possess." (vv. 10–13)

This passage suggests a progression in learning. First, the people were to listen to the commands of God. In a society that was at this point primarily illiterate, teaching and learning were conducted orally, so the law was to be read and listened to. It was understood that God had spoken to his people through the law and this law was to be heard. There was to be a ritual public reading of the law as a reminder that these were the covenant people of God.

But hearing is not the same as learning. It is quite possible to hear instruction and fail to learn it. Students in our time confirm this idea many times over. Moses states that he wanted the people to learn to fear the Lord. The word translated "learn" (*lamath*) is the most common Hebrew word for learning. It implies a subjective assimilation of the truth being learned, an integration of the truth into life.

Learning was to be demonstrated in two ways, by a change of attitude and by a change in action. The new attitude was that the people were to fear God. The fear of the Lord was both a literal fear of him as God and a proper respect for his authority over life. The fear of God is the beginning of knowledge (Prov. 1:7) and expresses the primary motivation for serving God. He was to be seen as a terrible God but also as a God to be loved. The Hebrew was to stand before this God in awe and reverence, in terror and in love.

Fear of the Lord was to be expressed through obedience to God's commands. A change of heart was to be expressed in a change in behavior. Only then could it be said that a person had learned the Law of

God. Learning God's law was not something divorced from life, but rather something that was to control all of life.

The function of the teacher in the Old Testament was to produce people of obedience, people motivated by a heartfelt respect for God. The teacher was to instruct others in God's commands so that the people would be recognized as having been set apart for God.

Eventually a group of professional teachers emerged in the Old Testament, but initially the whole nation was responsible for teaching. Through the various feasts and rituals, parents and elders were to teach the children the content of the Law and the need for obedience. The entire lifestyle was to be didactic in nature and function.

Later there emerged an enlarged teaching role for the priests and Levites. In addition, as Roland DeVaux explains, "teaching was given quite apart from worship, in the synagogues, and a new class arose, of scribes and teachers of the Law. This class was open to all, priests and Levites and layfolk alike, and eventually it displaced the priestly caste in the work of teaching."[1]

In a sense one could say that the breakdown of Israel's religious life constituted a breakdown in its educational system. People were to be taught to obey the Law and thus be the people of God. But there was a profound lack of obedience in the nation, and as a result God repeatedly administered discipline to bring the people back to obedience. Eventually the class of the Pharisees emerged, with their emphasis on teaching and obedience in an attempt to return the nation to God.

The relation of teacher to student in the Old Testament was the relation of parent to child. The terminology in Proverbs suggests that relationship. Education was not impersonal and detached, but personal and relational. Moreover, Jesus continued this pattern in his relationship with his disciples.

But the educational system established in Israel broke down. The prophet Jeremiah, proclaiming the coming judgment on the nation, asked:

> What fault did your fathers find in me, that they strayed so far from me? They followed worthless idols and became worthless themselves. They did not ask, "Where is the LORD, who brought us up out of Egypt and led us through the barren wilderness, through a land of deserts and rifts, a land of drought and darkness, a land where no one travels and no one lives?" I brought you into a fertile land to eat its fruit and rich produce. But you came and defiled my land and made my inheritance detestable. The priests did not ask, "Where is the LORD?" Those who deal with the law did not know me; the leaders rebelled against me. (Jer. 2:5–8)

Those in professional leadership positions had wandered so far from God that they no longer knew him. There was no personal relationship with him, so they were truly "blind guides." No educational system is above the people working in it. If the teachers do not fear the Lord and delight in him, the best educational system will fail.

TEACHING IN THE NEW TESTAMENT

At the time of the New Testament the Pharisees were attempting to restore Israel by their meticulous adherence to the Law. They were fanatical in their study and keeping of the Law but were ultimately misguided in their judgments. Much of our Lord's instruction regarding teaching was in response to the Pharisees and their mode of teaching.

Matthew 5:17–20 describes Jesus' relationship to the Law. He came to fulfill the Law and greatly valued its place in the kingdom of God. In this context he stated that whoever *practices and teaches* God's commands will be great in the kingdom (v. 19). The twofold responsibility of the follower of Christ is to obey God's commands and teach others to obey. Conversely, those who fail to obey and teach others to do the same will be the least in the kingdom.

The Christian educator is responsible to teach Scripture in a way that calls for response on the part of the learners. Bible classes that serve only to communicate information but do not change lives have no part in the kingdom. The Christian educator must be obedient and must teach others to be obedient also. Teaching for obedience, according to our Lord, is one of the most significant ministries possible, resulting in greatness within the kingdom.

The gospels provide pictures of the life of Jesus that help to determine his values. An incident recorded in Mark 6 demonstrates his view of teaching. When the apostles returned from their ministry, they were tired and in need of refreshment. Jesus suggested that they come away for a while to rest. But when the Son of God was walking incarnate in the land, it was impossible for him to avoid the crowds.

He led the Twelve to a quiet place, but the crowds arrived ahead of them. His response to the multitudes was not anger, frustration, or condemnation. He did not see them as an interruption, but rather as sheep without a shepherd (v. 34). He was moved with compassion for them because he saw them as both vulnerable and directionless. He looked at them through eyes of love.

How did Jesus express his compassion to the crowd? Mark tells us that "he

Properly understood, Christian education is a critical means of maintaining the life of the church and of moving the church forward. It was critical in the life of the Lord and became critical in the life of the church.

began teaching them many things" (v. 34). Since Jesus expressed his love by teaching, it follows that one of the most loving things we can do for others is to teach them. Helping people to know God and to be obedient to him is perhaps the greatest gift we can bestow. Understood in this way, Christian education can be one of the most compassionate ministries of the church.

The Great Commission of Jesus in Matthew 28:18–20 provides further insight into his understanding of the importance of teaching. He began by stating that all authority is rightfully his, proclaiming his lordship over all of creation. On the basis of this truth, the primary task of all Christians is to make disciples of all nations. The Gospel begins with and is motivated by the lordship of Christ. Any gospel that does not proclaim his lordship is a false gospel.

A disciple is one who is committed to the Lord with loyalty and devotion. The imperative of the command is that we are to be about the business of making disciples. As we go through life our task is always the same.

Regarding these verses, D. A. Carson observes:

> Baptizing and teaching are not the *means* of making disciples, but they characterize it. Envisaged is that proclamation of the gospel that will result in repentance and faith, for *matheteuo* ("I disciple") entails both preaching and

response. The response of discipleship is baptism and instruction. Therefore baptism and instruction are not coordinate— either grammatically or conceptually— with the action of making disciples.... The NT can scarcely conceive of a disciple who is not baptized or is not instructed. Indeed, the force of this command is to make Jesus' disciples responsible for making disciples of others, a task characterized by baptism and instruction.[2]

New disciples are first to be baptized in (or into) the name of the Father, Son, and Holy Spirit and then taught to obey everything the Lord has commanded. Baptism is the sign that people have been converted, and teaching is the means by which new converts are to be brought to maturity. Again, as in the Old Testament, obedience to the Lord's commands is the desired outcome of the teaching. The commission ends with the promise of Christ's presence with us until the end of the age.

Teaching is central to the Lord's plan, indicating its centrality in the life of the church. Properly understood, Christian education is a critical means of maintaining the life of the church and of moving the church forward. It was critical in the life of the Lord and became critical in the life of the church.

The early church continued with an emphasis on teaching. After the day of Pentecost, when three thousand were converted, Luke records that "they devoted themselves to the apostles' teaching"

(Acts 2:42). The means of building up the new converts were instruction, fellowship, worship, and community. By sharing material goods and meals together, by praying and worshiping together, and by learning together, believers were being built up and the people in the local community were seeing the reality of the Gospel being lived out before them. As a result of their teaching and relationships, both with God and each other, believers were being transformed into recognizably new creations in Christ.

Effective Christian education does not take place in a vacuum; it is best accomplished in the context of loving relationships and effective worship. The power of the Holy Spirit was upon the community of believers so that lives were being touched. The kingdom is not a matter of finding the newest educational techniques, but of believers being filled with love for God and each other. It is the power of the Holy Spirit in the lives of believers.

TEACHING IN THE EARLY CHURCH

Paul described himself as "a herald and an apostle and a teacher" of the gospel (2 Tim. 1:11). His ministry was to proclaim and to teach the Good News. Clearly, teaching was a critical aspect of his entire strategy for ministry.

Colossians 1:25–29 provides an important glimpse into the ministry strategy of the apostle. In the context of explaining how he labored on behalf of the church, Paul explains that his ministry was suffering (v. 24), proclamation (vv. 25–29), and intercession (2:1–5).

A central aspect of Paul's ministry was the proclamation of the Word of God. He was a servant of the church because he was first of all a steward of God. The only way anyone can effectively serve the church

is first to be committed to the Father. This was the source of Paul's motivation to give himself in ministry to the church.

The content of Paul's proclamation was the mystery of the fullness of the Word, the glorious mystery that had once been hidden but now was revealed. The mystery, Paul told the Colossians, "is Christ in you, the hope of glory" (1:27). The mystery is the key to spiritual life, the inner subjective experience of the indwelling Christ in all of his people, Jew and Gentile alike.

Paul's message was Christ, and his method was admonition and teaching with all wisdom, so that all might be presented complete in Christ. *Admonition* (a form of counseling) in this context probably refers to Paul's attempt to convince unbelievers of their need for Christ. The demands of the proclamation ran deep, with profound implications for how we are to live. This kind of proclamation must come with admonition.

Teaching was required because the mysteries of Christ are not easily understood and require instruction and explanation. So it was the practice of the apostle Paul to proclaim the gospel in a new territory and then remain to teach the converts the mysteries of Christ so that their lives might be changed. The apostle needed wisdom both to understand the message and to make it relevant to his hearers. Thus, to the Jews Paul became like a Jew to win them, and to the Gentiles he became like a Gentile to win them. Indeed, he became "all things to all men so that by all possible means [he] might save some" (1 Cor. 9:22).

The goal of this proclamation was that Paul might present everyone perfect, or mature and complete, in Christ. Faithful proclamation and instruction in the Word were done so that lives might be changed by obedience to the Word.

Effective Christian education must focus on the mysteries of God. For too long now, much of the church has lost this focus in its educational programs; instead, there has been content designed to speak to immediate needs but at the same time a neglect of the deep truths of God. People do not readily understand the truth of the Gospel, and for many theology has become irrelevant. As a result their faith is weak and their lives are defeated. They are ripe for the corruption of heresy and moral decay because there is no core of truth to their faith. The church has failed to proclaim the content of the faith, so people do not know what to believe.

Effective Christian educators proclaim the mysteries of God with all wisdom, making clear the relevance of biblical truth to life. The mysteries of God are not irrelevant to life, but they are in fact the only means of making sense of life. They provide the framework through which we can understand life and find ultimate meaning. The apostle stood with one foot firmly planted in the mysteries of God and the other in the experiences of life. As he taught the mysteries, Paul related theology to life experience, showing how a person must live in response to the truth. This task is the same for the modern Christian educator. We too must proclaim the truth of God and relate it to the lives of the people we teach.

Paul described this work as a *struggle* (Col. 1:29). It is not easy to understand the mysteries of God and relate them to the experiences of life. Christian educators must be soundly biblical and theological scholars, and they must also understand people. They do not have the luxury of studying only the text; they must also study people. Neither can they worry only about methods and organizational schemes without being concerned about the content they teach. Competent Christian education requires theological insight and understanding people both psychologically and culturally.

But the best of these insights will not produce a righteous people in and of themselves. God's power must be at work to bring about spiritual maturity. Paul struggled in his effort, but he realized that he was in partnership with Christ. Christ was at work in him. Productive Christian education is always a partnership between God and the educator.

As Paul worked to establish churches, the development of leadership was essential. Working to appoint elders in the various churches, Paul listed criteria that must be met by those who would lead the church. A critical concern was that they be "able to teach" (1 Tim. 3:2). Paul taught Timothy, who was in turn to "entrust to reliable men who [would] also be qualified to teach others" (2 Tim. 2:2) the truths he learned from Paul.

The church was to progress through evangelization and education. These twin themes are the heart of the ministry of the church. Both are critical for the growth and health of the church.

CONCLUSION

This brief overview demonstrates that teaching is not optional in the church; rather, it is a biblical imperative to be obeyed. The *form* of the teaching may vary. Sunday schools, for example, are not biblically mandated. They are a cultural form established in the last two centuries to fulfill the biblical mandate. *How* the church teaches is open to a variety of cultural expressions, but *that* the church teaches is nonnegotiable. The Scriptures demand that the church educate its people for spiritual maturity.

Notes

1. Roland DeVaux, *Ancient Israel* (New York: McGraw-Hill, 1961), 355.
2. D. A. Carson, "Matthew," in Frank E. Gaebelein, gen. ed., *The Expositor's Bible Commentary*, 12 vols. (Grand Rapids: Zondervan, 1984), 8:597.

3 | Modeling Our Teaching After Jesus

Jesus continues to be the premier example of the effective teacher. His influence is felt as powerfully today as it was two thousand years ago. His capacity to touch lives by his teaching and to help people see and understand spiritual matters serves as the ideal toward which we should strive. Jesus' teaching methods were culturally appropriate to his context, but still they are instructive for us in ours. Much of what he did and said serves as a model for Christian educators in the modern age.

THE PROBLEM OF NORMALCY

Before we examine Jesus' teaching methods, we must consider to what extent Jesus is truly normative for contemporary teachers. Is it realistic and appropriate to use Jesus as an example for contemporary teachers? We must consider two important issues before we can explore Jesus' approach to teaching.

Jesus had within him both the human and the divine nature. This hypostatic union of the two natures resulted in Jesus' being *sui generis* (in a class by himself). No other human possesses the powers and insights he possessed. Jesus could do miracles and understand the

---

Much of what Jesus did and said serves as a model for Christian educators in the modern age.

---

lives of people before he ever met them. Given these unique attributes, Jesus could teach in ways others could never hope to emulate.

This problem is somewhat solved through the *kenosis*—the emptying of himself described in Philippians 2:7. Perhaps as he "made himself nothing," Jesus limited his divine prerogatives in some ways, leaving himself dependent on the Father in the same ways we are. Jesus taught that if we had faith we could do greater miracles than he (Matt. 17:20). Theologians differ on the meaning of the kenosis, but the fact of Jesus' emptying himself suggests that while he was on earth his limitations might have been similar to ours.

A second concern is that Jesus' culture was completely different from ours. Jesus taught in open settings, traveling from place to place, bringing his disciples with him. Because itinerant rabbis were fairly common at that time, Jesus' approach was not unusual. But will that approach in any way transfer to today's culture?

Some authors believe there was a specific plan to his teaching, especially in regard to the training of the apostles—a plan that is transferable to our context.

For example, in his book *With Christ in the School of Discipleship*, Carl Wilson argues that there is a definite pattern in Jesus' work with the Twelve. In order to find the pattern, he says, we must first achieve a harmony of the gospels. Each of the four gospels must be integrated into a whole so that we attain a clear history of the life of Christ. Once we do this, Wilson believes, we can study the *pattern of experiences* for the Twelve and discover Jesus' method of discipleship.

Wilson's approach relies on successful harmonization of the gospels. But gospel harmonies are tenuous at best because the gospels were not written to provide a history of the life of Christ. Rather, the gospels were written as theological statements about Christ and are best understood when one reads them independently, seeking the internal message of each. When they are read as theological statements regarding Christ, no clear pattern of Jesus' approach to training the Twelve emerges. Instead, each writer presents a unique picture of Christ that reveals principles used by Christ as a teacher. Thus searching for a chronological pattern from which we may derive a specific pattern for discipleship is probably not appropriate.

To search for principles rather than patterns is to be more faithful to how the gospels were recorded. It seemed good to the Father not to provide us with a chronological history of the life of Christ, and therefore we need not seek one. But we can take the information each writer provides and use it to understand the primary principles that seemed to guide our Lord as a teacher.

Scripture teaches that Jesus serves as an example for us. We are told that we are to "walk as Jesus did" (1 John 2:6), living our lives according to the principles that guided him. Moreover, Luke tells us that he recorded "all that Jesus began to do and teach" (Acts 1:1). Luke was concerned not only with what Jesus said but also with what Jesus did. A study of Jesus as a teacher must consider both *what* he taught and *how* he taught. There are at least four major areas in which Jesus serves as a model for modern teachers.

OBJECTIVES: WHAT WAS JESUS' PRIMARY AIM AS A TEACHER?

Because this is a difficult question to answer, it is best first to answer it negatively—that is, to determine what his objectives were not. It seems clear that it was not Jesus' objective to leave behind a body of truth. Jesus was concerned with the communication of content, but this does not seem to be his primary concern. There were many times when, as a teacher, he seemed to be after something beyond the communication of new information.

Jesus reinterpreted the Old Testament, offering deeper insight into the meanings it contained. But he did not establish a whole new theology. Rather, Jesus' teaching was an extension of existing theology as he showed people whole new ways of thinking about the truths of the Old Testament and revealed who he was and his place in the Father's redemptive plan. He focused on the fulfillment of the Law, not a new theological interpretation of it.

Neither was it Jesus' objective as a teacher to systematize theology. Clearly he was concerned with coherent and congruent truth and with logical thought but not to the extent that these were his primary concerns. There are no examples of his organizing theological truth in new ways.[1] He did follow the traditional readings of the Old Testament according to Jewish custom, but we never read of his establishing "Bible classes" so that he could teach the whole counsel of God.[2] Jesus followed the normal religious traditions of his day, which assumed a study of Torah, but he did not offer commentary or interpretation on the Old Testament in any logical or sequential order.

What, then, was his objective as a teacher? Jesus said, "I have come that they may have life, and have it to the full" (John 10:10). His goal as a teacher was to change the quality of life of his students, raising them to a higher measure of obedience to God and a higher level of holiness. Because Jesus would lay down his life for them (v. 11), he was able to teach and enable them to live in new ways.

Jesus' purpose as a teacher was to influence the experiences of his students so that their lives would be different. He wanted them to experience God as their Father and to live in the reality of that relationship. Jesus wanted them to live righteously in obedience to the commands of God and to experience fullness of life in relationship to God. His objective as a teacher was to touch the lives of his students.

Some teachers confuse means with ends. They so focus on methods that they forget their objectives. Teaching the Bible is a method; changing lives is an objective. The reason we teach in the church is that lives may be changed. The reason we hold Bible studies is that lives may be changed. The reason we establish Sunday schools, youth groups, singles groups, and other educational programs is that lives may be changed.

When the objective becomes changing students' lives, the focus and activities of the teacher will be influenced. Jesus was not obsessed with "covering the content," because that was not his objective. He could take time to listen to students and interact with them because his agenda was their lives, not his content.

Modern teachers must learn from this example. We must remember that our objectives go beyond the communication of content to the life response of the student to the content we teach. We cannot be satisfied that our students "know the truth." Our students must live the truth. Only then can we say that our teaching has been successful.

But is it realistic to expect our teaching to bring about changed lives? Can we hope to touch the lives of others, causing them to be more righteous and more obe-

bring our students to maturity. Maturity, rightly understood, means a changed life.

Relationship With Students: On What Basis Did Jesus Accept and Reject Students?

Jesus responded differently to different people. To some, Jesus was gentle and forgiving, while to others he was harsh and condemning. Jesus was sought out by the multitudes and rejected by the religious leaders. The poor and oppressed

We cannot change lives, but our responsibility is to teach so that God can use our efforts to bring our students to maturity. Maturity, rightly understood, means a changed life.

dient to God? Can we really bring about this sort of response in our students? The simple answer is that we cannot change lives. But the content of Scripture taught in the power of the Holy Spirit does change lives. God can use our teaching to effect change.

Christian education is best understood as an educational partnership with God. We are responsible to teach others to the best of our abilities, striving to help them understand and obey God's Word. The Holy Spirit is responsible to use our efforts to touch the hearts of our students and lead them into obedient relationship with the Father. We are to teach as if it all depends on us, understanding that if students do respond it is because of the grace of God in their lives. We cannot change lives, but our responsibility is to teach so that God can use our efforts to

hailed Jesus as their hero, while the religious leaders condemned him as a heretic. People responded to him differently, and he responded to people in a variety of ways. What governed whether Jesus accepted or rejected people?

Jesus' encounter with Zacchaeus, recorded in Luke 19:1–10, provides insight into this question. Zacchaeus was a wealthy tax collector and by his own admission was a cheat. When Jesus saw Zacchaeus in the tree, he told him to come down so that he might dine in Zacchaeus's house.

The people complained because Zacchaeus was a "sinner" (v. 7). They were offended that Jesus would associate with such a man. They pointed out what was wrong with the man, calling him a sinner. But Jesus reflected on what was right about Zacchaeus, observing, "This man, too, is a son of Abraham" (v. 9). While the crowd saw Zacchaeus as a sinner, Jesus saw him as a descendent of Abraham.

Zacchaeus responded with true repentance. His life was so changed that immediately he pledged to sell his many possessions and give to the poor and to make restitution with interest for the wrongs he had committed. His conversion was so deep that even his wallet was affected! Jesus' acceptance of Zacchaeus while everyone else was rejecting him was a powerful statement that touched Zacchaeus deeply.

The pericope regarding the woman taken in adultery (John 8:3–11) is a somewhat disputed text, not appearing in the earliest manuscripts, but still it is considered reliable by many New Testament scholars.[3] Almost all agree that the story is authentic; it is the placement and exact wording that are in question. But the story helps us gain insight into how our Lord related to people.

The religious leaders brought to Jesus a woman who had been caught in the act of adultery. They let the man go, but the wicked woman was to be punished. (Even at that time the double standard regarding how women and men were treated was acceptable.) The leaders were only using the woman as a pawn in their game of entrapment. They wanted to place Jesus in the difficult position of having to choose between the Jewish law, which called for stoning, and the Roman government, which reserved the right of capital punishment for itself. If Jesus agreed that she must be stoned as Jewish law demanded, he would be in conflict with Rome. If he called for tolerance and forgiveness, he would be in conflict with Jewish law.

When confronted with this challenge, Jesus bent down and began to write on the ground with his finger. He then rose up and turned the accusation against the religious leaders, showing the hypocrisy of their actions. He challenged them by saying that he who was without sin should cast the first stone. Again Jesus bent down and wrote on the ground.

We are not told what he was writing. Dr. Rufus Jones, former general director of the Conservative Baptist Home Mission Society, suggests that perhaps Jesus was listing the names and dates of when these accusers had committed adultery themselves! Jesus' invitation for the one without sin to cast the first stone served to silence the crowd and to dismiss them.

Left alone with the woman, Jesus took great pity on her. Imagine the utter humiliation she had just endured. Jesus asked if there was anyone left to condemn her, and when she replied in the negative, Jesus offered his forgiveness, telling her to go and leave her life of sin. This does not imply that Jesus simply glossed over sin, but rather that although the law came through Moses, grace and truth came through Jesus (John 1:17).

What kind of effect would this have on the common person? People who were used to being condemned and rejected by the religious leaders were seeing them being made fools of by this new rabbi. They had to be cheering him on, seeing someone at last who could stand up to the religious tyranny they had suffered. Too long they had been trodden down by self-righteous Pharisees who laid more and more burdens on them without bringing them closer to God. At last there was someone who could be their advocate against organized and oppressive religion.

Jesus does not seem to be offended by sinful people. There is no doubt that both Zacchaeus and this woman were sinners and that they were painfully aware of their sinfulness. But Jesus offered them forgiveness in the midst of their pain. While the religious leaders called for their condemnation, he offered them redemption.

The same kind of story is told in the incident of the woman at the well, recorded in John 4. While everyone else shunned the woman because she had had five husbands and was now living with yet another man, Jesus had a natural and open conversation with her. He treated her with respect and told her that he was the Messiah (v. 26).

Jesus was a "friend of sinners" (Matt. 11:19), more accepting of them than he was of the religious leaders. Sinners knew Jesus was a man of God, yet they felt comfortable with him. The tax gatherers and prostitutes came to him freely, and he was their friend. But Jesus had strong conflicts with religious leaders.

The gospel of Mark records the degeneration of Jesus' relationship with the religious leaders. Mark 2:1–12 tells of the healing of the paralytic. Everyone rejoiced in the man's healing except the teachers of the law who were offended that Jesus had claimed to be able to forgive sins. To them, matters of law and religious propriety were more important than suffering and healing. Religious traditions were to supersede humanitarian concerns and compassionate response to human suffering. Indeed, their traditions were more important than even the miraculous setting aside of natural laws. They could not or would not see the miracle because of their theological position.

Mark 2:13–17 records the calling of Levi. He was a tax collector, a collaborator with the oppressive Roman occupiers. But Jesus called him and chose to eat with him. When Jesus was criticized for eating and drinking with sinners, he explained that he had come for sinners, using the analogy that it is the sick who need a physician, not the healthy. But the self-

righteous teachers of the law and the Pharisees did not accept this rationale. They did not see themselves as being in need of redemption.

The Jewish leaders also challenged Jesus because he did not follow the rituals of fasting (vv. 18–22). Other rabbis taught and practiced fasting, but Jesus taught that while he was present it was the time for feasting. This too did not meet their theological and religious standards.

Most of Jesus' conflicts with the Pharisees centered on their Sabbath laws. He allowed his disciples to pick grain on the Sabbath, and eventually Jesus challenged the religious leaders outright on the matter. Mark 3:1–6 tells how he brought a man with a shriveled hand up before the congregation. All of the eyes of the people were fixed on him because they understood that a direct confrontation was brewing. Their laws declared that no work could be done on the Sabbath, and healing was categorized as work.

Jesus raised the confrontation to the level of basic values by asking, "Which is lawful on the Sabbath: to do good or to do evil, to save a life or to kill?" (Mark 3:4). This was not a conflict about religious traditions but about basic values. Were people and their needs more important than human laws and traditions? Mark records that Jesus "looked around at them in anger . . . deeply distressed at their stubborn hearts" (Mark 3:5). Their rigid keeping of the Sabbath was more important to them than this man's deformity. So deeply did they hold this viewpoint that after Jesus healed the man they went out and began to plot how they might kill him.

It is evident that while Jesus was a friend of sinners, he would not tolerate religious hypocrisy. When people claimed to love God but were legalistically controlling others in the name of religion, this was more than he was willing to tolerate. The self-righteous attitude of these people incurred Jesus' anger rather than his forgiveness.

We modern Christian educators should learn from this example that we must never reject people because they are sinners. Rather, to be truly Christlike educators we must learn to love people as Jesus did. Educational programs should be havens for people who have been beaten down by religious establishments and religious leaders. Education that is Christian brings forgiveness and redemption, not condemnation and law.

It is sad that in some churches sinners are treated as objects—souls to be won rather than people to be loved. They are humiliated, talked down to, and treated disrespectfully, all in the name of Christ.

When I was a college professor, I was interviewing potential faculty members for a position in my department. I interviewed a woman who wanted to leave public education and enter Christian education. I asked her about her relationship with other teachers. She said there was one woman who was a good friend but did not know the Lord, and she was not yet able to get her to attend church with her. She went on to tell me that this woman's husband owned a tavern, and on several occasions she had been invited to have lunch at the tavern. "But," she told me, "of course I would never go into that 'beer joint' with her." I wondered how she ever expected to reach her friend if she would not even go to lunch with her to her husband's tavern. But to this woman, not being seen where liquor was served was more important than establishing a relationship with her friend. I decided then that I did not want her teaching in my department.

Jesus was a powerful teacher because he did not reject people just because they were sinners. He related to the downtrodden and the outcast, bringing them God's love not only in words but also in actions. He chose to eat with them, be seen with them, and teach them. And he refused to be controlled by a religious establishment characterized by arrogance rather than mercy.

The harshest words recorded from the lips of Jesus are found in Matthew 23—words directed at the religious leaders. He did not reject their authority as spokesmen of the Law (vv. 2–3), but he did condemn their lifestyle. They failed to live lives of compassion and care for the people around them. They were more concerned with maintaining religious traditions than with ministry to hurting people.

Every now and then the same problem emerges in our churches. We encounter those who are more concerned with traditions and propriety than with people. In the 1960s when God moved among the youth of our society in what was called The Jesus Movement, many churches could not accept the new converts because they did not dress in traditional ways. People were not welcomed into churches because they did not want to wear shoes or did not own a necktie. Some church members were more concerned with fashion than with people.

It can be a dangerous thing to love sinners and relate to them. Besides being exposed to the temptations inherent in their lifestyle, one can also risk incurring the wrath of other Christians. The idea of separation from the world is so ingrained in some believers that, like the Pharisees, they can only condemn those who reach out redemptively to the world. But to be obedient to Christ and to live truly righteously requires loving our neighbors as ourselves.

Methods: What Teaching Methods Seem Foremost in Jesus' Ministry?

Clearly Jesus used a great variety of teaching methods. Many are quite obvious, such as lectures, parables, object lessons, and discussions. Others are less obvious, such as using the life experiences of his students and designing "internships" for them. But the fact that Jesus used a great variety of teaching methods is indisputable.

The broad variety of teaching methods he used is instructive to us. Effective teaching requires a variety of methods, depending on the content, the student, and the situation. Just as Jesus varied the way he taught, so we too must vary our approach to teaching. There is no single best way to teach; neither is there a single "biblical" method of teaching. A wide variety of options exist, and the wise teacher will learn to teach in various ways.

Jesus seemed to stress informal rather than formal teaching. Clearly it was his practice to enter the synagogue on the Sabbath and teach in the formal setting; but the picture that dominates the gospels' portrayal of him as a teacher is informality. He is seen teaching in the countryside, along the road, on beaches, in homes, and in various other rather unexpected settings.

Stressing the informal does not imply that formal teaching is always ineffective. But it does mean that there is great power in informal modes of teaching. While classrooms can be important settings for some kinds of learning, life-changing sorts of education occur more often in less formal contexts. The close proximity of the teacher to the student in an informal or nonformal context tends to touch lives more effectively than the more dis-

tant relationship of the formal classroom.

As a seminary professor, I spend a good deal of my time in the formal context of the classroom. My teaching is controlled by clocks, academic schedules, accreditation standards, and a host of other matters normally associated with formal education. I accept these constraints on my teaching, but I also understand that the formal context of the classroom limits my ability to teach. The classroom is not a very effective context for touching lives in deep ways.

Responsible educators are always concerned with outcomes—the kinds of learning that result from our teaching. A helpful taxonomy of learning outcomes was suggested by Norman Steineker and M. Robert Bell.[4] Their taxonomy suggests the following levels of learning:

- Recall—I remember
- Recall and Approval—I like
- Recall and Speculation—I think
- Recall and Application—I try
- Recall and Adoption—I adopt

The lowest level is simple *recall*, by which the student is able to remember what has been taught. This is a simple cognitive exercise, unrelated to life. Recall is necessary for later higher levels of learning but is hardly capable of penetrating the life of the learner. Many students develop good memories and are quite successful at this kind of learning.

Approval involves not only the student's mind but also his or her *emotional* commitment to what has been learned. The student likes what has been remembered, feeling positive about the information. Effective learning that brings about life changes requires affective as well as cognitive involvement by the student.

Speculation is a voluntary cognitive involvement with the content. At this level the student thinks about how these ideas may be applied in his or her context. There is not yet a life response to the content, but there is active thinking about what has been learned. The affective involvement of level two has led to the cognitive activity of level three.

At the level of *application* the student *tries out* the concept in a real-life setting as a result of the thinking of level three. This step serves as a testing ground for the validity of the truth learned. Application may lead to a rejection of the content, or it may lead to the final level of learning if the concept "worked" in the crucible of life experience.

Adoption occurs when the student incorporates the concept into his or her life. The trial of level four proved positive, and the student now chooses to integrate this concept into the fabric of her or his thinking and doing. This is the ultimate step of effective learning.

Formal learning contexts are powerful for helping students achieve the first three levels of learning. Concepts can be communicated in winsome ways, and students can be led to consider possible applications in their daily lives. But formal education tends to be less effective than informal education in helping students reach the higher tiers of learning. The steps of application and adoption are generated better by more informal modes of teaching. The personal contact of informal instruction is ultimately more powerful than the more restrictive formal modes of teaching. Perhaps this is why our Lord chose to teach in informal modes.

Jesus also stressed establishing and maintaining relationships with students as a primary teaching method. He chose the Twelve that "they might be with him" (Mark 3:14), observing and interacting with him as he went about his ministry. As he taught, he entered into relationships with people, touching lives from the close proximity of intimacy.

John's gospel provides a striking portrait of the relational nature of Jesus' ministry. John's prologue introduces the idea of the Incarnation providing the remarkable observation that "the Word [logos] became flesh and lived for a while among us" (John 1:14). Sent into the world by the Father, the Word took on human form and entered into relationship with us by moving into our neighborhood and living like one of us.

But what was the educational program of the Son of God? How did he go about his task of teaching humanity of the Father and of the Gospel of the Son? John 2 tells us that he went to a wedding feast. Perhaps what is most remarkable is that we do not know who got married. It was an unnamed couple in Cana of Galilee, a small and unimportant town. The couple could not afford adequate wine supplies (a problem no doubt multiplied by the arrival of an itinerant rabbi and his thirsty disciples).

While at this wedding, Jesus chose to do the first of his miraculous signs. His turning of the water into wine had much greater implications than providing refreshment at the wedding reception. The mere fact that he came to the wedding is instructive in itself. When he could have been holding large public meetings or important conferences with religious and political leaders, he chose to attend the wedding of friends of the family.

Chapter 3 of John's gospel tells us that he held an all-night conversation with one man about his need of regeneration. Nicodemus was a member of the Jewish ruling council, but the focus of their conversation was highly personal. Rather than choosing to address the political body, Jesus spoke with one man alone at night. This conversation yields immensely powerful theology for the church, but it is significant that the context in which it is given is private conversation with one man. The picture emerging from the gospel narrative is of a relational approach to ministry.

Chapter 4 records another intimate conversation, this time with a woman whose personal life was in shambles and whose morality was bankrupt. The Samaritan woman had had five husbands and was currently living with a sixth man. No doubt she was a social outcast, a person to be avoided by respectable citizens. But when the Word became flesh, he chose to enter into relationship with her, telling her that he was the promised Messiah (John 4:26). No Jews had dealings with Samaritans, let alone with a Samaritan of this ilk. Nonetheless, it is to her that he went, and to her he told of the living water.

The outcome of this relationship was that many Samaritans believed in him. They first heard her description of the encounter, but then they experienced Jesus themselves. They heard his words in the context of his relationship with them, and this proved the truthfulness of his teaching.

Chapter 5 records his entrance into Jerusalem. It seems only logical that when the Word entered human history he should go to the seat of power in the region where he lived. But John tells us that when he entered Jerusalem he went to the pool of Bethesda and talked with a *paralytic*, a man who had been in that condition for thirty-eight years! Even in the urban center of his world, he chose to enter into relationship with one of the lowliest people there.

The modern Christian educator must learn from this example that effective ministry involves relationships as well as content. Teaching ministries devoid of personal contact are only partially successful in their ability to change lives. Powerful communicators can be effective in instructing others on matters of doctrine and Christian living, but the deeper life-changing results normally occur in the context of human relationships. Because we are called to love, we are called to relational involvement with others. It is impossible to love persons without that involvement.

There is a subtle temptation to establish educational programs in our churches, demand that the people support them, and insist that attendance will be a mark of spirituality. This attitude reverses the notion of education as service to people; it forces people to serve education. Education that is Christian proceeds from the base of loving people, seeking their best interests and concern, not demanding that they serve the programs.

CONTENT: WHAT WAS THE ROLE OF CONTENT IN JESUS' TEACHING?

Although it was not Jesus' primary concern to leave behind a body of doctrine, he did have propositional truth to communicate. Content played an important role in his ministry as he sought to reach his generation and the generations to come. Several observations can be made about the use of content in his teaching ministry.

Jesus referred to the Old Testament regularly, and it is evident that he believed it to be true. He accepted the authority of Scripture over human conduct, regularly arguing, "It is written . . . ," thus indicating the authoritative nature of God's Word. In addition, he believed the truthfulness of the Old Testament stories. For example, he taught his own resurrection from the dead by using the analogy of Jonah in the belly of the fish (Matt. 12:39–42). He regularly taught from the

Scriptures. Never is there any indication that he doubted the truthfulness or historical accuracy of the text.

Jesus believed that the witness of Scripture was the witness of God, that God was the true author of the Scripture. He recognized the human authors but believed that behind them was the divine author. Therefore he could either say, "Moses said" or "God said," because to him both were the same. Moreover, he argued that "Scripture cannot be broken" (John 10:35) and that "not the smallest letter, not the least stroke of a pen, will by any means disappear from the Law until everything is accomplished" (Matt. 5:18).

Perhaps he made his most stinging attacks on the religious leaders when he asked them, "Haven't you read . . . ?" (Matt. 12:3, 5). His message was clear: If they were to lead the people, they must know the Scripture. If they were to be the people of God, they must know the Word of God.

Conflict also arose on the issue of authority. The Pharisees equated their traditions with the authority of Scripture, believing that both were to be obeyed. But our Lord made strong distinctions between the traditions of men and the commands of God (Mark 7:1–13), distinguishing between what Moses said (v. 10) and what the Pharisees said (v. 11). The Pharisees believed that Moses and "the elders" (the historic founders of the Pharisees) were not only compatible but were in fact equal. Jesus saw this as a conflict between God's authority and human authority.

Jesus was concerned with teaching content, but the content was to be God's Word as revealed in Scripture. In an age when some Christians are questioning the truthfulness of Scripture, it is instructive to remember that our Lord both believed the Scripture to be true and taught it to

be true. He was not bothered by issues of "lower or higher criticism," but believed the Scripture at face value. Moreover, he

> *Effective Christian education leads people into Bible study as a means of growth, not as an end in itself. Faithful study of the Bible must be a means of learning to know and obey God.*

made a distinction between the religious traditions of the Pharisees and the Word of God. The former was seen as human, but the latter was divine.

Educators who follow Jesus' way of teaching will teach the Bible with confidence and authority and will distinguish between church traditions and God's Word. Effective Christian educators must be convinced of the validity of Scripture and be able to distinguish God's Word from human traditions.

Jesus believed the Scripture to be true, but he understood it to be a means to an end, and not an end in itself. He warned against the possibility of overexalting it by making it an end in itself (John 5:39–40). The purpose of Scripture is to point people to Christ. It is true that today many people have too low a view of Scripture, not accepting it as the actual written Word of God. But there are others with too high a view of Scripture, seeing it almost as an object of reverence. John Stott observes that these "become so absorbed in Scripture itself that they lose sight of its purpose, which is to manifest Christ to them."[5]

It is also possible to use Bible study as a way of escaping our responsibility as believers. It can be "safe" to rush off to yet another Bible study, thus effectively removing ourselves from any active ministry or involvement with people. The last thing some Christians need is another Bible study; rather, what is needed is to have our lives changed by the Bible. Effective Christian education leads people into Bible study as a means of growth, not as an end in itself. Faithful study of the Bible must be a means of learning to know and obey God.

When Jesus was brought to Pilate for his trial, Pilate examined him to determine if there was warrant for his execution. He concluded, "I find no basis for a charge against this man" (Luke 23:4). But the Jews screamed for his crucifixion, insisting, "He stirs up the people all over Judea by his teaching" (v. 5). The accusation brought against him was that he was a dynamic teacher! His teaching stirred people up, making them think and behave differently.

Unfortunately that accusation is rarely brought against the teaching ministry of our churches. We are charged with incompetence and irrelevance—two charges that can be painfully accurate. We teach lessons unrelated to life, and we do it poorly. We fail to engage people's hearts and minds as our Lord did and tend to insulate them rather than influence them for God. I look at the teaching ministry of Jesus and see principles that made him a dynamic teacher. These same principles can be incorporated into educational ministry today. We need conscious application of these matters in our teaching, so that by God's grace we too may stir up the people by our teaching.

Notes

1. This in no way should be construed to imply that systematic theology is unimportant. Given that humans are logical beings and that laws of communication require logic, it is absolutely necessary for the church to systematize its understanding of divine revelation. The only point I am making is that this was not a critical concern for our Lord's agenda as a teacher.

2. Again, this is not to imply that the systematic teaching of Scripture is unimportant or unbiblical. It only serves to point out that this was not a primary concern of our Lord.

3. See, for example, R. V. G. Tasker, *The Gospel According to St. John* (Grand Rapids: Eerdmans, 1960), 110; D. A. Carson, *The Gospel According to John* (Grand Rapids: Eerdmans, 1991), 333–34.

4. Norman W. Steineker and M. Robert Bell. *The Experiential Taxonomy: A New Approach to Teaching and Learning* (New York: Academic Press, 1979).

5. John R. W. Stott, *Christ the Controversialist* (Downers Grove: InterVarsity Press, 1972), 90.

4 | Understanding God, Understanding People

Modern Christian educators have worked hard to understand humankind—how we learn, how we develop, why we respond in the ways we do. Clearly the modern Christian educator must understand something of psychology, striving to comprehend the nature of persons. But there has not been equal effort to understand the nature of the God we serve and whose character we are to emulate. No wonder our faith is often feeble and our worship uninspired. We tend to put more emphasis on understanding people than on understanding God. We must learn to do both with equal fervor.

Attempts at building a theology of Christian education have normally begun in the arena of ecclesiology because the church is the context of spiritual growth.[1] Context is an important consideration, but this emphasis has been at the expense of deeper issues—the nature of spiritual maturity and the character of God. First we must explore the more foundational concept of what God is like; then we can move on to consider context. Understanding what God is like will shape our understanding of what it means to be spiritually mature and how we should help believers to grow toward maturity. Moreover, knowledge of

that God's holiness has been ignored in contemporary theologies of Christian education. But what does the Scripture say?

Isaiah's vision of the presence of God

Understanding what God is like will shape our understanding of what it means to be spiritually mature and how we should help believers to grow toward maturity.

---

what God is like helps believers keep themselves from idolatry, specifically the idolatry of creating God in our image, rather than accepting him as he is.

THE HOLINESS OF GOD

In a sense God's attribute of holiness is central to all his other attributes. It can be understood as the modifier or discriptor of all that God is. His love is a holy love; his grace, a holy grace; his anger, a holy anger; his justice, a holy justice.

Contemporary theology tends to stress God's love as his central characteristic. Indeed Scripture does stress the wonder of the depth and breadth and height of God's love (Eph. 3:18–19). But we have so focused on God's love that we have failed to understand that beneath his love resides his holiness. His love is so wondrous because it is a holy love.

Perhaps God's holiness has been ignored in recent years because of its necessary association with his justice. If God is truly holy, he must also be just, punishing sin as an affront to his moral purity. It seems much safer to believe in a gentle and loving God than in a holy and just God who judges sinfulness according to his justice. It may be for this reason

included seraphim who called out, "Holy, holy, holy is the LORD Almighty; the whole earth is full of his glory" (Isa. 6:3). Similarly, when John looked into the courts of heaven, he heard the four living creatures around the throne ceaselessly saying, "Holy, holy, holy is the Lord God Almighty, who was, and is, and is to come" (Rev. 4:8).

The focus of the worship in heaven is God and his holiness. It is the attribute of holiness, above all others, that prompts the heavenly worship. Only the attribute of holiness is raised to the level of triple pronouncement, showing the importance placed on it. Scripture uses repetition as a literary device for emphasis. R. C. Sproul observes:

> Only once in sacred Scripture is an attribute of God elevated to the third degree. . . . Only once is a characteristic of God mentioned three times in succession. The Bible says that God is holy, holy, holy. . . . The Bible never says that God is love, love, love, or mercy, mercy, mercy, or wrath, wrath, wrath, or justice, justice, justice. It does say that He is holy, holy, holy, the whole earth is full of His glory.[2]

Especially in the Old Testament, God seems to want this attribute known above all others. Thiessen wrote that God's holiness

> is emphasized by the bounds set about Mount Sinai when God came down upon the mountain . . . , by the division of the tabernacle and temple into the holy and most holy places . . . , by the prescribed offerings that must be brought if an Israelite would approach God . . . , by the institution of a special priesthood to mediate between God and the people . . . , by the many laws about impurity . . . , by the set feasts of Israel . . . , and by the isolation of Israel in Palestine.[3]

The central place given to the concept of holiness causes this attribute to be the regulatory principle of all that God is. He establishes his throne on the basis of his holiness (Ps. 47:8), and holiness defines above all else what God is like.

There are two aspects to the concept of holiness, both of which are central to understanding the main idea. The first aspect is that holiness indicates God's position or relationship to all else. It denotes that God is *separate and absolutely distinct* from all his creation.

The psalmist refers to God's majesty (Ps. 93:1), and Peter uses this term to refer to the greatness of Christ (2 Peter 1:16). References to divine majesty are rooted in the concept of this first meaning of holiness, and are always invitations to worship. Apprehending something of the majesty of God requires worship as the only appropriate response.

The second aspect of God's holiness, closely related to the first, is that of absolute moral perfection. That is, God is unlike all else in that he is completely without sin and is morally pure and righteous in all that he is and does. God's ethical holiness means that he is absolutely separate from any evil or injustice. This is why he demands that he be treated in special ways—to remind us that he is

unlike anything else we can ever encounter.

It is striking to contrast the Old Testament's strict guidelines for approaching God with the rather casual and almost cavalier ways people approach him today. In some contemporary worship there is almost no sense that God is holy, that he is to be revered and feared because of his terrible holiness. Rather, the tame God of some Christians can be approached in any way and with any attitude they desire. As a result they are unimpressed with God and see him as almost incidental to their daily lives. Focus turns to self. Happiness and fulfillment become all-consuming, and the biblical calls to deny ourselves and follow God are only faintly heard.

THE TRAUMA OF ENCOUNTERING HOLINESS

Encounters with holiness are always terrifying. When a human is allowed to see something of what God is like, there is always a response of terror and despair, because the presence of a holy God forces us to see the extent of our sinfulness.

When Isaiah had a vision of a holy God, he responded by turning the prophetic "oracle of doom" upon himself, proclaiming, "Woe to me!" (Isa. 6:5). "Woe to you" was the formula used by the prophets to pronounce judgement on God's enemies. But now Isaiah proclaimed doom on himself. The reason is clear. He cries, "I am ruined! For I am a man of unclean lips, and I live among a people of unclean lips, and my eyes have seen the King, the LORD Almighty" (Isa. 6:5). When people are allowed to see something of the glory of God, the response is invariably a profound sense of sadness and helplessness because of their sinfulness. True piety will always be accompanied by a sense of shame and despair because of one's sinfulness.

When Habakkuk was upset that God was not responding to his cries regarding injustice (Hab. 1:2–4), God told him to wait and see what he would do to the nations. But Habakkuk complained a second time, saying that God was being unjust to use the Babylonians to execute judgment on his people (Hab. 1:12–2:1). He set himself up as a judge of God's righteousness. The Lord's reply was powerful, vindicating his own righteousness and asking who this man was to question him. Habakkuk responded in a repentant prayer (ch. 3), confessing, "I heard and my heart pounded, my lips quivered at the sound; decay crept into my bones, and my legs trembled" (3:16).

After Habakkuk's encounter with the holiness of God, his bravado was replaced with fear, and his anger with despair. He now understood who he was, and his argument was ended.

Job also experienced the trauma of encountering God's holiness. Job was a blameless and upright man who feared God (Job 1:1). But God allowed Satan to test Job, removing his wealth, his family, and his health. Job's wife counseled him, "Curse God and die!" (Job 2:9). Job refused to do so and remained faithful to God. But his friends brought Job to the point of utter frustration as they accused him of unrighteousness and sin. Job finally cried out in anger that if only God would come down, he would personally argue his case before his Creator. The implication was that God was treating Job unfairly.

God answered Job by subjecting him to a terrible inquisition. We read in chapter after chapter how God questioned Job, challenging him to defend himself. The thrust of God's questioning was "Who are you to question me?" God asked, "Would you discredit my justice? Would you condemn me to justify yourself?" (Job 40:8).

Job then understood his unworthiness before God and made no further attempt to justify himself. But the ordeal continued as again God questioned Job. Finally, when Job responded, it was with the despair of one who has encountered a holy God. His reply in part was "My ears had heard of you, but now my eyes have seen you. Therefore I despise myself and repent in dust and ashes" (Job 42:5–6).

Similar experiences are recorded in the New Testament. As people encountered the holiness of Christ, they too were made painfully aware of their own sinfulness. Luke 5 records the calling of the first disciples. The setting was on the shores of the Sea of Galilee. After the disciples had fished all night and had caught nothing, Jesus told Peter to set out and cast their nets. Somewhat skeptically, Peter obeyed, and the catch was phenomenal. Recognizing that this was no ordinary rabbi, Peter's response was "Go away from me, Lord; I am a sinful man!" (Luke 5:8). Peter recognized that Jesus was holy, distinct from all other humans, and in doing so he was forced to confront his own sinfulness. Peter's rather strange response becomes understandable in light of the trauma of encountering holiness.

A similar response is seen in the people who witnessed the healing of the demon-possessed man whose story is recorded in Luke 8. After Jesus restored the man to his right mind, the people were "overcome with fear" (Luke 8:37). They asked Jesus to leave their shores. The Gerasenes recognized Jesus' holiness as a threat to them because somehow his uniqueness made them aware of their own sinfulness. If they had known—as Peter and the other disciples came to know—that the awesome holiness of God was counterbalanced by

God's amazing grace, they might have begged Jesus to stay among them.

THE GRACE OF GOD

Grace and Fear

In each of the encounters mentioned above, God's response is merciful. For Isaiah, he directs one of the seraphs (the creatures surrounding the throne) to bring a hot coal from the altar. With it Isaiah's lips are cleansed, his sin is atoned for, and his guilt is taken away (Isa. 6:7). God responds to the repentance of Habakkuk and Job also with mercy. Yet the fear of God is an appropriate response to an awareness of his holiness. It is a good gift from God because it is essential to spiritual change and growth in maturity. Indeed, "The fear of the LORD is the

A great frustration for many Christian educators is trying to motivate people to serve God. The primary motivator for serving God is a thankful heart.

beginning of knowledge, but fools despise wisdom and discipline" (Prov. 1:7).

The starting place for a relationship with God is a proper fear. The fear of God serves to purify the lives of his people. When God revealed himself in the terrible thunder and smoke on the mountain in

Exodus 19 and 20, Moses encouraged the people by telling them, "The fear of God will be with you to keep you from sinning" (Ex. 20:20).

There are at least two detrimental results of not having a proper fear of God. First, sin will more easily abound without the fear of God to restrain it. When the apostle Paul established that all people, Jew and Gentile alike, stood condemned before God's holiness, he summarized his argument by selected quotations from the Old Testament. He concluded by declaring, "There is no fear of God before their eyes" (Rom. 3:18). The terrible litany of sins recorded in Romans 1:18–3:20 reveals that humankind had lost any notion of the fear of God.

It is the grace of God that allows us to fear him as we should. Temptation is sometimes defeated simply because we are afraid to sin. Fear can be an important motivation to do right. Ultimately we should serve God from grateful hearts, but this response is learned first through the process of fearing God.

Second, not fearing God reduces our appreciation of God's mercy. Until we understand the desperate condition of sinners before a holy God, we cannot understand the magnitude and wonder of the grace he has shown us in Christ. The sad truth is that some people are not impressed with their salvation, not properly thankful for what God has done for them. Their lack of gratitude is rooted in a lack of understanding of what has been done on their behalf. As we grow in understanding who God is, we will also grow in understanding the wonders of his grace toward those who believe.

Grace and gratitude

Since the goal of the educational ministry of the church is to produce people who are spiritually mature, Christian educators must understand that the fear of God is the necessary starting place for a relationship with God. Because God is holy and we are sinful, we naturally respond in fear to who he is. But the fear is redemptive because it produces spiritual purity and gratitude in our hearts.

A great frustration for many Christian educators is trying to motivate people to serve God. Some Christians seem to believe that God exists to serve them, rather than seeing themselves as grateful servants of the most high God. The primary motivator for serving God is a thankful heart.

The narrative regarding Isaiah's vision of God shows that after Isaiah had been reduced to terror by seeing God's holiness, the Lord responded in grace, offering atonement for his sins and calling him to service. Isaiah's response to all of this was his grateful cry, "Here am I. Send me!" (Isa. 6:8).

The dimensions of God's love become more apparent when we understand that his justice requires the punishment of sin and that in his grace he sent his Son to die in our place. The mercy of the cross becomes utterly incomprehensible when it is seen against the backdrop of a holy and wrathful God. When the fear of God is in our hearts, we understand his grace more completely, and thankfulness will then lead us to service. The apostle Paul rooted his appeal to his readers to serve God in the fact that God had been merciful to them (Rom. 12:1–2).

Grace and Human Dignity

The creation account of Genesis 1 states that "God created man in his own image, in the image of God he created him; male and female he created them" (Gen. 1:26–27). All human beings have great worth and dignity because they are made in the image of God. We all bear the likeness of God in our beings and therefore are to be treated with respect. Moreover, regardless of ability, wealth, race, sex, or any other factor, we are to reflect the holiness of God. We are to be holy because he is holy.

Since all people have dignity because they bear God's image, Christian education must use educational techniques that are respectful of persons. Approaches that are manipulative or demeaning must be avoided. Even approaches that may produce impressive results but do not value or respect persons must not be used. Rather, the holiness of God and the resultant dignity of his sixth-day creation demand educational techniques that respect all people as having great worth.

It is only the grace of God that can restore human dignity and guarantee the eternal worth of a human being. We were made in the image of God, "crowned . . . with glory and honor" (Ps. 8:5), but we are bent on self-destruction, and only God's grace can bring us back to wholeness. "Therefore, if anyone is in Christ, he is a new creation; the old has gone, the new has come!" (2 Cor. 5:17).

THE PROBLEM OF HUMAN SINFULNESS

Because all people are made in God's image, they have dignity and worth. But Scripture and experience also teach us that human beings are sinful, failing to live up to the potential they have been given by God. Scripture relates not only the account of creation but also the story of the Fall. Therefore any theology of sanctification and spiritual growth must include within it a proper view of human sinfulness.

In the modern era, both education as a whole and Christian education in particular have tended either to reduce or ignore the biblical teaching on sin. But critical to a well-developed approach to Christian education is a proper understanding of human sinfulness. This will help shape both how we view the educational process and our understanding of God's work in the life of his people.

The Biblical Teaching on Sin

Scripture declares that "everyone who sins breaks the law; in fact, sin is lawlessness" (1 John 3:4). God has given us laws to be obeyed, and sin is the breaking of God's law. Properly understood, sin is *cosmic treason* against the authority of God. It is a willful defiance of his authority.

Sin may be either an active disobedience or a passive ignoring of God. Active sin is the willful disobedience of God's law, whereas passive sin is neglecting responsibility or unintentionally violating God's law. James wrote, "Anyone, then, who knows the good he ought to do and doesn't do it, sins" (James 4:17). Chapters 4 and 5 of Leviticus contain instructions for the cleansing of those who *unintentionally* sin against God. Our Lord carried this teaching into the New Testament, teaching that even those who do not know what is expected of them will be punished, but their punishment will be less severe than the punishment of those who willfully disobey (Luke 12:47–48).

All people understand that human beings behave badly at times, but there is disagreement regarding what causes people to sin. The contemporary concept regarding the origin of sin is that it comes from our environment. When this thought is carried over to the moral realm, it contends that our primary problem is our environment—bad homes, bad schools, or bad backgrounds.

If this is true, then no one is responsible for his or her behavior. "It's not my fault" becomes the proper explanation for all that we do, because we are only products of our environment. Modern society helps people avoid responsibility for their behavior by arguing a form of determinism that teaches it is environment that leads us astray, never our innate sinfulness. For this reason, governments put millions of dollars into housing projects and other efforts to create environments that will produce "good" people.

Clearly, as Christians we must be concerned with the social needs of people and be involved with helping people live in better environments. But we must also understand that human needs are deeper than economics and environment. Improving environmental conditions is a necessary step to helping people, but it is not sufficient to change people at the core of their being.

Scripture offers a different explanation for radical human sinfulness. It contends that sinfulness is a *family disease* in that it is inherited from our first parents, but it also insists that we are responsible for our own rebellion against God. The origin of sin was in the Garden of Eden, where Adam rebelled against God. Paul wrote, "Therefore, just as sin entered the world through one man, and death through sin, and in this way death came to all men, because all sinned . . . ," (Rom. 5:12) teaching that the propensity to sin is passed on to all humans. In this sense sin is more than our willful rebellion against God; it is also a condition that is carried by the entire race.[4] Contrary to the contemporary assessment that humans are inherently good or are passive reactors to environment, Scripture contends that in our hearts we are sinful, ever rebelling against God.

Scripture presents graphic descriptions of our condition. For example, Genesis reports, "The LORD saw how great man's wickedness on the earth had become, and that every inclination of the thoughts of his heart was only evil all the time" (Gen. 6:5). Jeremiah said, "The heart is deceitful above all things and beyond cure" (Jer. 17:9).

Scripture teaches that humans are infected throughout with sin and that there is no good within us. The result is that we stand guilty before a holy God, utterly condemned and without hope. In fact we are enemies of God and "by nature objects of wrath" (Eph. 2:1–3). The strongest indication of the seriousness of our sin is the death of Christ. How serious must our guilt be that only the blood of Christ could cleanse us from sin! Christ's agony on the cross indicates not only the extent of God's love for us but also the seriousness of our condition before him.

Modern society has become quite adept at denying sinfulness. We use psychological and sociological categories to describe our sinfulness.[5] People are described as having weaknesses or making or suffering lapses rather than as sinning against God. But Scripture exposes sin for what it is—rebellion against God and a destructive force in human lives.

Theology describes human sinfulness as *radical corruption* or *total depravity*. The use of these terms is an attempt to capture the thrust of the Bible's teaching on sinfulness. The terms do *not* mean that human beings are as bad as they can possibly be. Rather, they imply that sinfulness extends to the total being. Berkhof describes it this way:

> The immediate concomitant of the first sin . . . was the total depravity of human nature. The contagion of his sin at once spread through the entire man, leaving no part of his nature untouched, but vitiating every power and faculty of body and soul. . . . Total depravity here does not mean that human nature was at once as thoroughly depraved as it could possibly become. In the will this depravity manifested itself as spiritual inability.[6]

Some of the Bible's strong statements regarding human sinfulness seem overstated when we consider actual people we know. We all know people who are "good"—decent people, both Christian and pagan, who live exemplary lives, helping others and promoting moral purity. In what sense can we say that these people are not good?

Good and *bad* are relative terms, taking their definition from comparisons. They are understood in relation to some standard of comparison. For example, our family had a dog named Maggie who was a good dog. By that I mean that she had a pleasant nature, a pretty dog, and quite well-behaved. She was sort of a cocker spaniel. Her legs were too long, her tail was not clipped, and her ears were too small for a normal spaniel. If we had attempted to show our "good" dog at a kennel club, we would have been laughed out of the show. She was only "good" when compared to nonprofessional standards held by those who are just interested in a good family pet. But according to the standards of professional breeders, she was not "good" at all. She would be useless as a show dog.

Likewise, the biblical standard of "goodness" is God's moral character. While there are many "good" people when compared to other people, their "goodness" pales to nothing when compared to the goodness of God. It is in this sense that the Bible concludes that "there is no one who does good" (Rom. 3:12). Only the most mature believers will understand the radical nature of their sinfulness. Most tend to be blissfully unaware of their true nature before a holy God.

Goodness is comprised of two aspects—action and motive. A good deed is one that corresponds to the will and law of God and proceeds from a heart that is seeking to please God and loves God. Therefore righteousness is a matter of both external conformity and internal motivation. The problem with the Pharisees was that *externally* they conformed to the law, but *internally* they were corrupt (Matt. 23:27–28). The problem is that many times people will do the right thing but for the wrong reason. Their actions appear to be good, but in reality, in reference to their motivation, they are not good.

Several years ago a large group of rock musicians created a song-and-video tape entitled "We Are the World." The music was written and performed to help raise funds because of a famine in West Africa. One of the musicians was asked why she performed in the video. Her response was that it was good to help other people, "and besides," she said, "it makes you feel good when you can help someone else." What appeared on the surface to be a wonderful humanitarian deed—and indeed the music did provide funds to help alleviate starvation—was in the end also another form of self-serving: helping others so that she could feel good herself. The bottom line was still self-happiness and self-fulfillment.

Enlightened self-interest is the process of doing good to others as a means of helping oneself. But Scripture tells us that the only acceptable motivation for any action is *pleasing God* and bringing glory to him (Col. 3:17). This is why the Bible concludes that "all our righteous acts are like filthy rags" (Isa. 64:6). Even the best acts of human kindness are many times tainted by improper actions.

My wife and I have chosen to be foster parents as a means of expressing our Christian faith. As of this writing we have taken twenty-five children into our home and raised them for various lengths of time. I wish I could say that our motivation has always been completely pure—that we desired only to please God and serve children. But because of our own sinful hearts, other motives such as pride or the desire for recognition have also influenced us. The children have still been served, but such actions can hardly be called righteous. They are "good" according to human standards, but they still fall short of God's standards.

The outcome of the sinfulness of human beings is that in one sense they actually *hate* God because of the threat of his holiness. This hatred is not in the sense of a conscious emotional state but rather in the sense of indifference toward God, which is the absence of love. Human beings flee *from* God rather than *to* him because of the threat of holiness. This is what Paul means when he says, "There is no one who seeks God" (Rom. 3:11, paraphrasing Ps. 53:2). Separation from God is imbedded deep in our beings and is expressed through the aversion some people feel toward religion or faith. Depravity can be seen in the actions and attitudes of all people, both Christians and pagans. Only God is good.

Charles Hodge believed that all people are aware of their sinfulness:

> Every man in virtue of his being a moral creature, and because he is a sinner, has therefore in his own consciousness the knowledge of sin. . . . He knows that sin is not simply limitation of his nature; not merely a subjective state of his own mind, having no character in the sight of God; that it is not only something which is unwise, or derogatory to his own dignity; or simply inexpedient because hurtful

to his own interests, or injurious to the welfare of others.[7]

Human depravity is not just an abstract doctrine; it has direct relevance to how people behave and how we must think about and approach the ministry of Christian education.

IMPLICATIONS FOR CHRISTIAN EDUCATION

Human beings left to themselves would never seek God. But the mercy of God is greater than our sin. The essence of mercy is that it is voluntary. God has chosen to call people to himself and enable them to believe in him.

As a theology of Christian education is developed, it must include a proper view of human sinfulness and a proper view of God's redemptive involvement with his people. We must understand both the extent of human sinfulness and the magnitude of God's grace. Only then can we move toward a proper understanding of the educational ministry of the church.

Several implications for Christian education can be drawn. First, we must understand that *unredeemed people cannot understand spiritual truth.* "The man without the Spirit does not accept the things that come from the Spirit of God, for they are foolishness to him, and he cannot understand them, because they are spiritually discerned" (1 Cor. 2:14).

The unredeemed are incapable of understanding spiritual truth because they do not have the Holy Spirit in them. Spiritual truth is understood by means of the Holy Spirit. Just as a person without eyes cannot be expected to see, so those without the Spirit of God within them cannot be expected to understand spiritual truth. The apostle Paul asks, "Who among men knows the thoughts of a man except the man's spirit within him? In the same way no one knows the thoughts of God except the Spirit of God" (1 Cor. 2:11).

Our family used to have a particularly obstinate cat named Dolores. She insisted on sharpening her claws on our couch. She believed that it was a "dog eat cat" world out there and that sharp claws were essential for survival. I believed that couches were for sitting and that sharpening claws on them was unacceptable behavior. Dolores and I never clearly communicated on this matter because she had the spirit of a cat, and I had the spirit of a man in me.

In the same way, there will never be clear communication regarding spiritual matters between those who have the Spirit of God and those who do not. It is not a matter of educational gimmickry or powerful persuasion. Unless the Spirit of God enters a person, he or she is incapable of understanding spiritual truth.

I have spent hours explaining the Gospel to a particular friend, making the facts of salvation as plain as possible. Her response has usually been "I don't know what you mean." Without the Spirit of God in her, she cannot understand even the simple truths of the cross of Christ. To her the cross is foolishness.

Second, *there must be supernatural intervention in our ministry for lives to be touched.* As educators we are able to entertain, enlighten, teach, and lead people, but to enable a person to grow in faith requires the touch of God. Human beings cannot cause others to grow in their faith. We can only create a context in which a person can grow.

Christian education is more than an educational endeavor; it is a spiritual battle. We dare not trivialize the work by creating silly little gimmicks to help people learn. Rather, we must understand that we are dependent on the Father to be merciful to his people and to send his Spirit to help them learn.

Prayer in the educational ministry of the church is not optional; it is imperative. When we recognize that unless *God* is at work our effort is in vain, then we grasp the essential place of prayer in the teaching ministry of the church.

Christian education is best understood as both a natural and a supernatural process.

Third, *Christian education is a partnership between God and the educator.* Although we are absolutely dependent on God for our results, still we have a responsibility to teach in the best ways possible. God uses the efforts of human beings to build up his people. We are commanded to teach, with the understanding that God will use our efforts and by his Spirit cause people to grow.

Christian education is best understood as both a natural and a supernatural process. God has created the world to function according to natural law; and we are responsible to study and discover the natural order of things. Learning is part of the natural order and therefore requires that we understand the process of learning. As learning is understood, principles of teaching may be extrapolated. Behind this process is the assumption that God has created humankind to learn in certain ways and that the educator is responsible to understand and work with the ways people learn.

Therefore, being fully aware of the fact that they are totally dependent on the supernatural work of God to allow their teaching to touch a person spiritually, Christian educators are responsible to teach well and to pray well. They are in dynamic partnership with God, working in both the natural and the supernatural realms simultaneously.

Notes

1. See, for example, Gene Getz, *Sharpening the Focus of the Church* (Chicago: Moody Press, 1974); Lawrence O. Richards, *A Theology of Christian Education* (Grand Rapids: Zondervan, 1975).
2. R. C. Sproul, *The Holiness of God* (Wheaton, Ill.: Tyndale House, 1985), 40.
3. Henry Clarence Thiessen, *Introductory Lectures in Systematic Theology* (Grand Rapids: Eerdmans, 1949), 129.
4. Some people believe that this is unfair because we are being blamed for something we did not do. The assumption is that God made a "bad choice" when he designated Adam our representative in the Garden. But the fact is that we would have done exactly the same had we been in his position. Moreover, if we reject the idea of Adam's federal headship for sinfulness, so also must we reject the idea of Jesus' federal headship for salvation.
5. I do not mean to deny the validity of psychology or sociology; but I do mean to warn about seeing *fundamental theological issues* in categories other than the way Scripture describes them. While there is great value in the social sciences, we must not become so enamored with them that we lose our theological moorings.
6. Louis Berkhof, *Systematic Theology*, 2d ed. (Grand Rapids: Eerdmans, 1941), 225–26.
7. Charles Hodge, *Systematic Theology*, vol. 2 (Grand Rapids: Eerdmans, 1977), 181.

The Renewal of the Mind

CHAPTER
5

The Renewal of the Mind

W e don't have any theology; we just love the Lord," a young Christian said recently. He explained that his group was "not into head trips" about their faith. What a person believed was of little consequence to them—they only wanted to love Jesus. Is this an adequate and helpful perspective on what it means to be a Christian?

Christian faith is a matter of what we believe, whom we love, and how we behave. Its components are rational, relational, and behavioral, all combining to make up the substance of faith. Spiritual maturity, then, is a matter of holding to correct beliefs, loving God more deeply, and living in growing obedience to God. Together these three aspects are necessary for spiritual maturity.

Unfortunately, Christianity experienced a highly "scholastic" period when faith was reduced to a series of intricate theological/philosophical propositions that were to be memorized, mastered, and argued. The charge of "dead orthodoxy" was rightly earned because it was entirely possible to play this sort of academic game and never

59

have one's heart touched by the love of God and the depth of his grace. Moreover, this sort of thinking led people to a faith devoid of compassion and soul; rather, Christianity became, for some, the ability to argue doctrine effectively.

Sadly, vestiges of this tradition remain in some groups, where effective Christian education is understood to be training people to learn these arguments and then wield them against those who believe differently. Theology is reduced to matters of no consequence—matters that can be debated and discussed, but hardly lived. As a backlash against this kind of reli-

> *If Christian education is to be effective, it must recapture a proper understanding of the role of the mind in spiritual growth.*

gion, Christianity for many has become anything but a matter for the mind. For these people, beliefs are rooted in one's experience rather than in God's self-revelation in Scripture. Matters of *orthodoxy* (right belief) are considered irrelevant as long as people "love God." How God is perceived is not considered important; only the fact that one loves God is deemed of consequence. The result is that the mind is left out of Christian faith and experience, and thinking is deemed peripheral to being a Christian. When people consider issues of orthodoxy and heresy to be of no consequence, they open the door to all sorts of trouble.

Ultimately maturity is a matter of lifestyle. When we stand before God to be judged, it will be on the basis of our works—how we have lived our lives in light of our faith in Christ. Paul warns, "For we must all appear before the judgment seat of Christ, that each one may receive what is due him for the things done while in the body, whether good or bad" (2 Cor. 5:10). Therefore the final purpose of the educational ministry of the church is to change lives. But the mind is not uninvolved with this process; Scripture asserts that part of the transformation is to be in our thinking. Paul warns the Ephesians that they "must no longer live as the Gentiles do, in the futility of their thinking. They are darkened in their understanding and separated from the life of God because of the ignorance that is in them" (Eph. 4:17–18).

If Christian education is to be effective, it must recapture a proper understanding of the role of the mind in spiritual growth. The church must again value the way people think as an important aspect of being the people of God. We must learn to follow the biblical imperatives regarding the relationship of thinking and acting, valuing both the cognitive and the volitional in Christian living.

The apostle Paul wrote:

Therefore, I urge you, brothers, in view of God's mercy, to offer your bodies as living sacrifices, holy and pleasing to God— which is your spiritual worship. Do not conform any longer to the pattern of this world, but be transformed *by the renewing of your mind.* Then you will be able to test and approve what God's will is—his good, pleasing and perfect will (Rom. 12:1–2, italics mine).

This passage provides a paradigm for spiritual growth and a clear mandate for the educational ministry of the church.

The book of Romans is central in its doctrinal clarity and importance. Calvin wrote regarding Romans, "When anyone gains a knowledge of this Epistle he has an entrance opened to him to all the most hidden treasures of Scripture."[1]

Romans 12:1–2 functions as the transitional point from the doctrinal or ethical portion of the epistle to the practical or imperative portion. As he does in all of his writings, the apostle Paul leads his readers from theological foundations to the outworking of lifestyle. The word "therefore" indicates that the following section grows out of the preceding teaching.

There is always a danger of holding a theology unrelated to practice, or of following a practice unrelated to theology. Theory and practice must always go together, both in education and in life. Scripture knows nothing of abstract theological discussion, nor of ungrounded lifestyle demands. Theological truth is ultimately to be expressed in living that is consistent with it. After developing the doctrines of God's mercy, Paul now turns his attention to matters of living.

His ultimate call to the Romans is that they must experience such a radical change as to be transformed. The transformation is to be a *metamorphosis*, literally a "change of form." When a caterpillar changes its form into a butterfly, it is metamorphosed into a new creature. So the Christian is to be metamorphosed from sinner to saint. Luther commented on this idea, observing that

> man [the Christian] is always in the condition of nakedness, always in the state of becoming, always in the state of potentiality, always in the condition of activity. He is always in sin and always in justification. He is always a sinner, but also always repentant and so always righteous. We are in part sinners, and in part righteous, and so nothing else than penitents.[2]

The process of transformation in the life of the believer is the process of sanctification, or growing in Christ. It is God's will for his people that they continue to become mature and holy (1 Thess. 4:3). It is therefore imperative that believers be transformed.

The theological basis for this appeal is the *mercy of God*. The first eleven chapters of the epistle describe how all people are condemned because of sin before a holy God, but they also declare that God has been merciful, sending his own Son to die in our place. By faith alone we can be justified, and by faith we can be freed from the laws of sin and death. In light of this mercy our response should be to be transformed.

Our primary need as we stand condemned before a holy God is to be forgiven. Only after we understand something of God's holiness and our sinfulness can we understand something of the mysteries of his grace. If we comprehend that God is merciful to us as sinners, thankfulness functions as a motivation to serve him. But if we view his grace as cheap and inconsequential, we are hardly motivated to transformed living.

The contemporary problem is, of course, that we have lost any notion of God's holiness, our sinfulness, and the magnitude of God's grace. Rooted in a theological vacuum regarding God's holiness, contemporary theology has little to say regarding God's mercy. As a result, believers are not highly motivated to serve God out of thankful hearts. They turn to the pragmatic question, "What will I get from this?" rather than the more appropriate "How can I serve God?" Believers must be taught to understand and respond to God's mercy.

The transformed life is to be expressed by a radical new dedication to God. Paul uses the terminology of sacrificial offering, urging us to offer our bodies as "living sacrifices," which he sees as a reasonable form of worship. Stuart Briscoe observes:

Paul's use of the words *present* (the verb used is the technical expression for presenting a victim for sacrifice) and *sacrifice* show clearly that he expects believers to hand over their bodies to God in a manner resembling the way people of Israel presented their offerings to the Lord. There were, of course, two main kinds of offerings: first, those which led to reconciliation; and, second, those which were an expression of celebration after reconciliation had been accomplished.[3]

The living sacrifice is the ultimate worship of God. Rather than being a matter of liturgy or music, worship that is pleasing to God is lived out in the arena of life. Doxology is ultimately a matter of obedience. It is no good to praise God with raised hands and glad singing and then deny him in actions. Worship concerns how we live, not the style of our church services. Jim Guyer, pastor of the Beulah Presbyterian Church in Pittsburgh, often dismisses his worship services with the declaration "The service is over; let the worship begin." He reminds his people that worship is carried out ultimately in life.

Barclay wrote:

True worship is the offering to God of one's body, and all that one does every day with it. Real worship is not the offering to God of a liturgy, however noble, and a ritual, however magnificent. *Real worship is the offering of everyday life to him*, not something transacted in a church, but something which sees the whole world as the temple of the living God (italics his).[4]

Moreover, Paul calls us to moral purity, reminding us that our sacrifice to God must be holy. Some Christians believe they can be related to God and yet remain sinful in their practice. But true believers will be holy—striving to please God in *all* they do, avoiding sin and recognizing immorality in all its modern forms.

Radical dedication to God requires nonconformity to the world. Here the term *world* refers to the sentiments and morals of the society.[5] It means that we are not to accept nor be controlled by those values of our society that are opposed to the values of the kingdom of God. Worldliness is being controlled by lust, greed, power, or any other value common to sinful humanity. But those who are being transformed are resisting these values and striving first to seek God's kingdom and his righteousness (Matt. 6:33).

It is dangerous to reduce the concept of worldliness to matters of clothing or entertainment without confronting the larger issue of values. It is lamentable that there are people who would never think of smoking or drinking alcohol, but who are racists or materialists and see no conflict between those values and their Christian faith. But such values come from the world and have no place in the kingdom of God.

The educational issue at stake here is that this transformation is to be accomplished by the renewing of our minds. When people learn to think in new ways, with new values and new categories in place, their minds are renewed. The task of Christian education is to teach so that people's minds may be renewed.

In one sense, God's act of regeneration creates a renewed mind at the time of the new birth. But it is also true that renewal is to be an ongoing process in the lives of believers. This continual process of renewal is expressed several places in Scripture. Second Corinthians 4:16 refers to being inwardly renewed day by day, and Colossians 3:10 speaks of putting on "the new self, which is being renewed in knowledge in the image of its Creator."

Educational ministry in the church is not only for the acquisition of knowledge but also so that people may learn to think Christianly about all matters of life. Having our minds renewed means learning to think in new ways, according to the teachings of Scripture, about all things so that we may "take captive every thought to make it obedient to Christ" (2 Cor. 10:5).

If people do not hold to or understand the biblical categories regarding reality and ethical matters, they can scarcely be expected to think in conformity with them. If a person has never heard of righteousness, for example, it is not surprising that he or she would not think about an issue as it relates to matters of righteousness. We cannot expect people to think or act like Christians if they do not even know Christian categories.

For example, some may say, "We want to love God." But what is the nature of the God they want to love? If they have not been taught the Bible, they may not have any sense of God's wrath toward sin and may totally omit that aspect of the character of God. Then when they encounter his justice toward those who oppose him, they will have no categories in which to think about or make sense of the occurrence of God's wrath. But if they have been having their minds renewed by instruction in biblical constructs and ways of thinking, they will be able to understand better how God works in his world.

The outcome of transformation and radical dedication is that the believer will "be able to test and approve what God's will is" (Rom. 12:2). Many believers accept the idea of the will of God in theory, but in practice they do not have the faintest idea of what his will might be. God's will is thought of as some mystical reality that one can never quite find or follow, sort of like the plot of a good mystery novel. Paul resists that idea, insisting that the will of God is knowable and provable through the process of radical dedication to God. Those who will be transformed, radically giving themselves to God in moral purity, resisting the influences of the world around them, will know with assurance the goodness of the will of God.

John Murray wrote that to test or approve the will of God means

> to discover, to find out or learn by experience what the will of God is. It is a will that will never fail or be found wanting. If life is aimless, stagnant, fruitless, lacking in content, it is because we are not entering by experience into the richness of God's will. The commandment of God is exceedingly broad. There is not a moment of life that the will of God does not command, no circumstance that it does not fill with meaning if we are responsive to the fullness of his revealed counsel for us.[6]

Knowing the will of God is contingent upon obeying God's word revealed in Scripture. Those who genuinely do what is required of them in Scripture will find in their own experience the goodness of God's will. It is not a matter of mystical insight; rather, discerning the will of God grows out of having a mind transformed by learning and obeying Scripture.

EDUCATIONAL IMPLICATIONS

Many implications for Christian education can be drawn from this passage, but four seem especially compelling. Each is rather broad in its scope but serves to provide a foundation for education that leads toward spiritual maturity.

First, *instruction in God's Word is essential to help people renew their minds.* If people are to learn to think and act according to God's Word, it is obvious that they must know his Word. We must learn to obey both the prompting of the Holy Spirit within us and the clear commands that do not teach the Word of God. Our minds must be brought into captivity to Christ, and this can be accomplished only as the Word of God is learned.

If people are to act like Christians, they must think like Christians. If people are to think like Christians, they must first know what Scripture says and what it requires of them.

---

of Scripture. In a fine essay "Putting the Renewed Mind to Work," Douglas Moo observes:

> Certainly the New Testament strongly emphasizes the role of the Holy Spirit in directing the steps of the believer. Jesus promised that he would send "the Counselor, the Holy Spirit" to "teach you all things" (John 14:25–26, NIV). And Paul says to the Galatians: "Live by the Spirit, and you will not gratify the desires of your sinful nature" (Gal. 5:16, NIV). But it is important to recognize that the New Testament does not stop there. In the same passage in which He promised the gift of the Spirit, Jesus also told his disciples: "Whoever has my commands and obeys them, he is the one who loves me" (John 14:21, NIV). And Paul, the great apostle of freedom in the Spirit, reminded the wayward Corinthians that "keeping God's commands is what counts" (1 Cor. 7:19, NIV).[7]

Education that leads to spiritual growth must communicate the truths of Scripture clearly. If people are to act like Christians, they must think like Christians. If people are to think like Christians, they must first know what Scripture says and what it requires of them. It is irresponsible to offer in the church any educational programs

Recent trends in church education have been away from Bible and theology and toward "life issues" and need-oriented courses. These can be helpful to a certain degree, but the ultimate help resides in teaching people the themes and issues of Scripture so that they may think about life from the broad perspectives offered in the Bible. Only through learning such themes as holiness and justice, sin and redemption, grace and forgiveness can the people of God have their minds renewed to think in biblical ways.

Responsible Christian education teaches Scripture in ways that help people discover its themes and concerns. Bible studies that are purely informational or fail to explore application to life will not be effective. But studies controlled by sound exegesis and sensitive to the contemporary culture can do much to help people learn to see life according to the intent of Scripture. The value of theology in this regard is that it delineates profound and timeless concepts essential to spiritual growth and development. Christian education must value the insights of both biblical and systematic theology and teach these insights in the context of real life issues so that people can learn to think and act Christianly.

Christian education must avoid teaching Bible and theology as ends in themselves, reducing them to purely cognitive constructs. Rather, studies must be designed so that students learn to *think* in biblical ways, using theology as a guide to categories of thinking. Instructional approaches that lead people into analysis and problem-solving activities, using theological insights, will do much to help them have their minds renewed.

Second, *adult converts must be taught to understand life in new ways*. The adult who has been converted must learn to reject old ways of thinking and be trained to think according to scriptural principles. New ways of understanding reality and new ways of relating to people and to God will be required.

Referring to the title of his book *Born Again*, Chuck Colson observes, "For me it is anything but a cliché suggesting that someone has arrived at some state of spiritual superiority; it means only a fresh start at putting my life in order—but it had to come with the renewing of my spirit."[8]

He goes on to chronicle his salvation experience and the process of his learning to think in new ways. His subsequent books provide insight into the process of how a superior mind such as his has been retrained to think about life from new perspectives. Seeing, for example, that there is actually spiritual warfare taking place and that indeed there are kingdoms in conflict is the result of having his thinking and perceptions shaped by biblical truth.

The ancient practice of *catechesis* was the instruction of adult converts in the truths of Christianity. In a sense, when adults are converted, they must be catechized. It is not enough that they have a "born-again experience"; they must now be taught to think and live according to the realities of the kingdom of God.

Having their minds renewed means teaching them to reject their former ways of thinking and to replace these with new, biblical ways of thinking. This was the work of Jesus with his disciples and the work of Paul with his converts. This is also the work of the educational ministries of the church.

Too often in the contemporary era, Christians have believed that Christ could simply be "added to" their existing beliefs. Jesus becomes one more thing to believe in, one more addition to a life philosophy. But Jesus is much more than that, and being a Christian is more than adding Christian principles to our lives. Jesus requires full allegiance to his teachings, and being a Christian means having our lives radically transformed by the Gospel and God's Spirit within us. Being a Christian is a matter of both adopting God's perspective and letting go of our own flawed perspectives. For the adult convert, this requires training in the things of God.

Third, *children can be taught from the beginning to think Christianly*. Paul's admonition to "bring them up in the training and instruction of the Lord" (Eph. 6:4) means in part that parents should train their children to think like Christians. The wonderful privilege of Christian parents is that we can teach our children God's truth. Rather than having to fight the battles of flushing errors in perception from their minds, we can from the beginning teach them the truth.

Writing to Christian parents, Horace Bushnell in his classic *Christian Nurture* wrote that the aim of his argument was to establish

> that the child is to grow up a Christian, and never know himself as being otherwise. In other words, the aim, effort, and expectation should be . . . that he is to open on the world as one that is spiritu-

ally renewed, not remembering the time he went through a technical experience [of conversion], but seeming to have loved what is good from his earliest years.[9]

The strength of Bushnell's position is that he valued and encouraged Christian parents to train their children to be Christians. From their earliest days they

> *If the educational task is to teach a Christian worldview, we dare not trivialize childhood education.*

can be taught a Christian worldview, seeing and understanding the world around them from a Christian perspective.

All people, including the children of believers, must be regenerated by God to have their minds renewed. But the educational task in regard to these children does not have to include the *retraining* of their minds. They, like Timothy, can be taught from infancy the holy Scriptures, which are able to make them wise for salvation through faith in Jesus Christ (2 Tim. 3:15).

The problem of how to relate to public schools is not a new one. In the third century Tertullian wrote a treatise entitled *On Idolatry*. In it he discussed how the church should relate to the pagan literature of his day. No compromiser, Tertullian made it clear that he hated the poets who advocated idolatry, extolling the myths of the gods. But he was also a realist, knowing that children must understand this literature to function in their society. Having great faith in the power of the Christian home to counteract the

influences of the society, Tertullian came to the conclusion that believers should send their children to pagan schools, but that no true believer should ever be a schoolmaster. As a teacher, the Christian would be asked to advocate paganism as a valid worldview, and this would be unacceptable.[10]

Training children to think Christianly does not require alternative school systems. While many believers value either home schooling or private Christian schools, it is also possible to train a child to adopt values different from the values of the public schools. Scripture does not demand alternative school systems, but it does require nurturing children in the Lord. Conscious and careful education by parents and the church working in concert can easily counteract the negative influences of a secular school system. This requires that parents and Sunday school teachers be aware of what is being taught in the public schools and that they open discussion with the child about these issues. Like Tertullian, we too can and should have confidence in the power of the Christian family to shape the minds of the children for the good of the kingdom.

If the educational task is to teach children a Christian worldview, we dare not trivialize childhood education. Too often we allow the educational ministry to children to be entertainment rather than education. And unfortunately, it is poor entertainment at best. But the training of children can be both enjoyable and meaningful as we teach them to look at life through the lens of Christian truth. Teachers who love children and understand theology can do much to shape the way a child thinks about life. Parents who will take the time to talk respectfully with a child can do much to fashion that child's thinking in ways appropriate to the kingdom. Robert Coles has shown that children do think in strongly theological modes.[11] Christian parents and teachers can tap this resource and mold it into an important aspect of Christian maturity for the child.

Fourth, *Scripture is essential for renewing the mind and must be taught in relation to life.* There is a difference between having biblical knowledge and having biblical understanding. Biblical knowledge means that people have biblical information stored away in their memories. It means that there are facts and data to be drawn upon, perhaps even verses or portions of Scripture that have been memorized. But it is possible to be knowledgeable about the Bible without having understanding of it.

One of the problems with the Pharisees was that they had knowledge but not understanding. They knew a great amount of detail, but they missed the broader implications. They could "strain out a gnat but swallow a camel" (Matt. 23:24) when it came to their biblical understanding. Jesus taught the people very little regarding the *content* of the Old Testament, but he taught them much regarding the *meaning* of the Scriptures. The Pharisees did not understand the meaning of his teachings.

The purpose of learning Scripture is that our minds may be renewed. Scripture is a means to an end, not an end in itself. When we stand before God, he will not check our memory verses; rather, we will give an account of how we lived (2 Cor. 5:10). Scripture is to be a guide to living, teaching us how to think about life issues. Therefore biblical education not related to life serves only to delay the process of having our minds renewed.

Responsible Bible teaching explores the truth of a passage but also explores how that truth relates to life. It teaches people not only content but also meaning. The process of thinking biblically must be modeled in the classroom, and then the students must gain experience in thinking through issues themselves.

CONCLUSION

Christian faith can never be reduced only to matters of the mind; but neither can the mind be removed from faith. How we think about things does matter, and as believers we are to have our minds renewed so that our lives may be transformed. The educational task of the church starts with helping people have their minds renewed, teaching them that theology interacts with all of life and that we must think Christianly about all we see and do.

Too long now Christian education has failed to engage the minds of the people. How we think about things does matter. Spiritual maturity is more than how we think; it is never less. Teaching people how to *think* like Christians is an important aspect of helping them learn to live like Christians.

Notes

1. John Calvin, *Calvin's Commentaries on Romans* (Grand Rapids: Eerdmans, 1947), xxix.
2. Martin Luther, *Commentary on the Epistle to the Romans* (Grand Rapids: Zondervan, 1954), 152.
3. D. Stuart Briscoe, *The Communicator's Commentary: Romans* (Waco, Tex.: Word, 1982), 215.
4. William Barclay, *The Letter to the Romans* (Philadelphia: Westminster, 1975), 157.
5. Calvin, *Romans,* 453.
6. John Murray, *The Epistle to the Romans* (Grand Rapids: Eerdmans, 1965), 2:115.
7. Douglas Moo in John D. Woodbridge, ed., *Renewing Your Mind in a Secular World* (Chicago: Moody Press, 1985), 146.
8. Charles W. Colson, *Born Again.* (Lincoln, Va.: Chosen Books, 1975), 11.
9. Horace Bushnell, *Christian Nurture* (1861; reprint, Grand Rapids: Baker, 1979), 10.
10. William Barclay, *Educational Ideals in the Ancient World* (Grand Rapids: Baker, 1959), 239.
11. Robert Coles, *The Spiritual Life of Children* (Boston: Houghton Mifflin, 1990).

CHAPTER

6

Developmentalism

Effective Christian education is concerned not only with what the Bible teaches but also with God's design of people. Christian educators must understand both theology and people if they are to have a productive educational ministry. Rooted in the theology of Creation, which teaches that people have worth and dignity, education that is distinctly Christian will evidence respect for God's sixth-day creation and Christian educators will attempt to understand how people learn and what motivates their behavior. It is incredibly disrespectful to assume that people are simply empty vessels to be filled with knowledge, even if that knowledge is the content of Scripture. Developmentalism provides a framework for understanding the process of educating for spiritual growth.

Christian education is concerned with teaching for spiritual growth, assuming that learning is an integral part of becoming spiritually mature. Since learning is a *human* phenomenon, it is incumbent upon the educator to understand how people learn. This question can be cast as pure-

It is the responsibility of Christian educators to use the social sciences wisely, integrating psychology properly into their philosophy of Christian education.

ly psychological: How do people learn? It can also be cast more integratively: How has God created people to learn? By casting the question in the latter way, we are assuming that *all truth is God's truth* and that both the social sciences and theology are important for understanding human beings.

INTEGRATING SOCIAL SCIENCES AND THEOLOGY

Taking an integrative approach to Christian education is necessary, but it is also difficult. It is necessary to develop a complete understanding of ministry, but it is difficult because of the human tendency to separate and compartmentalize truth. We must come to the place where we realize that there are larger questions than Is it biblical? We must also ask, Is it true?

Truth that exists outside of Scripture must be considered. For example, no one attempts to develop a *biblical* approach to electronics. The study of electronics is rooted in physics, which is a study of God's created order. The Christian understands that creation is orderly, and part of the divine mandate to humans is that we are to understand God's creation.

But can the same approach be taken regarding psychology? Is the study of people the same as the study of electricity? In one sense it is, because both are inquiries into God's created order. But the issue becomes confused when scientists con-

ducting the inquiry hold presuppositions that control the way they conduct their inquiry. If, for example, the psychologist is a committed naturalist, it would be impossible for him or her ever to acknowledge that anything supernatural occurs. Every phenomenon has to be explained naturally.

The key for the Christian is first to understand the presuppositions of the scientist and, second, to integrate them properly. It is the responsibility of Christian educators to use the social sciences wisely, integrating psychology properly into their philosophy of Christian education.

Three broad streams or approaches to psychology exist. Each of these has elements of truth, but one stands above the others in terms of the validity of its presuppositions and usefulness to Christian education. In each of these there are many variations, but all approaches can be placed into one of the following three positions.

Psychoanalysis or Depth Psychologies

The first primary approach is a mode of therapy that emphasizes unconscious forces in the mind. The *primary assumption* of the depth psychologies is that human beings are primarily *proactive* toward their environment. That is, human behavior is best understood as a result of the *internal forces* operative within people.

Those who hold this approach believe that rather than waiting for environmental stimuli, human activity is initiated from within the person.

First developed by Sigmund Freud and later adapted by Carl Jung, Anna Freud, and Erik Erikson, these psychoanalytic schools see people as being comprised of various internal forces that shape the personality and activity of the individual. Classical psychoanalytic psychology believes that within all people are the id, the ego, and the superego, regulating and controlling the person's behavior and feelings and seeking balance within the human psyche. While behaviorism stresses human behavior, depth psychologies stress the inner working of the human being.

The primary contribution of this "first force" psychology is that it offers an attempt at understanding the inner workings of the human personality. There is a certain respect for the person and with it an awareness of "mystery." Human beings are not easily reduced to a series of stimuli and responses as in behaviorism. Rather, they are seen as a complex interworking of various energies operative within the human personality.

While psychoanalysis can be a helpful mode of therapy, it is not particularly helpful for the purposes of education. There is a growing distrust of psychoanalysis among psychologists and little use of its theories outside of the realm of counseling. The work of Erik Erikson has been most helpful, describing a series of epigenetic stages through which people progress as they move toward psychosocial maturity. Understanding these stages is especially helpful for those working in youth ministry, but they are not directly relevant for educational questions.

The fundamental weakness of psychoanalytic perspective is the overemphasis on internal forces, without an adequate emphasis on the person's ability to *control* his or her behavior. There are some important insights offered for therapy, but not a great deal is useful for the educator. The stress on the *unconscious* aspects of the personality render it not particularly helpful for the educator.

Behaviorism

First introduced by the Russian physiologist Ivan P. Pavlov and then applied to psychology by John B. Watson and Edward L. Thorndike, the "second force" psychology of behaviorism came to the forefront under the influence of B. F. Skinner (1904–1990). The *primary assumption* of behaviorism is that human behavior is explained in terms of environmental stimuli. People are best described as being *reactive* to their environment. First there is environmental stimulation, which is followed by human behavior.

Behaviorists offer an empirical approach to psychology. They are interested only in those phenomena that can be empirically observed. Such nonobservable issues as motives, emotions, or values are not considered because they do not yield to empirical observation. The presuppositions of behaviorism immediately hamper its usefulness because it is limited by its own rules. There is no room for the inner person, or for such issues as conviction by the Holy Spirit.

Behaviorism is highly popular, especially in the United States. Its popularity can be traced to several factors. First, it is highly "scientific," being guided by the rules of empirical inquiry. It yields nicely to statistical analysis and is easily reduced to hard data. The American population has been trained to value this kind of information.

Second, it provides a wonderful escape from responsibility. If it is true that human behavior is wholly determined by environment, then everything we do is a result of factors outside of ourselves and we can in no way be held responsible. "I'm not responsible" has become the cry of our age, and it is rooted in the psychology of behaviorism.[1]

Third, in many instances behaviorism works. For certain kinds of learning in which behaviors need to be acquired, behaviorism can be highly effective. Anyone who has ever trained an animal by using rewards and punishments to get the desired effects has seen the power of behaviorism. Moreover, *behavior modification*, the approach to discipline that ignores negative behavior and rewards positive behavior, can be an effective means of disciplining children.

But behaviorism must be rejected by the Christian as ultimately inadequate and incomplete as a means of understanding human beings. It is inadequate because it fails to allow for those aspects of reality that cannot be empirically observed (referred to by Immanuel Kant as the "noumenal" aspects of reality). The cosmos is more than the material world, and human beings are more than behavior. While it is true that people respond to environmental stimuli, that does not explain *all* of human behavior.

Behaviorism is incomplete for the Christian because of its fundamental disrespect of human beings. It is a mode of manipulation that attempts to *control* others. Even the term *behavior modification* indicates the intent of changing people, and it assumes that the person doing the "modifying" knows best how the other person should behave. Behaviorist researchers move directly from a study of rats and mice to a study of humans, *assuming* that all organisms learn the same way. In fact Skinner directly taught that we must get beyond the romantic notions of human freedom and dignity and understand that people are no different from the animals. Skinner believed that people can and should be controlled by manipulating the environment.[2]

Unfortunately, behaviorism is so ingrained in our society that it has been used inadvertently in many Christian ministries. Approaches to ministry rooted in methods of rewards and punishments, or in highly individualized approaches to teaching and learning are being controlled by behaviorism. Clearly the Scriptures appeal to humans by offering rewards and punishments for corresponding behaviors, but this is not the *only* means of teaching suggested by Scripture. While aspects of behaviorism can be helpful, Christians must adopt a more complete approach to understanding people and their behavior.

Humanistic Psychologies

"Third force" psychologies, generally categorized as "humanistic" approaches, offer a more balanced perspective.[3] These psychologies are called humanistic because, more than either behaviorism or the depth psychologies, they value human beings as being thoughtful and purposeful. First made popular by Carl Rogers, Abraham Maslow, and Erich Fromm, these psychologies also include the works of Jean Piaget, Lawrence Kohlberg, and James Fowler.

Third-force psychologists understand humans as *interactive* with their environment, recognizing that people not only are influenced by, but also exert influence on their environments. An organismic understanding recognizes that there are times when people are definitely reacting to their environments and other times when they are acting upon their environments. From this perspective emerges a more complete picture of why people do the things they do.

Some of the movements within humanistic psychology have been at odds with a Christian worldview and have been destructive to our society. The "values clarification" movement, for example, with its myth of "value-free" education has been detrimental to social structures and needs to be opposed by thoughtful people. But not all of the approaches included in this group of psychologies are negative. For example, *developmentalism* is an approach that is highly compatible with a Christian perspective and offers helpful insights for the educational ministry of the church.

DEVELOPMENTAL ASSUMPTIONS

There are various approaches to developmental psychology, with different emphases in each approach. Broadly speaking, however, all developmental approaches will hold to most, if not all, of the following ten assumptions.[4] These are assumptions about the nature of human beings and, for the Christian, can be understood as descriptions of how God has designed people to develop.

1. In essential attributes human beings are more similar than dissimilar.

Flying in the face of the individualism prevalent in the United States, developmentalists contend that there is more that makes us alike than makes us unalike. While our society likes to stress our differences, developmentalism stresses our similarities.

We sometimes tell our children, "You are unique. There is no one in the whole world just like you." In a sense, this is true because there are no *exact* duplicates of people. But there is more that makes us "just like" other people our age than makes us different from them. Because people have similar attributes at each stage of life, it is possible to generalize about them. For example, we can conduct a seminar on adolescent development because there are very *predictable patterns* to the process of growth in adolescence. Developmental psychology recognizes and describes the similarities in human beings.

This assumption is difficult for Americans to accept because we like to think of ourselves as "special." When we discover that an experience we are having is actually quite common to people of our age, it can become for some, a depressing discovery. But in cultures in which commonalities are accepted, with the group emphasized over the individual, people easily accept the fact that we are more similar than dissimilar.

2. The essence of humanness is carried in genetic structure and is in every respect inherent.

What makes us "human" is not environment, but genetics. That is, humanity is a matter of *internal* structure (carried in the DNA) and not a matter of where or how we were raised. Human beings are more than products of environmental stimuli but are genetically unique creatures.

Periodically we discover that a child has been placed in a chicken coop or some other such horrible environment and raised as an animal. Called "feral children," such children will many times behave in ways more appropriate to the animals with which they lived than to children of their own age. But apart from their behavior, they are still distinctly and completely human, because their genetic structure is human.

The point of this assumption is that environmental influences are inadequate to explain the basic nature of persons. Environment influences us in certain ways, but it does not control who we are. From a Christian perspective, genetics is simply the means God has used to design his creation.

3. The patterns of human development are in the nature of humankind.

Humans develop in predictable ways because of genetic structure. For example, with the exception of certain birth defects, all babies are born small and then grow larger throughout childhood. All over the world, in every race and culture, the pattern of physical development is to start small and then grow larger.

When my friends had a baby, I asked, "How big was she?" The mother responded "Six-eight." "That's tall for a baby!" was my witty reply. Of course my observation was ridiculous because I knew she was referring to her daughter's weight, not her height. The reason I knew was that the *pattern* of development for all people everywhere is the same, and babies are not born six feet eight inches tall. This is true because of the genetic structure of human beings.

4. The patterns of development cannot be significantly altered.

Referred to as *predeterminism*, this assumption indicates that we are *genetically programmed* to move through predictable patterns in our development. These patterns are part and parcel of being human and are not normally susceptible to external influences.

Because there are predictable patterns that cannot be easily altered, we can predict and generalize about human development. Recently a friend came to me, concerned about some traits she was seeing emerge in her preadolescent daughter. As we talked, I was able to assure her that the things she was seeing were quite normal for a child of that age and would probably not last too long. I was able to give this assurance because the patterns of development in people are quite secure.

Developmental stages are *invariant* and *sequential*. All people go through the same stages in the same order. Some move more quickly through the stages and are called advanced or gifted, while others move more slowly and are usually called developmentally delayed. The pattern remains in place, but the rate of development varies.

5. Development can be seen in several interwoven aspects—physical, cognitive, affective, social, and moral.

Five aspects of the human personality yield to empirical inquiry and demonstrate predictable stages of development. For the sake of study and discussion, each is considered separately; but human beings are integrated wholes and each aspect interacts with and influences the others.

The *physical* aspect of the human being is obvious, and the developmental patterns are easily seen. Even though people may try to stop or hide the normal patterns of bodily growth and decline by coloring their hair or going on frantic "fitness programs," the physical aspect moves through clear stages as a person ages.

The *cognitive* aspect is concerned with how people know and think about things.

> *Development can be seen in several interwoven aspects— physical, cognitive, affective, social, and moral.*

Scripture acknowledges that children think differently from adults (1 Cor. 13:11) and that it is inappropriate for adults to continue to think like children. Cognitive developmentalists work to understand the patterns of reasoning through which people progress as they move toward adulthood.

The *affective* aspect of human beings refers to their emotional development and is closely related to the values they hold. People move through stages of emotional development as they progress from the child's absolute need to receive love to the adult's capacity to live interdependently with others, both giving and receiving love.

Social development refers to the stages through which people move as they grow to be responsible social beings. The need of adolescents to be simultaneously independent from parents and dependent on peers is a predictable part of social development. Some societies (such as in the United States) allow for great freedom in this realm, while others put much greater control on how this process is worked out. But all people move through predictable patterns from the dependency of childhood to the interdependency of adulthood.

The *moral* aspect of development refers to the changing ways people sort out right from wrong. Children make moral decisions based on highly self-centered criteria, whereas morally mature adults see larger issues or principles as important. Between these extremes adolescents make moral decisions on the basis of societal expectations. But again, there are predictable patterns in the progress of this development.

Common to much Christian education literature are discussions of the "spiritual" aspect of people.[5] But it is more appropriate to see the "spiritual" as the *essence* of what humans are, rather than as an aspect. Scripture describes us as spiritual in the core of our beings. Ted Ward uses the illustration of the human hand, with each finger representing an aspect of the human personality. In his illustration the spiritual essence of the person resides in the palm of the hand, indicating that each aspect of the person interacts with and is influenced by the spiritual.

When Christians speak of ministering "spiritually" to someone, I often wonder how this may be done. The only means of ministering spiritually is *through* one of the five aspects described above. The spiritual is not an aspect of our humanity; it is the essence of what we are. Therefore we feed and clothe people, reason with them, love them, relate to them, and treat them justly, all as a means of ministering to them spiritually. The aspects of the human personality are the avenues through which we minister to people spiritually.

6. Development must be understood holistically.

Rather than taking an atomistic approach to persons, viewing them as unrelated parts, we should recognize the organic functional relation between parts and wholes. Human beings are complete and must ultimately be understood as integrated wholes. The old fundamentalist reference to people as "souls" (as in "How many souls came forward?") really does a disservice to how people should be seen. Likewise, people in the medical profession may refer to a patient as "the hip in room 214" (referring to the surgery performed) rather than seeing the whole person.

The intertwining of aspects of the human personality is critical to understanding people. For example, a child with cerebral palsy has a physical condition—brain damage—that usually occurs at or near birth. The physical problem may cause a cognitive problem of mental retardation. Because the child is affected cognitively, emotions may also be involved, slowing emotional development. Lack of physical ability related to the brain damage will influence the child socially, affecting his or her ability to play with and generally relate to other children. Finally, the cognitive problem will have an effect in the moral realm, probably inhibiting moral development.

In the same way, the various aspects of the human personality may have an influence on a person spiritually. A physical problem may cause a person to be angry with God. Inability to relate socially cuts people off from the influence of the church. Emotional problems will influence how a person relates to and understands God.

For the sake of research and discussion, development is described in relation to the various aspects of the human personality. But to be both realistic and respectful of people, development must be understood holistically.[6]

7. Environment facilitates or represses development.

Environment does matter, either helping or hindering the developmental process. It *influences* development but does not *control* it. Environment plays a role in the developmental process, but it is not as profound as behaviorists claim.

On several occasions I have watched my neighbor plant a garden. Deciding that planting a garden is a good idea, I dutifully dig up a plot of ground and plant some seeds and put in a few small plants. Unfortunately, that is usually as far as my gardening efforts go. As a result, while my plants are recognizably tomatoes or lettuce or carrots, they are usually not very healthy or impressive. The role of the gardener is *to create an environment in which development is facilitated.* Weeding, fertilizing, and watering all serve to create such an environment. My garden, however, consists of an environment that hinders development.

The task of the educator, parent, or youth worker is to help create an environment in which people can grow. There is nothing we can do to change the pattern of development. We are responsible to create the environment that facilitates God's natural order and his supernatural intervention in the lives of his people. The behaviorist manipulates the environment in order to change people. The developmentalist also works with the environment but does so with a completely different motive. His or her motive is to create an environment that facilitates the *inborn* developmental program.

8. Development is best understood as a matter of losing limitations.

Preformationism is the assumption that the completed stages of development are inherent in the individual. From the time of conception (more properly than at birth) the person is a complete, yet limited human being. Inherent in the person is all

> *It is God's will that people made in his image develop in all aspects of their personality.*

that is necessary to becoming a fully functioning adult.

When babies are born, they cannot walk, talk, eat solid foods, think conceptually, or do a myriad of other things appropriate to adults. They are *complete* human beings but are *limited* by their development. It is more appropriate to think about the developmental process as *losing limitations* than it is to think in terms of *adding to* the person. They gain knowledge and skills but are already whole people.

Preformationism helps us to look at people respectfully, seeing them as complete, yet limited. Children need to lose the limitations of childish thinking—not somehow become more human. Our task is to help people lose the limitations of the lower stages so that they may enjoy the fullness of their God-given human potential.

Preformationism can also be helpful for Christian nurture. When persons are *born again* into Christ, they too are now complete, yet limited. They may not know how to pray, share their faith with others, or walk by means of the Holy Spirit and are therefore limited as Christians. But they are complete in Christ and need only to be "set free" from the limitations of spiritual immaturity. We do not "add to" them as we teach them; rather, we help them to be "set free" in Christ.

9. Development can be stalemated by adverse conditions.

Sometimes environment can be so destructive that the developmental process is stopped. Children who are abused or starved may be so profoundly damaged by the environment that their development in some aspects is arrested. The various aspects of the human personality differ in their susceptibility to environmental influence. The relative strength of the developmental process progresses in descending order, with the physical being the least susceptible to environmental influence and the moral being the most susceptible. This is why, for example, the moral climate in our nation is poor. The environment of moral decay is slowing or even stalemating people's moral growth.

Overall, the developmental process can be relied on, being trusted to progress apart from environmental control. But in extreme situations, development can be thwarted.

10. Fulfilling the continuing pattern of human development throughout life is a requisite for fulfilling humanness.

To develop is natural; not to develop is pathological. Inherent in human beings is great potential and great worth. Christians understand that this potential is written by the finger of God. Being human means, among other things, to become mature, fully developed in all aspects of the personality. It is a terrible thing to see people held back from development, because there is great potential in all human beings. To cast this in Christian terms, it is God's will that people made in his image develop in all aspects of their personality.

Certain sicknesses inhibit development, and there are people who, through no direct fault of their own, never develop. Such is part of living in a fallen world. But this must be seen as pathological and evil, not as part of God's intended order. Fulfilling the privileges of humanness means fulfilling our potential for development.

EDUCATIONAL IMPLICATIONS

If it is true that God has created people to develop according to predictable patterns and that these patterns are inherent in people, several important implications can be drawn. First, *Christian educators must understand the developmental process*. Although they are not developmental psychologists per se, Christian educators must understand the patterns of development. The various stages shape the way people learn and will also influence how they experience their faith. Understanding the patterns will help the educator design learning experiences that are appropriate to the developmental stage of the person.

Second, *the developmental process must be respected*. Rather than rushing people through the various stages of development, or holding them back from the natural developmental process, the process must be allowed to progress at its own rate. People need time to live in and experience each stage of development. American society tends to rush the process, attempting to accelerate development. Children are pushed ahead, hardly allowed to be children. Unfortunately, Christians too get caught up in this trap, worried that their children will be left behind if they are not pushed ahead in their development.

Conversely, some people want to fight the developmental process, not allowing others to grow and develop. Especially during adolescence, some parents are frightened of the natural social progress of breaking free of parental controls, and they try to hold their children back. The tug of war between development and parental control can create tension in the home and confusion in the life of the teenager.

Developmental stages are best pictured as *large rooms* rather than *confining boxes*. Each stage needs to be explored and experienced, exhausted of its potential before it is left behind for the next stage. If we attempt to rush people through the developmental process, we are demonstrating our distrust of God's design for people and probably creating undue stress for the people involved. Respect for the developmental process allows people to be who they are at any given time and trusts God's design for individual growth. It allows for the rate of development to progress normally, neither forcing people ahead nor holding them back.

It can be difficult to watch another person progress through a developmental stage. Parents of teenagers sometimes agonize as they watch their children grow up. "It's only a stage" can be a pat answer to a difficult situation, or it can be an honest appraisal of what is taking place. Respecting the developmental process means allowing people to be at the stage appropriate for their age.

Third, *we should desire to see growth in the people we serve*. Too many educators settle for the acquisition of information as the purpose of education. But education, best understood, is about development, not simply the gaining of information or the acquiring of new skills. Information and skills are *part* of the process, but development is the key outcome. Developmentalism defines higher stages and helps us to understand the ways in which our people need to grow. The goal of development can help set the agenda for educational outcomes, especially when the findings of developmentalism are integrated with theological perspective.

Development as a goal is a lens through which people can be understood. Used improperly it becomes another means of control by which the educator forces people into predetermined "boxes" and disregards the uniqueness of each individual. But properly understood, human development becomes a "map" of God's design of human beings, charting the broad movements through which people move as they grow toward maturity. With proper controls in place, developmentalism can be a very "Christian" way of understanding people. When integrated with theological understanding, it can provide helpful insights into teaching for spiritual growth.

Fourth, *development will interact with a person's growth as a Christian.* Because human beings are whole entities, their spiritual lives are not separated from the rest of their existence. Development interacts with and influences how we will experience our faith, and it helps educators understand the sorts of teaching strategies appropriate to the different age groups. Understanding development is an important key for understanding teaching. Developmentalism is not the only way to understand people (every system is flawed in some way), but it is a helpful way of understanding what people are like. It provides important insights for working with people and allows educators to play the role of facilitator rather than controller. It recognizes the orderliness of God's creation and strives to cooperate with the process of human growth.

Notes

1. For a fine explanation and critique of behaviorism, see Mark P. Cosgrove, *B. F. Skinner's Behaviorism: An Analysis* (Grand Rapids: Zondervan, 1982).

2. B. F. Skinner, *Beyond Freedom and Dignity* (New York: Knopf, 1971).

3. Humanistic psychologies should not be confused with secular humanism. Secular humanism is an anti-Christian movement rooted in a naturalistic philosophy that sets human beings up as the ultimate of all that is. However, humanistic psychologies emphasize the dignity of humanity and were originally rooted in Christianity. Historically, humanism was a *Christian* movement that attempted to restore the inherent dignity of all people as made in the image of God and was in no way anti-Christian.

4. These assumptions are adapted from lectures by and discussions with Ted Ward and are used with his permission.

5. See, for example, the chapter by Robert E. Clark in Robert E. Clark, Lin Johnson, and Allyn K. Sloat, eds., *Christian Education Foundations for the Future* (Chicago: Moody Press, 1991), 233–48. Clark describes the "spiritual development" of elementary-age children.

6. At the time of this writing, the term *holistic* is quite popular among certain New Age groups. Although this association may be confusing, I choose to use the word because it is readily descriptive of the concept and does not *necessarily* carry with it any of the improper connotations of the New Age movements.

7

Cognitive Development

"We want our children to know the Bible" is a common and appropriate concern of Christian parents and leaders. Because knowledge of Scripture is central to Christian growth and maturity, any person who desires to help children grow in faith will want them to learn Scripture. But there is a problem with the child's capacity to know and understand this distinctly adult book. The problem is that children *know* and *think* about things differently from adults. Essential to effective ministry is an understanding of the ways children think and know.

Ronald Goldman,[1] a British religious educator who wrote from a theologically liberal perspective, pointed out the problems with how children understand Scripture. Because they do not think in the same ways as adults, they will often re-form biblical concepts and terms into meanings that make sense to them. "Hallowed be thy name" became "Harold be thy name" in the mind of a child so that this incomprehensible phrase made sense to him. Goldman concluded "that the Bible is not a children's

> *The problem is that children know and think about things differently from adults. Essential to effective ministry is an understanding of the ways children think and know.*

book, that the teaching of large areas of it may do more damage than good to a child's religious understanding and that too much biblical material is used too soon and too frequently."[2]

But the Bible demands that we teach our children its content. Much of the Old Testament was recorded so that the stories could be passed on *to the children* so that they might know of God's faithfulness on their behalf. Strategies were established to prompt the children to ask questions so parents could tell them the stories of God's faithful care. Clearly it is God's intention that children be taught biblical truth.

From a theological point of view it is important to teach the Bible to children, but from a psychological point of view it is important to see that children understand differently from adults. How can we bring these two concerns together so that we can teach the Bible responsibly to children?

JEAN PIAGET AND COGNITIVE DEVELOPMENT

Goldman's writings were predicated on the work of Jean Piaget (1896-1980), the Swiss "genetic epistemologist" who first described the cognitive developmental process in children. While his name is readily recognized, a brief overview of his life and work is appropriate.[3]

Born in Switzerland, Piaget was raised by a father who was a scholar and by a mother who was intelligent and devoutly religious. He learned early the values of systematic thinking and at the age of ten published his first paper—a description of a partly albino sparrow he had observed in a park.

He was trained in biology, with an emphasis on malacology (the branch of zoology that deals with mollusks), receiving his Ph.D. in 1918 from the University of Neuchatel. During his adolescence his godfather, Samuel Cornut, spent a few summers teaching him the philosophy of Henri Bergson, who wrote on creative evolution. This opened the young scientist to the world of ideas and the broader questions of epistemology. As a result, he began to read in the areas of philosophy, religion, and logic, asking, "What is knowledge?" and, "How is it achieved?"

The dual concerns of biology and philosophy led him to try to find a biological explanation of knowledge. The commitment he made to biology and philosophy in adolescence never waned through his entire life. Fred McCormick states:

> He was continually casting his biological pursuits against the backdrop of philosophy and epistemology. He avidly read Kant, Spencer, Cante, Durkheim, Tarde, James, Ribot, and Janet, as well as other philosophers and psychologists, and he came to the conclusion that the most viable explanation of reality existed in the relationship of the parts to the whole, ideas he garnered from the dispute between Durkheim and Tarde. Piaget concluded that particulars do not exist in isolated fashion, but in dependency upon

the other parts and upon the whole. From this system of logic stemmed Piaget's concept of equilibrium (or equilibration).[4]

Piaget used the term *genetic epistemology* to describe the interplay between body and mind that was to be the focus of his thought. He was convinced that intellectual development and how we come to know are "firmly rooted in the biological development of the individual, as expressed by the term 'genetic.'"[5]

While doing postgraduate studies at the Sorbonne, Piaget worked with Theophile Simon, who with Alfred Binet developed the first intelligence test. As he attempted to standardize certain aspects of the test, he discovered that *children of similar ages systematically missed the same questions in the same way.* He began to wonder why this was so and became increasingly interested in how children thought about issues. He hoped to discover how they reasoned. As a result of early publications on these findings, he was offered a position as director of research at the Institut Jean Jacques Rousseau in Geneva. He was twenty-five at the time.

His career progressed at amazing speed as his prodigious writing and remarkable theories advanced. Through detailed observation, first of his own children and then of children from all over the world, he developed and refined his theories on logic, moral reasoning, and cognitive stages in children. In 1950 he published his three-volume theory of knowledge, which was a summary of his life's work to that point. At the time of his death in 1980 he had published forty books and hundreds of journal articles.

Adaptation

Piaget believed that *adaptation* is the essence of how a person functions cognitively, just as it is the essence of biological functioning. Adaptation is the capacity to organize the sensory stimuli we receive into some sort of order and then to adapt ourselves to our context.

Adaptation consists of two processes, *assimilation* and *accommodation*. Assimilation is the processes by which we incorporate ideas, people, customs, manners, and all sorts of other things into our own activities. For example, the young child who desires to bring a Bible to church because mommy and daddy do has assimilated this custom into her life.

Accommodation is the balance to assimilation, the adjusting of how we reach out to our environment. The young child who learns to raise his hands in praise can be said to have accommodated to his environment by learning the behavior of the people around him.

The deer population in northern Illinois where I live has gotten out of control because of increased size of the herds and decreased land area in which they can live. As a result, the deer have had to *accommodate* their behavior by grazing along the highways in full view of passing humans, and they have learned to *assimilate* new kinds of food as their normal feeding areas have disappeared.

Likewise, humans learn to accommodate and assimilate to their environment. Babies learn to put new things into their mouths as parents teach them to eat solid food. But they must also learn that not everything they find should go into their mouths. Therefore, as the baby functions adaptively to her environment, she also develops cognitively as she establishes categories of *things that do go into my mouth* and *things that do not go into my mouth.*

Children continue to reach out actively and explore their environments. One can almost watch them learn as they explore their world and organize it cognitively into meaningful systems. Meanwhile, they adapt their behavior to what they are learning, always trying to maintain a balance between what they are learning and how they behave.

Equilibration

The regulatory force between assimilation and accommodation is *equilibration.* The human mind seeks to understand, to keep ideas in balance; so young children find simple ways to explain their world, offering childish explanations for what they experience. But as their world grows and their ability to understand develops, children seek better, more adequate levels of equilibrium. The explanations of childhood fail to satisfy the sophisticated mind of the adult, so the force of seeking equilibration stimulates the mind to higher levels of reasoning.

Piaget believed that three factors stimulate cognitive development: maturation, experience, and social transmission. First, *maturation* is more than a biological force; it is also cognitive. Just as the body matures, so the mind matures, developing new capacities for thinking and reasoning. Children exercise growing muscles, strengthening them through use. Likewise, they must use their minds to strengthen them at each level of development. But the mind is more than a muscle to be strengthened; it is a developing aspect of the human personality, growing in predictable ways.

Experience also prompts cognitive development by providing sensory input for children. Active involvement with their environment allows children to gain information necessary for later cognitive development. Experience of direct sensory involvement with the environment is what Piaget had in mind—not a sterile sort of "academic" involvement, but a direct touching, tasting, smelling, hearing, and seeing sort of involvement. Because of this need, Piaget believed that "play is the work of the child." It is through playing that the child is able to gain this type of experience.

Social transmission is the third factor that stimulates cognitive development. The verbal instructions offered by parents and teachers are critical stimulations for cognitive growth. Children must make sense of the various things said to them, reconciling the various messages they receive. When they hear contradictory messages, *cognitive conflict* is experienced as their sense of equilibration is disturbed. In this sense they may be *disequilibrated* (not a term used by Piaget, but descriptive of the state) and will seek to find higher levels of understanding that may serve to resolve the conflict and restore them to a state of equilibration.

The young child is taught that "Jesus is the Christmas baby" who was laid in a manger by his mother. Later the same child is taught that "Jesus was God's Son who died on the cross for our sins." These strange, conflicting messages can be resolved only as the child realizes that the baby *grew up* to become the man who died on the cross. Equilibration is reestablished when the higher level of thinking is gained.

STAGES OF COGNITIVE DEVELOPMENT

Piaget's work was remarkable because he saw children, not as miniature adults, but as being cognitively different from adults. He understood that they saw the world in ways different from those of adults and that these different modes of understanding should be respected. Moreover, rather than seeking to understand individual differences, he worked to describe *ways in which children are the same.* He believed that in all ages and in all cultures there were predictable patterns to the ways children made sense of their environment. There were "invariant and sequential stages of cognitive development" through which all children must pass on their journey toward adulthood.[6]

Through extensive observations and interviews with children, Piaget described and refined the stages of cognitive development through which children progress. Only a brief summary of these stages can be offered here.[7]

Sensorimotor Period

The first two years of life are characterized by increasingly sophisticated sensory input and the rudimentary beginnings of cognitive thought. The stage is called *sensorimotor* because children demonstrate their intelligence through sensory input and motor activity. Parents delight when their children first demonstrate visual recognition of them through motor activity—smiling or kicking their feet in excitement when the parents come into sight.

Children begin life exclusively egocentric—aware only of themselves. There is little sensitivity to a world outside of themselves and no clear means of making sense of the wide array of sensory stimuli they receive. But as they mature, they establish new behavior patterns as means of interacting with their world. Usually focused around sucking, infants progress to behaviors (motor activities) designed to help them find new things to suck.

Piaget describes six substages in the sensorimotor period that provide the movement toward completion of this cognitive stage. The child's primary need at this level is to be cared for both physically and emotionally. Children need a safe environment and the sensory input of being touched and held. This assures them that the world is a safe place. This is not the time to teach content; rather, it is the time to allow children to explore their world and to discover the basic "rules" of existence.

Children decrease their egocentrism, learning that others exist in the world, and these others too must be taken into consideration. They learn that specific actions can produce specific results and that they can influence their environments. Animals are capable of this kind of learning also, but at the age of two the child is progressing far beyond the ability of the animals as God's design for human beings continues to emerge.

Preoperational Period

Ages two to seven constitute the period of transition from the sensorimotor period of the infant to the thinking world of the school-age child. Internal mental activities or *operations* begun in the later stages of infancy are refined and developed in early childhood.

A primary task of this stage is to learn to use the *symbols* of thought as a replacement for the *actual object.* Language replaces motor activity as the children's means of getting what they want, and they learn to think about things rather than always needing them in their immediate environment. Piaget and Inhelder wrote:

> At the end of the sensorimotor period, at about one and a half to two years, there appears a function that is fundamental to the development of later behavior patterns. It consists in the ability to represent something (a signified something: object, event, conceptual scheme, etc.) by means of a "signifier" which is differentiated and which serves only a

representative purpose: language, mental image, symbolic gesture and so on . . . we generally refer to this function that gives rise to representation as "symbolic."[8]

"Make-believe" play is critical for children at this stage, because this activity provides important experience in using objects as symbols for other objects. Children use a stick for a gun, or a leaf for a plate, pretending that the substitute object is the real thing. Or they "dress up" in different clothes, acting out symbolic thinking by pretending to be someone else in a different time or place.

Collective monologue is the primary speech pattern of the preoperational child. Children talk more to themselves than to others, providing a commentary on their own actions and thoughts. It is only at the later portion of this stage that children actually interact verbally with any consistency with other children.

The preoperational child looks at the world in ways quite different from those of the adult. Everything is seen to exist specifically for the child, and everyone shares the child's point of view. A marble rolls down the hill because *it knows you are down there* and therefore desires to come to you. Explanations are still strongly egocentric, and much of the world functions by a sort of magic the child can control.

Egocentrism does not allow the child to take another's point of view. When Piaget took his son for a ride in the car, he observed that the boy did not recognize a familiar mountain when it was seen from a different vantage point. The boy believed that the mountain, rather than his point of view, had changed.

Conservation is the ability to understand that certain attributes of an object remain constant. In a classic experiment, Piaget showed children two equal balls of clay. When one ball was rolled into the shape of a hot dog, the children believed that it now contained more clay because it was "longer." They could not *conserve* the fact that it was only shape, not volume, that had changed.

Centration is the tendency to focus only on certain aspects of an object, idea, or event and to ignore the rest. Children in this stage tend to centrate their perspective to one aspect of their perceptual field, failing to perceive other aspects or relationships of the phenomenon under investigation.

Parents may ask their daughter what she did in Sunday school. She reports, "We had cookies." "Yes, but what did you learn about?" the parents reply. "The cookies were good!" is the child's answer. "But did you talk about Jesus?" the father interjects (indicating a growing concern for the lack of content being taught in Sunday school). "The cookies were chocolate" is their daughter's final word on the matter. Mom and Dad decide that either Sunday school has to be revamped or their daughter just has no heart for spiritual matters. Clearly something has to be done.

Of course, what has really happened is that the child has centrated, focusing only on that aspect of the Sunday school hour that was most sensory and most satisfying to her. As she matures she will learn to "decenter," or focus on greater complexities in her perceptual environment. But for the moment, her stage of cognitive development limits her capacity to perceive the broad picture.

The preoperational period is a time of relearning things previously learned in the sensorimotor stage. Now they are perceived in new ways and can be thought about symbolically, rather than being expressed only through motor activity. But another epistemological revolution is ahead as the child develops into concrete operations.

Concrete Operations

The period of concrete operations involves children from ages seven to eleven. In this period of their lives the limitations of centration, egocentrism, and irreversibility (the inability to reason backwards from effect to cause) are removed through continued assimilation, accommodation, and equilibration. Mary Ann Spencer Pulaski wrote,

The preoperational child can form mental pictures or symbolic representations, as evidenced by his drawings, his make-believe play, and his use of language. However, he functions not logically but intuitively, depending on immediate perception and direct experience. In the experiment with the clay balls, for example, the reasoning of the preoperational child is: I perceive them to be different; therefore they must be different. The child who is operating logically reasons: They were the same to begin with, so they must be the same now, even though they look different.[9]

The logical ability of children in this stage allows them to understand the world in new and remarkable ways. With these new cognitive abilities concepts that were previously mysteries, known only to older children and adults, can now be understood. Concrete Operations is a stage of exciting and intense learning. In this stage children are no longer limited to perceptual data to make judgments regarding concrete, real problems; they now can use logical operational thinking that is capable of reversible, decentered perceptions.

Several new cognitive abilities serve to liberate thinking in the concrete operations stage. *Group* is the mathematical construct referring to a set of elements that utilize the principles of composition, associativity, identity, and reversibility. Those who are familiar with the logic of the "new math" will recognize these terms. Piaget used these constructs to explain the logic of concrete operations.

Pulaski explained the concept this way:

A very simple fundamental grouping is concerned with the relationship of identity or equivalence. If A = B, and B = C, then A = C. As an example of this, Piaget asked a group of boys if they had brothers. One little boy named Paul said yes, he had a brother named Etienne. Asked if Etienne had a brother, the boy said he did not. His limited point of view prevented him from realizing that he bore the same relationship to Etienne as Etienne did to him.[10]

Conservation, which was absent in preoperations, is evident in this stage. In another classic experiment, children were shown two rows of eight pennies, with one row being spread out further than the other. When asked which row had the most pennies, the preoperational children would usually choose the row with the most space between the pennies. Children in the concrete operations stage quickly counted the pennies, conserving the idea that the number did not change, only the spacing.

Classification is the ability to overcome slight perceptual differences and maintain similarities according to a classification scheme. Children were shown twenty wooden beads—eighteen brown and two white. The children were asked to separate out the brown beads, providing them with the classification "brown." They were then asked if there were more brown beads or more wooden beads. Most preoperational children responded that there are more brown beads because perceptually the classification of brown was the strongest. Children in the concrete operations stage included the white beads in their classification of wooden beads, showing their ability to combine classes to form a new category.

Seriation also emerges in the concrete operations stage, allowing children to number and to place objects, events, and ideas in logical order. The preoperational child has great difficulty in placing historical events, such as those recorded in the Bible, into sequential order. "Who came first,

content the subject becomes capable of reasoning correctly about propositions he does not believe, or at least not yet; that is, propositions that he considers pure hypothesis. He becomes capable of drawing the necessary conclusions from truths which are merely possible, which constitutes the beginning of hypothetico-deductive or formal thought.[11]

In the long run, questioning is much better than never questioning, because questioning means thinking, and thinking is necessary for spiritual growth.

Jesus or Moses?" is a question beyond the logical ability of the four-year-old. But the nine-year-old now has the ability to seriate, along with the ability to grasp concepts of time, space, and speed. These new abilities allow children to unscramble much of the information acquired but not really understood in earlier years.

These sorts of logical groupings allow children to order and understand their perceptual environments in most satisfying ways. But they are still limited to that which is concrete—what they actually see and experience. Movement to the next stage opens the world of *possibility* and *hypothesis* to children. As they move into adolescence, the final liberation of their thinking emerges.

Formal Operations

Somewhere around the age of eleven or twelve, children move into *formal operations*, the last stage of their cognitive development. Piaget and Inhelder introduced the stage as follows:

The great novelty of this stage is that by means of a differentiation of form and

In the formal operations stage adolescents and adults begin to think in the purely theoretical vein, imagining possibilities and reasoning in pure logic, apart from the constraints of content. A problem such as "If a car is bigger than a house, and a house is bigger than a truck—which is bigger, a car or a truck?" need not be solved by the constraints of reality but can be solved on the basis of the information given.

Also in this stage a person can now imagine other possibilities than those that actually exist. The ability to imagine perfect situations gives rise to the idealism of adolescence. Moreover, the questioning of adolescence is born of the ability to think in new ways.

Development into the formal operations stage may influence religious thinking. Adolescent agnosticism may emerge as the youth of the church wonder if God really does exist. Other questions of faith, such as the trustworthiness of Scripture or the exclusivity of Jesus as the only means of salvation may emerge. These questions do not indicate a crises in faith but rather are indicative of the fact that young people are using their new cognitive capacities to think about their faith. In the long run, questioning is much better than never questioning, because questioning means thinking, and thinking is necessary for spiritual growth.

IMPLICATIONS FOR CHRISTIAN EDUCATION

When Goldman burst on the scene advocating a revised approach to the religious education of children, he was prompted by the state of religious education in Great Britain. There religious training is part of the public school curriculum. The problem was that children seemed to become *less* religious as a result of their training. Attempting to speak to this problem and to take Piaget seriously, he ended up advocating that the Bible *not* be taught until children have developed a proper "readiness for religion."

Goldman's perspective was rooted as strongly in theology as it was in psychology. His assumption about Scripture was that it is a human document, recording myths, legends, and ancient perceptions of how God has communicated with humankind. It is not the divinely inspired and authoritative Word of God. Given this understanding, it is not surprising that he considered it expendable for the religious training of children. He wrote, "Bible-centered religious education emphasizes that the Bible must be taught because it is the Bible. Child-centered religious education, however, focuses upon the fact that it is the child as a growing person who should be our central concern."[12]

Goldman set up a false dichotomy, asking the reader to choose between the Bible and the child. Rather than making that choice, which is inappropriate, we must determine how to consider *both* the theological importance of the Bible *and* the cognitive development of the child. Goldman is correct in trying to take Piaget's work seriously, but wrong in his conclusion. What then are the implications of cognitive development to education for spiritual growth? How can we use Piaget's insights to help us teach children more effectively? The following implications can be drawn:

1. Teaching is a matter of stimulating equilibration.

Given the processes of assimilation and accommodation, we can develop an approach to effective teaching. Effective teaching begins by activating the existing cognitive structures through the introduction of familiar concepts. Beginning with what is known engages the mind and provides a framework for what will follow.

Second, the teacher should introduce new concepts or facts that the existing cognitive structures cannot accommodate. This disruption of the cognitive equilibration may cause a certain degree of discomfort, but it is necessary to the learning process. The slight level of anxiety generated by being disequilibrated provides the "energy" necessary for learning.

Students who have been disturbed by a class know well the feeling of not being equilibrated. There is an uneasiness that can be helpful to learning, not allowing the person to rest until the issue has been solved. But when the disequilibration becomes too severe, it serves as a detriment to learning. The student who says, "I don't want to think about it" is saying, "I don't want to be disequilibrated." The wise teacher is sensitive to the proper level of discomfort appropriate for effective learning.

Third, the teacher helps the student create new cognitive structures that can assimilate the new ideas. Teaching is a matter of helping people think in more adequate ways about the subject matter being presented.

Jesus' parables served this purpose. He began by talking about a familiar concept, introduced a new idea that shattered the religious categories of his audience, and then resolved the conflict by suggesting better ways to think about the kingdom of God. Likewise, teaching is a matter of introducing new data or concepts and helping students restructure their thinking to include the new information in responsible ways.

2. Cognitive stages control what the child can learn.

Learning is subordinate to the level of cognitive development. Concepts beyond the cognitive ability of the child cannot be grasped until the appropriate cognitive stage necessary for the concept has been reached. Children like to please adults; they learn to give the answers they believe we want to hear, but that is different from comprehending what they are saying.

Years ago I visited a class of two- and three-year-olds in a church in Florida. The teacher was reviewing the previous week's lesson with the children. She reminded them, "Remember last week when we studied that b-i-i-i-g word 'propitiation'?" Propitiation is central to the gospel, affirming that the death of Christ has satisfied God's justice and appeased his wrath against sin, but it is not a concept that can be grasped by children barely preoperational in their cognitive development.

Piaget's research teaches us to consider the content we teach, making it appropriate to the way our children think. Chil-

Theology tells us the content we need to teach, but psychology helps us know when and how we should teach it.

dren need to be taught the truth, but it must be presented in ways they can understand.

Larry Richards offers a helpful distinction between *exhaustive* versus *true* meaning. He states:

> Sometimes the possibility of knowing Truth is rejected because we cannot know all the Truth. But it is not necessary to know Truth perfectly to know Truth. Certainly a child cannot "understand" omnipresence. But he can understand that "Jesus is always with me." The vast Truth of omnipresence has come to have true meaning for him . . . however limited his understanding of "Jesus," of "always," or of "with" may be.[13]

Theology tells us the content we need to teach, but psychology helps us know when and how we should teach it. Paul reminded Timothy, "From infancy you have known the holy Scriptures, which are able to make you wise for salvation through faith in Christ Jesus" (2 Tim. 3:15). But we must also remember that when the boy Jesus went to the temple at the age of twelve and sat among the teachers to listen and to question, "Everyone who heard him was amazed at his understanding and his answers" (Luke 2:47). What was amazing at this encounter was that the boy did not think like a child.

Christian education needs to be respectful of Scripture, valuing it as the Word of God. But it must also be respectful of children, recognizing that God has designed them to think differently from adults. Certainly the Holy Spirit can give unusual understanding to children, but in the normal flow of events, we should not expect him to violate his design of children.

3. Avoid multisymbolic abstractions for children under twelve.

Much of our Christian talk is based on complex concepts. Using terms such as "Ask Jesus into your heart" or "Give your all to God" requires more cognitive sophistication than most children can deliver. These concepts are based on a variety of symbolic meanings that are beyond the grasp of children. Indeed, some are beyond the grasp of adults. (What *does* it mean to "ask Jesus into your heart"?)

Clearly children are capable of *faith*. In Matthew 18:3 our Lord used the humility of the child as a model for the kingdom person, affirming that such humility would be the basis for a childlike trust. But that is different from assuming that children understand all of our terminology and abstract concepts. Especially those who work with children must be aware of how things are said, considering the cognitive ability of the child.

4. Concrete learning is necessary for later abstract thinking.

Rather than not teaching Bible as Goldman suggested, we should strive to teach children Bible stories so that as they move into the formal operations stage they have biblical data with which to form their new modes of thinking. As Richards has properly observed:

> This process of reconstructing one's perception of reality *from the data possessed* continues as the child moves from one stage to another. But *data which is not possessed* (and by "data" I mean concepts, terms, symbols, etc.) *cannot be handled in this restructuring process! The child will build a world view with the data he has . . . and if theological and moral content is not part of his data bank, his construct of reality will leave it out!* (italics his)[14]

It is probably better to tell the Bible stories to children than to read them. They were *meant* to be told, and by telling them we can fit them to the cognitive level of the child. We can choose language that is appropriate to the child's cognitive level and bring the story to life by inflection and oral interpretation.

Of course, not all of Scripture is appropriate for the young child. We must choose content that is understandable and applicable to the life of the child. Especially appropriate are stories that teach of God's character—his goodness, greatness, majesty, and holiness. Also, stories that tell of God's mighty acts on behalf of his people have special meaning to children.

5. Emphasize social interaction and environmental stimulation.

Learning is accomplished through interaction with the environment. "Sit down and be quiet" should be said only to gain control in the classroom. Children learn best through active involvement—touching, tasting, smelling, feeling, and doing. Because of the processes of adaptation, children need active and interactive learning environments.

Effective teachers think in terms of *learning activities* for children. Activity is directed and controlled so that learning outcomes may be attained. Children are directed into active involvement with their environment to stimulate learning.

6. Focus on one central aspect of the lesson for children under seven.

Because of the child's tendency to centrate, well-designed lessons focus on one key idea. All of the activities of the day center on one idea, which is taught in a variety of ways. A simple concept such as "God helps us" is taught through stories, songs, play, and pictures. The built-in repetition allows the child to engage the concept in a variety of ways, increasing the probability of learning.

7. Abstractions for a child under the age of twelve must always be tied to a concrete referent.

Children in the concrete operations stage are capable of abstract reasoning if the abstraction is related to something real. Math is taught, for example, using "apples and oranges" to tie the abstract concepts to real-life objects. Rather than asking the child to reason only in the theoretical domain, the teacher makes the concept concrete by tying it to reality.

Likewise, theological concepts must be tied to real-life situations. God's love, for example, must be discussed on the basis of actual examples of his love for us. If the concept is left totally abstract, the child will have difficulty grasping it, but when it is tied to actual ways God expresses love,

the concept can become "alive" and meaningful to the child. Many adults enjoy theoretical discussions, but children think such discussions are "dumb" because they cannot see relevance to their life. Only when theory is tied to actual experience can the child appreciate the importance of the concept being discussed.

8. Allow for questions and dialogue to correct misconceptions.

Because children think differently from adults, their perceptions need to be checked to monitor how they are understanding concepts being taught. Teaching must be dialogical with children, allowing them to express their understanding and to raise questions. Because Christian education is concerned with thinking correctly, it is especially important that children understand what is being taught. Misconceptions can lead to inappropriate fears or other conclusions that might hinder spiritual growth.

Teaching is a matter of listening as well as talking. Especially when our students think in ways different from ours, we need to hear what they are saying and help them to understand correctly. Through questions and dialogue we can correct the misconceptions of children and lead them toward better understanding of their faith.

The Bible is meant to be taught to children, but it must be taught in ways that grow out of how children learn and process information. Piaget has helped us understand the way children think, and this is critical to understanding how to teach them in responsible ways. Christian education needs to consider the cognitive development of children.

Notes

1. Ronald Goldman, *Religious Thinking From Childhood to Adolescence* (New York: Seabury, 1964).
2. From Ronald Goldman, *Readiness for Religion* (New York: Seabury, 1965), cited in Lawrence O. Richards, *A Theology of Christian Education* (Grand Rapids: Zondervan, 1975).
3. This overview is based on Mary Ann Spencer Pulaski's excellent introduction to Piaget, *Understanding Piaget* (New York: Harper & Row, 1971).
4. Fred D. McCormick, "Implications of the Conceptual Developmental Theory of Jean Piaget for Teaching Biblical/Theological Concepts to Children," master's thesis, Trinity Evangelical Divinity School, 1981, 13.
5. Pulaski, *Understanding Piaget*, 3.
6. Piaget used the philosophical mode of *structuralism*, which had never before been applied to psychology. Structuralism seeks to understand the parts in relation to the whole, which is the opposite of normal scientific inquiry. It looks for patterns of relationships, seeking to find the underlying structure of a culture, language, literary work, or, in Piaget's case, the child's epistemology. His extensive use of algebraic equations to explain the outworking of a child's logic is an attempt to define relationships of thoughts in the mind of the child. It is his remarkable power of structural analysis that allowed him to draw his exceptional conclusions.
7. Almost always literature about Piaget's stages will describe four stages of cognitive development—the sensorimotor, preoperations, concrete operations, and formal operations. In Piaget's writings preoperations is actually a significant substage of concrete operations. However, most writers discussing his theory separate preoperations into a distinct substage because of the amount of activity included here. I am choosing to follow this accepted trend and describe four stages of cognitive development.
8. Jean Piaget and Barbel Inhelder, *The Psychology of the Child* (New York: Basic Books, 1969), 51.
9. Pulaski, *Understanding Piaget*, 53.
10. Ibid., 57.
11. Piaget and Inhelder, *The Psychology of the Child*, 132.
12. Goldman, *Religious Thinking*, 68.
13. Richards, *Theology of Christian Education*, 185.
14. Ibid., 186.

CHAPTER 8

Moral Development

Scripture affirms that God is holy and that human beings are sinful and fall short of the glory of God's moral perfection. Only the most naïve, those who cannot bear or are not willing to see human sinfulness, argue the basic goodness of humankind. People have great worth and great dignity, but not great goodness. We are bound to and controlled by moral natures that rebel against God and do injustice to fellow human beings. As a race, human beings have been corrupted by sin.

The educational myth that the only things people need are a proper environment and proper stimulation to be good has been challenged by many. It is becoming increasingly obvious that more than a good environment is needed. Education that helps people grow morally and make sound moral decisions is needed. The whole realm of moral education is gaining increased attention in the public sector as the twentieth century comes to a close.

The church has always been concerned with morality because it is an important corollary to faith. God wants us

The church has always been concerned with morality because it is an important corollary to faith. God wants us to know right from wrong and wants us to do what is right and avoid what is wrong.

to know right from wrong and wants us to do what is right and avoid what is wrong.

Morality is, to a large extent, a matter of values. What a person values will shape the moral decisions he or she makes. So the church has been concerned with teaching people to value what God values and to hate what God hates. Unfortunately, the approach normally used by the church of naming and communicating Christian values has not always proved successful. People may *know* the right thing to do but still fail to *do* it. Or, worse yet, they change their minds, deciding the values learned in church are not appropriate or valid for their current life context.

Many churches have experienced the pain and surprise of sending students off to college well equipped with a knowledge of Christian lifestyle and values, only to have them return to announce, "We don't believe that anymore." The values and moral perspective so carefully taught at home and at church were abandoned with relative ease when challenged by a secular society. Moral education by parents and the church did not equip them adequately for living in a society of moral relativity and anti-Christian values.

The problem resides at the fundamental level of an assumption held by the church, namely that *moral education means teaching people to believe the right things*. Inherent in this assumption is that if people *know* the right thing they

will *do* the right thing. But is that a proper assumption?

THE CONNECTIONS BETWEEN KNOWING AND DOING

If it were true that to know is to do, all we would have to do is teach people the truth and they would then do it. But both experience and Scripture teach that knowledge does not automatically lead to action. We all have times when we know what we should do but for a variety of reasons choose not to do it. We sin by failing to live up to the knowledge we have. Not only must people *know* what to do; they must also be *willing* to do it.

Sometimes we have no real idea of what the right thing to do is. We need moral knowledge at that point, telling us what is good and right to do. But at other times we know what we should do, but out of fear or pure sinfulness, we simply do not want to do it. The Scripture warns of this possibility and concludes, "Anyone, then, who knows the good he ought to do and doesn't do it, sins" (James 4:17).

But the problem is compounded further when we both *know* what we should do and *want* to do it but do not have the *ability* to do it. Paul spoke of this condition when he wrote, "For I have the desire to do what is good, but I cannot carry it out" (Rom. 7:18). His problem was not at the level of *desire*, but rather at the level of *ability*. In order for people to do the right thing, they must have (1) moral knowledge of what is right, (2) be willing to do what is right, and (3) have moral strength to actually carry out their desire. The line from moral knowledge to moral action is not direct; included are also the will and the strength to do the right thing (see figure 3).

Educationally, it is not enough to teach moral values. Surely the church has moral content to communicate, but she must also speak to the will and the power to do that which is right. An educational strategy that enables people to grow in moral action is needed.

INADEQUATE APPROACHES TO MORAL DEVELOPMENT

Infants are born separated from God because of sin but without any moral awareness. They are born unable to comprehend moral issues because of their limited cognitive abilities. But they must learn to become moral beings. Adults who are *amoral* are sociopathic, unable to grasp ideas of morality and therefore unable to determine right from wrong. They function in society outside the bounds of accepted moral behavior, usually as terrible criminals, bound by no moral code. If people are to function in society, they must develop into moral beings capable of moral reasoning and willing to behave morally.

The question of moral development is, *How does the amoral infant become capable of moral behavior?*[1] How this question is answered will serve to shape the way we educate for morality. Several approaches to moral education have been offered by educators and psychologists alike.

Character Education

Probably the oldest approach to moral education is *character education*. This is a

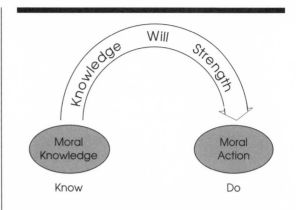

Figure 3

method of indoctrination that seeks to transmit a certain set of values to the next generation. The task of the adults is to *tell* the children what good morals are. Sometimes referred to as the "bag of virtues" approach to moral education, this approach stresses *knowing right from wrong* and the *passing of values* from one generation to the next.

The most difficult problem with this approach is determining what virtues should be taught. In societies governed by firm traditions, the selection of virtues or values to be passed on is already in place. The role of education, according to those who take this approach, is to pass these values on to the next generation.

Many Christian institutions take this approach to moral development. Believing their values are biblical, they feel compelled to pass them on to the next generation. Difficulty arises when different Christian groups teach different values, each claiming its own to be biblical. This becomes a hermeneutical problem, to be solved on the level of theology.

But in today's society traditions have been cast aside, and even Christians are interpreting Scripture in new ways. More-

Some Christians fall into the trap of believing Christian living is only a matter of lifestyle. But theologically, righteousness is a matter of action and motive. *God wants his people to do the right thing for the right reason.*

over, Christians are facing moral dilemmas never faced by previous generations. Traditional answers do not exist because these question have never been faced before. People need to think about moral issues so they can decide properly about the questions facing them in contemporary society.

Values Clarification

A second approach, rooted in the philosophy of moral relativity, is *values clarification*. This approach is based on the presupposition that all morals are relative and that the only correct value is tolerance. Therefore the task of the educator is to help people clarify their values and to hear and respect the differing values of others. Values clarification assumes the equality of all values and specifically resists the direct communication of any value system. Diametrically opposed to character education, values clarification seeks to allow all people to decide for themselves what their values will be.

Moral Behavior

The third approach, *moral behavior*, is based on the assumption that morality is only a matter of behavior. Rooted in the psychology of behaviorism, this approach focuses on observable behavior, taking a *learning* approach to morality. Children must be taught to *do* the right thing so that they can be moral.

Some Christians fall into the trap of believing Christian living is only a matter of lifestyle. But theologically, righteousness is a matter of *action and motive*. God wants his people to do the right thing for the right reason. A righteous act is an act that is in complete agreement with the will of God and proceeds from a heart that desires only to please God. Anything less cannot be considered righteous.

Sometimes pagans live better lives than do Christians, being kinder, gentler, and more forgiving than those who name the Name as their own. But because their *actions* are more "Christian" than ours may be does not mean they are more "righteous." Motives may be self-serving and not emanating from a desire to please God.

The moral-behavior approach can be helpful in shaping behaviors, but it cannot be accepted by Christians as ultimately helpful for moral education.

Moral Conflict

Growing out of psychoanalytic understandings of human behavior, the *moral conflict* approach to moral development is based on the belief that within all people resides a conflict between the *id*, or the basic instincts and drives of the person, and the *super ego*, which learns the expectations of society. This conflict is regulated by the *ego*, which is that part of the inner personality that must actually deal with the real context in which the person lives. The psychoanalytic method helps people develop a "favorable combination of the ego and superego characteristics so that the person will be able to cope both with a world of reality and with the realm of the moral."[2]

There is little that is educative in this approach to moral development. Rather, the concern is individualized, focusing on the phenomenological perspectives of each individual. It can be helpful as a therapy mode for those experiencing difficulties but is not especially beneficial for educators.

THE COGNITIVE-DEVELOPMENTAL APPROACH

Lawrence Kohlberg (1927–1987) was the director for the Center for Moral Development at Harvard University from 1968 until his death in 1987. Following in the line of Dewey and Piaget, Kohlberg was the first to identify clear stages in the development of moral reasoning. His research has been hailed by some as the most influential work in moral development ever and attacked by others as completely incompetent. The truth lies somewhere in between.

Raised in a privileged home, Kohlberg was educated in a private preparatory school. Rather than attend college, he chose to serve in the merchant marines and ended up helping to smuggle Jews from Europe into Palestine. He was detained on the island of Cyprus for this work and there faced the question of how what he perceived to be moral (the saving of the Jews from Nazi Germany) could be declared illegal by the British. He wondered, *How can one justify disobeying the law and legitimate authorities?*

His interest in moral issues led him to the University of Chicago where he com-

pleted his bachelors degree in one year. He continued his studies in psychology, interested in the possibility of moral stages of reasoning, posited but never validated by John Dewey. His doctoral dissertation became the foundation for his life's work, the study of the stages of moral development.

Research Terminology

To understand the cognitive-developmental approach one must understand what is being studied. Kohlberg distinguished between *moral judgment* and *moral action,* recognizing the possibility discussed above of a discrepancy between moral thinking and moral action. His research was in the cognitive realm, focusing on how people think about moral issues.

Moral judgment has both a moral content and a moral structure. Moral content focuses on *what* a person believes to be right or wrong. "Stealing is wrong" is a content statement, declaring the "what" aspect of a moral judgment. Moral structure focuses on the reasoning supporting a moral content, stating *why* a particular content is right or wrong. "I believe stealing is wrong because it is against the law" is a structure statement. Kohlberg studied the development of moral structure, identifying six stages of moral reasoning through which people may develop.

Because Kohlberg did not focus on content, some think he was a moral relativist. Nothing could be further from the truth. He believed strongly in the centrality of *justice* as the key moral content to be believed and upheld by moral people. In fact, the emergence of constructs of justice serve for Kohlberg as a key indicator of moral development. What Kohlberg did not accept was the possibility of ethical absolutes being rooted in divine revelation.

Kohlberg believed that philosophy had to come prior to psychology in the study of moral development. He rejected the psychological assumption of moral relativity and argued for the absolute necessity of ethical absolutes. His problem was where to find these absolutes. In a critical essay entitled "From Is to Ought: How to Commit the Naturalistic Fallacy and Get Away with It in the Study of Moral Development,"[3] he argued that it is possible to derive philosophical conclusions from nonphilosophical premises. The naturalistic fallacy specifically is reasoning from *what is* (morality or accepted moral behaviors that are nonabsolute) to *what ought to be* (ethical conclusions that carry with them a sense of imperative for all times and all people).

The need for ethical absolutes stems from his acceptance of the "formalistic" or "deontological" line of thinking running from Immanuel Kant to John Rawls.[4] This tradition contends that the best morality is *principled*, making moral judgments on the basis of universal ethical principles. Principles are different from *rules* (which are primarily prescriptions of behaviors) in that they are universal guides for making moral decisions.

Some Christians have criticized Kohlberg for his stand on justice as a primary ethical norm. Most notably Craig Dykstra[5] and Paul Vitz[6] challenge the use of justice as the controlling issue of moral content. But neither Vitz nor Dykstra interact with the theme of justice from a biblical perspective, nor do they acknowledge the centrality of this issue in Scripture. Given the biblical emphasis on justice, it seems to me that Kohlberg's concern is sound. I disagree with how he reaches his conclusion by means of the naturalistic fallacy rooted in deontological ethics, but I do believe that justice is an adequate and appropriate concern for moral judgment.

The prophet Micah's statement "He has showed you, O man, what is good. And what does the LORD require of you? To act justly and to love mercy and to walk humbly with your God" (Mic. 6:8) provides an important summary of the Old Testament's ethical requirements for the nation of Israel. Clearly God is concerned with justice, and his judgment of the nations for acting unjustly (see Ezek. 16:49) is indicative of the centrality of this issue.

STAGES OF MORAL DEVELOPMENT

The empirical study of moral development as a part of cognitive development began with Piaget. As part of his study of children's reasoning, he examined how they made moral judgments. Focusing on the game of marbles, Piaget had children teach him the rules. As he listened carefully to their reasoning about rules, he identified two distinct moralities that emerged in developmental sequence—moralities first of *constraint* and then of *cooperation*. The morality of constraint was *heteronomous* with its almost mythical respect for rules, while the latter was *autonomous*, recognizing that rules could be changed. Initial concepts of justice were rooted in the notion of obedience to the rules. Later this developed into understandings of cooperation and fairness, with a focus on equality and reciprocity.[7]

Kohlberg continued this line of research but focused originally on a sample of eighty-four boys aged ten to sixteen whom he followed for twenty years, testing them at three-year intervals. The obvious sampling bias of all males has been challenged by Carol Gilligan,[8] who contends that females will see other issues besides justice as controlling factors in moral reasoning. Since the original study, Kohlberg included women in his samples and interacted with Gilligan regarding this concern.[9]

Using the ancient technique of discussing moral dilemmas, Kohlberg constructed hypothetical situations that placed socially accepted values in conflict—such as the value of life versus the value of property—and then attempted to understand how these conflicts might be resolved by people at different ages. He identified six different stages in their conception of justice, which appeared in invariant sequence. Each stage accomplished a hierarchical reorganization of the moral concepts of the preceding stage, leading to a more differentiated and nuanced understanding of the dilemma and hence a more just resolution.

Each stage of the sequence identified by Kohlberg was signified by an expansion of the social unit to which moral judgment applied and a more complete understanding of how justice might be worked out in a growing social context. Thus the egocentrism of childhood is replaced by a group awareness in adolescence, which is subsequently expanded to a principled morality in adulthood. The stages are grouped into three levels consisting of preconventional, conventional, and postconventional reasoning. *Preconventional* reasoning is egocentric, drawing moral judgments from individual needs. *Conventional* reasoning is based on shared moral values held by groups, communities, or societies. *Postconventional* reasoning takes a prior-to-society perspective, drawing on principles that have universal application. Each level consists of two distinct stages, which emerge in invariant sequential order.

PRECOVENTIONAL MORALITY

Stage One—
Heteronomous Morality[10]

In this stage people make moral judgments on the basis of the physical consequences of their actions, seeking primarily to avoid punishment. Feeling vulnerable to the retribution of powerful authorities, they try to survive by staying out of trouble. Obedience for its own sake, as a means of avoiding punishment, is the controlling factor in making moral decisions.

The moral content "It is wrong to steal" is supported by the structure "You get in trouble if you steal." The rightness or wrongness of an act is determined by the consequences it may bring to the individual. There is virtually no awareness of issues of justice at this stage of development.

Stage Two—
Individualism, Instrumental Purpose, and Exchange

Judgment at this stage is still egocentric, but external authorities are no longer considered all-powerful. Experience has taught that wrong actions are not always immediately punished and right actions are not always immediately rewarded. Right action is now seen to be that which instrumentally satisfies one's own needs. Rules are followed only when it is in one's best interest to obey. The emergent autonomy is reflected in moral judgments based on concepts of reciprocity and fair exchange, with justice being identified with *fairness*.

Reciprocity is understood as "You scratch my back, and I'll scratch yours," apart from any deeper understanding. The moral content of "It is wrong to steal" is supported by a structure that may reason " ' Cause if you steal, people will probably steal from you, and you'll just lose everything anyway."

CONVENTIONAL MORALITY

Stage Three— Mutual Interpersonal Expectations

As the first stage to be distinctly societal in its orientation, stage three reasons from stereotypic and conventional conceptions of goodness, with the person seeking to be perceived as "nice." Sometimes called the "good boy–nice girl" orientation to morality, the expectations of others becomes very important. A new awareness of relationship with others now means that issues of loyalty, respect, and gratitude must be considered.

"It is wrong to steal" is now supported by the logic that states, "Everybody would think you were a crook." The intention behind an action now comes into play, and "He meant well" becomes a consideration when judging actions.

Stage Four— Social System and Conscience

In this stage people consider the welfare of society as a whole, having a high regard for maintaining the authority of societal rules. Right behavior means doing one's duty, showing respect for authority, and maintaining the current social order. The welfare of the individual is linked to the welfare of the group, and its rules are binding because they serve to prescribe the nature and extent of one's moral obligation.

Stealing is wrong because "Stealing is against the law, and anarchy could result if stealing were tolerated." Society's point of view is maintained over the individual perspective, and rules can be broken only when they conflict with other rules of equal or greater importance.

POSTCONVENTIONAL MORALITY

Stage Five— Social Contract and Individual Rights

Stage five marks the transcendence of societal expectations by the discovery of universal ethical principles. Social contract and individual rights become all important, with the possibility of changing laws to make them more equitable being realized. Societal standards must be critically examined and agreed upon by the whole society. While people in this stage recognize that most societal rules are relative to a given culture, they are now aware that certain rights such as those of *life* and *liberty* must be upheld in any society, regardless of majority opinion.

"It is wrong to steal" may be called into question *if stealing can enable the protection of individual rights.* There may be times when stealing is warranted to serve the greater good. If stealing might enhance the well-being of the entire group, the principle of greatest good would supersede the law.

Stage Six— Universal Ethical Principles

Moral judgments at this level are determined on the basis of personal obligation to self-chosen ethical principles that apply to all humankind regardless of race, sex, nationality, or socioeconomic status. Human rights and the worth and dignity of all people is emphasized. "Stealing is wrong" is based on the principle that *to steal would violate the rights of others and therefore be unjust.* Human laws are valid only to the extent that they are based on universal ethical principles that serve to protect persons and enhance justice. The

Golden Rule is now extended to its fullest implications as a categorical imperative for all people at all times.

Because these stages are recognized according to the capacity to reason cognitively, they are dependent on Piaget's stages of cognitive development. People cannot be capable of postconventional morality until they are capable of understanding formal operations. Kohlberg's understanding of moral development is contingent upon Piaget's stages of cognitive development.

COMPATIBILITY WITH SCRIPTURE

While some people have argued that Kohlberg's work is only a reflection of his own political stance and not supported by hard data,[11] it seems to me that the extensive research data does indicate a validity to his findings. But is this understanding of how people reason morally and the sequence of development indicated by this research compatible with Scripture? How does the Bible speak to us about moral issues?

Clearly Scripture makes moral appeals on all three levels of moral development. Preconventional morality is attuned to rewards and punishments. Scripture appeals to the human heart through the promises of rewards and punishments when God states in effect, "Obey me and I will bless you; disobey me and I will curse you." Appeals to heaven and hell, blessing and cursing, are appeals that would have meaning to the person who reasons in a level one, preconventional way. These persons would follow the Lord because of what they could gain or avoid by means of their obedience.

Some preaching and teaching is aimed at this level by offering "health and wealth" if we will follow the Lord. Scripture also speaks in these ways, but there are higher-level appeals to be found in the Scripture as well.

Conventional morality is concerned with obedience to authority. Much of Scripture calls for obedience *because God has spoken.* Such appeals as "Thus says the LORD" and Jesus' often-repeated observation "It is written" assume that there is an external authority to be obeyed. The Bible is filled with appeals at this level, teaching that God is to be obeyed because he is God. Obedience is not contingent on reward or punishment but on the fact that God is to be respected for who he is.

It would be a wonderful thing to get our churches up to a level-two morality where obedience to God is valued in and of itself. Too many Christians obey only those parts of Scripture that seem good to them, those parts that seem to promise reward or success. Scripture calls us to obey God because he is God, regardless of the outcome in our lives. Sometimes obedience will bring pain and suffering (Luke 14:25–35), but still we are called to obey, because he is Lord. In level-two morality people accept external authority, recognizing that there are larger issues than "What is in it for me?"

Postconventional morality goes beyond the letter of the law and seeks the underlying principle that the law expresses. Scripture ultimately subsumes all law under principle, telling us that if we can live by the principle we will fulfill the law. Hosea's instruction "For I desire mercy, not sacrifice, and acknowledgment of God rather than burnt offerings" (Hosea 6:6—repeated by our Lord in Matthew 9:13 and 12:7) and Micah 6:8, quoted earlier, are indicative of God's ultimate intention for his people. Much of the thrust of the Sermon on the Mount is to help people move beyond the letter of the law to the principles it is affirming.

Jesus' conflict with the Pharisees was to a great extent over their failure to grasp the larger principles of the law. They were so locked into thinking only in legalistic terms that they missed the larger issues of justice, mercy, and faithfulness (Matt. 23:23).

On several occasions Paul teaches that "love is the fulfilling of the law" (Rom. 13:8, 10; Gal. 5:14). Moreover, our Lord taught that all of God's law could be summarized in the two commands to love God with all our hearts and to love our neighbors as ourselves (Matt. 22:37–40).

The ultimate appeals of Scripture are made on the level of principle. After God has changed our hearts to desire to please him, we are finally moved to the place where law ceases to be the issue. The problem with law is that it does not cover every possibility. The Pharisees ended up creating additional laws that spoke to matters not clearly defined in Scripture. For example, they created extensive rulings on what constituted "work" so that they might be sure not to violate Sabbath. But they missed the principle that "the Sabbath was made for man, not man for the Sabbath" (Mark 2:27). They were never liberated to the level of principled morality, never discovering that there is a higher order than the written code.

Paul instructed the Romans in this regard, teaching them, "But now, by dying to what once bound us, we have been released from the law so that we serve in the new way of the Spirit, and not in the old way of the written code" (Rom. 7:6). When God promises to write his law on our hearts (2 Cor. 3:3), it is at the level of principle that his word is internalized. To hide God's word in our hearts is much more than a matter of memorization ("Thy word have I hid in my heart, that I might

win a free week at camp")—it is a matter of internalizing the principles of Scripture and applying them to daily life.

The question is not, "Is Kohlberg biblical?" (He did not examine Scripture; he studied people.) Rather, the question is, "Are his findings compatible with Scripture?" I think his research has the "ring of truth" both biblically and experientially and can be understood in biblical perspective.[12]

IMPLICATIONS FOR CHRISTIAN EDUCATION

Christian education needs to move past the "bag of virtues" approach to moral education and help believers learn to think well about moral issues. Morality is about more than moral judgment; it is also about moral action. But included in morality is the cognitive aspect of moral judgment. Regarding the relationship of moral judgment to moral action, Kohlberg wrote:

> If logical reasoning is a necessary but not sufficient condition for mature moral judgment, mature moral judgment is a necessary but not sufficient condition for mature moral action. One cannot follow moral principles if one does not understand (or believe in) moral principles. However, one can reason in terms of principles and not live up to those principles.[13]

Several educational principles, rooted both in theology and the findings of Kohlberg, can be drawn from this research.

Ask "why" questions regarding moral issues.

Because moral content is supported by moral structure, we cannot be satisfied

> *We must never teach theology apart from life implications and never make ethical demands apart from theological basis.*

when those we teach merely know the right answer. We all know the empty feeling of realizing that the people we are teaching have learned the "correct answers" without really engaging the issues.

Ted Ward tells a delightful story of the pastor who was asked to stop in and address the first-grade class of the Christian school meeting in his church. "I am thinking of one of God's creatures," he told the class. "It lives in the trees and gathers acorns for the winter. It has a large bushy tail and is grey. Who can tell me what I'm thinking about?" he asked. After a long and rather painful silence, he asked a deacon's son for the answer. "I know the answer is 'Jesus,' " the boy replied, "but it sure sounds a lot like a squirrel!"

The danger of dealing only with content but not structure is that if there is not adequate structure, the content may be abandoned. Teenagers may go off to college well equipped with all the right answers but not equipped to defend them. When their moral *reasoning* is attacked and they have not developed adequate reasons for *why* they believe, their moral content will be quickly abandoned.

When my own daughters were growing up, I would often ask them if they would ever take illegal drugs. "No, Dad," was their stock reply. "But why not?" would

always be my follow-up question. "Because you would kill us!" was their level-one answer as children. But as they grew older, they knew and I knew that they could sneak the drugs, and that I would be greatly disappointed, but I would not "kill" them. They needed a higher-level reason for not doing drugs. Asking the "why" questions allows parents and educators to explore and stimulate the structure of moral reasoning.

Understand that the "whys" of Christian living are rooted in theology, primarily in the character of God.

The ethical demands of Scripture emanate from the principle that we are to reflect the holiness of God to the rest of creation. We are to be loving because God first loved us. We are to be morally pure because God is morally pure. We are to be concerned for justice because God is concerned for justice. We are to be merciful because God is merciful.

Christians do not have to find their ethical imperatives from the best of society, as did Plato, Kant, and Kohlberg. Our imperatives are found in God and his Word. Christian educators must think theologically about life issues, finding a structural basis in the nature and character of God. We must never teach theology apart from life implications and never make ethical demands apart from theological basis.

I was exposed early in my Christian life to people who were vitally concerned with eschatology, arguing and exploring biblical passages that speak of the "end times." But much of this "prophetic teaching" was concerned only with future "time lines" as an attempt to prove various eschatological schemes. The schemes were taught devoid of any ethics, and we rarely discussed how we should live in light of these truths. But Scripture never discusses the future apart from ethical imperatives. The point of prophecy is not to map out the future in some careful way but to teach us how to live in light of the Lord's return.

Enabling moral development for the Christian means helping people make connections between ethical values and faith. It means teaching people to think Christianly, helping them to reason from theology to ethics and discover the underlying structure for moral behavior. Moral development will mean moving beyond the egocentric concerns of childhood into the more fully developed concerns of society and finally on to ethical principles. Proper theological interaction regarding these matters is essential to having our minds renewed.

Recognize that the structure of people's judgments do not improve by telling or teaching but by their own experience in moral-value problem solving.

Moral development is not a matter of listening to lectures but of actually doing the work of a moral philosopher. All people are forced by life experiences to think about moral issues and to determine how they will behave. Kohlberg constructed hypothetical moral dilemmas to study people's moral reasoning. But life is filled with real moral dilemmas that must be resolved if we are to function morally in society.

Children encounter moral dilemmas at school when they know their friends have cheated and they are tempted to cheat also. Teenagers live in a world filled with

moral decisions as they try to negotiate the tricky road of adolescence. Adults face continual moral issues as they try to sort out how to be Christian in a fundamentally pagan society.

Christian educators must be willing to confront and discuss the hard moral issues of the day in order to help students learn to think. Rather than denying the moral conflicts we face ("Christians don't think about those things") or trying to solve them with content alone ("The Bible says"), we must be willing to allow our students to struggle with the issues and help them learn to think in higher moral ways about them.

People become frustrated (disequilibrated) when their mode of thinking cannot accommodate a moral problem. It is this process of *living the struggle* that is the stuff of moral growth. But if we attempt to cut off or deny the struggle, or try to "fix it" with a lesson or two, we fail to allow people to have the experiences necessary for growth.

Some approaches to Christian education actually hinder moral development. Always promising a reward for serving God will lock a person into a preconventional morality. We serve God because he is God, not because of what we will get from serving him. Giving is to be sacrificial, not because he will "bless" our 90 percent if we give him 10 percent.

Some groups lock their people into conventional morality by passing rules and regulations on all sorts of issues. It is much more risky to offer people a principle rather than a rule, but it is necessary to help them move beyond a rules-and-regulations mode of moral reasoning. But Christian groups that have numerous rules and regulations will actually hinder the liberation of their people into postconventional thinking.

Adjust moral appeals to the developmental level of the students.

Moral appeals must be made at the level at which the student functions. Asking young children to "do what Jesus would do" is appealing to the more conventional sort of reasoning appropriate to adolescents. Children understand the language of rewards and punishments, so these have a definite place in working with children. But if we try to motivate teenagers and adults in these ways, we will have to raise the level of rewards and punishments to unreasonable and inappropriate heights.

Public schools place armed guards in the hallways because teenagers are still thinking like children in the moral realm. The punishment for disobedience must be raised to the level of arrest or injury because they have not learned to take a perspective broader than their own interests. This is a profoundly sad commentary on our society and is indicative of our lack of adequate moral development.

Older children need examples, models, and fair rules to help in their moral growth. Parents, youth leaders, teachers, and children's workers can work with the children to help them grow in a sense of fair play and reciprocity, which is critical for later moral reasoning.

Adults need more than a "prooftexting" approach to moral education. They need dialogue and exploration of moral issues to help them identify the differing sources of ethical constructs and the various values they represent. Rather than simply receiving correct content, they need experience in reflecting on and analyzing contemporary situations. The news is full of moral issues that can be used as case studies to determine how we ought to think about these matters and how we should respond. When adults exercise their capacity for formal operations regarding actual moral issues they face, they will be able to discover and explore ethical principles taught in Scripture.

Do not try to rush people through the levels of moral development.

Each level of development and its substages need to be explored and lived before a person can move on. The only way people can respect authority outside of themselves is first to have lived out an egocentric perspective and discovered its inadequacies. The only way a person can faithfully follow principle is first to have lived under external authority and experienced the outworking of the principle in the laws of the group. Each level is the necessary foundation and safeguard for the next level.

The stages of moral reasoning should not be thought of as totally discrete. That is, people will usually live in several stages simultaneously. Their reasoning will be predominantly in one stage but will also move back and ahead as the developmental process takes place. As with all of the developmental processes, we must trust God's design for his people and allow the process to develop normally.

An atmosphere of mutual respect can greatly contribute to a person's moral development.

Because moral development is concerned with justice, an environment in which justice prevails will greatly enhance growth. If people are treated with respect, not forced into positions they do not desire, they can have the freedom necessary for moral development. Environments that rigidly control, with only those in authority having power, will inhibit moral development. Listening to other people, hearing their perspectives and integrating them into decisions, helps children and youth learn to think in more mature ways.

A prison is a rigidly controlled environment that does little to help its inmates grow. Prisoners are punished for their crimes, but the context is hardly redemptive. A distinctly Christian context does not set moral constraints aside, but it will treat all people respectfully as moral issues are explored.

John Dewey called for democratic experimental schools nearly eighty years ago. Kohlberg followed his lead, setting up experimental "just moral communities" as laboratories in which to test his theories. He was able to produce students who did well in moral reasoning, but they were not particularly successful in translating this ability into moral action. But this does not negate the importance of treating people respectfully. Christian education needs to go beyond Kohlberg, using his insights but adding to them the theological foundations necessary for more complete moral maturity.

Our nation is in moral crisis because we have focused only on the lowest levels of moral reasoning, valuing individual rights and freedoms above any other moral principle. But the kingdom of God is about holiness and justice. It values the principles of Scripture. We need a Christian education that helps people develop in moral reasoning so that the principles of Scripture can be applied to contemporary settings. A task of Christian education is to produce people who are well developed morally.

Notes

1. Bonnidell Clouse, *Moral Development* (Grand Rapids: Baker, 1985), 20.
2. Ibid., 26.
3. In Lawrence Kohlberg, *The Philosophy of Moral Development* (San Francisco: Harper & Row, 1981), 101–89.
4. John Rawls, *A Theory of Justice* (Cambridge, Mass.: Harvard University Press, 1971).
5. Craig Dykstra, *Vision and Character* (New York: Paulist Press, 1981).
6. Paul Vitz, *Psychology as Religion: The Cult of Self-Worship* (Grand Rapids: Eerdmans, 1977).
7. Jean Piaget, *The Moral Judgment of the Child* (1932; reprint, New York: Free Press, 1965).
8. Carol Gilligan, *In Another Voice: Psychological Theory and Women's Development* (Cambridge, Mass.: Harvard University Press, 1982).
9. Lawrence Kohlberg, *The Psychology of Moral Development* (San Francisco: Harper & Row, 1984), 320–86.
10. A variety of names have been used by Kohlberg and others for these stages. I am choosing to use the names designated by Kohlberg in *The Psychology of Moral Development.*
11. See, for example, R. Shweder, "Review of Lawrence Kohlberg's *Essays on Moral Development, Volume I: The Philosophy of Moral Development*," in *Contemporary Psychology* (June 1982).
12. Again, I am indebted to my colleague Ted Ward for his unpublished essay "The Meaning of Value Development in Biblical Perspective" for helping to shape my thinking on this issue. However, he should not be held responsible for my perspective.
13. Lawrence Kohlberg, "The Cognitive-Developmental Approach to Moral Education," *Phi Delta Kappa* 56, no. 10 (June 1975): 670–77.

9

Faith Development

Why is it that most children are captivated by Bible stories and love to hear them over and over again? Why is it that adolescents may suddenly begin to question their faith and even announce that they no longer believe what their parents believe? Why is it that young adults sometimes make dramatic new discoveries about their faith, realizing that Christianity is more than doctrines and regulations, that it is, rather, an intimate personal relationship with God?

Each of these tendencies and other similar ones can be explained by means of faith-development theory. Just as there are stages of cognitive development and stages of moral development, faith-development theory presents the possibility of stages of faith—that is, *the way people understand and experience their faith will emerge through predictable stages.* If this theory is true, it offers some important insights into how we should educate for spiritual growth.

A REASONABLE THEORY?

Scripture affirms that faith is a gift from God (Eph. 2:8–9; cf. Rom. 12:3; 1 Cor. 12:9). But if our faith is a personal matter, one that is given by God, can it be reduced to predictable stages? Where is the mystery and serendipity of experiences of faith? Doesn't a stage-theory of faith do injustice to that which is in the realm of the Spirit?

Efforts to protect the supernatural essence of faith compel critics of faith-development theory to raise these questions. The application of *cognitive*, *developmental*, and *structural* elements to faith seems to be too limiting and predictable to be appropriate for describing faith; for these critics, stages are perceived to be like *boxes* that do not allow for the unique work of God.

But thinking about growth in faith in predictable ways is not a new idea. Scripture uses numerous metaphors of growth to describe how our faith should come to maturity. Metaphors of milk and solid food imply that spiritual development is like physical development. The Hebrews were rebuked because they still needed milk rather than solid food (Heb. 5:11–14). Also, metaphors of seeds and plants indicate that spiritual growth is like botanical growth, moving from a preliminary stage to a later mature stage. The calls of Scripture to maturity are calls for growth, and the pattern of growth is to some extent predictable.

Christian writers from all ages have spoken of predictable stages of faith. In the twelfth century Bernard of Clairvaux wrote,

> As one star differs from another, or as one cell from the next, so the spirit of the beginner, the spirit of the one making progress, and the spirit of the mature can be distinguished. The state of the beginner may be called "animal," the state of the one making progress "rational," and the state of the more mature "spiritual."
>
> Every religious institution is made up of these three categories of men. Those in the state called "animal" are those who are not yet governed by reason nor yet by the affections. They are stimulated by authority and good teaching and are led by teaching. But they are still like blind men led by the hand, acquiescing in the good where they find it, and following and imitating others.
>
> Then there are the "rational" who judge by their reason and the discernment that comes from natural learning. They know the good and are desirous of it. But they are still without love.
>
> Finally, there are the spiritually mature who are led by the spirit and are more abundantly enlightened by the Holy Spirit. They are called "spiritual" because the Holy Spirit rests upon them as He dwelt with Gideon.[1]

This ancient Christian mystic believed that people progress in their faith and that there are predictable patterns to the progression. We might choose to use different descriptions of these stages, but the validity of such stages seems obvious.

Influenced by the Reformation, a variety of more modern writers acknowledged the reality of stages of faith.[2] Educational understandings rooted in the Enlightenment offered new assessments of children, acknowledging that they learn differently from adults and that their mode of learning also influences their religious experiences. Both John Locke's *Some Thoughts Concerning Education* (published in 1693) and Jean-Jacques Rousseau's' *Emile* (published in 1762) indicate preliminary understandings of child development and its implications for religious training.[3] Moreover, Luther, Comenius, and Francke all acknowledged the existence of, and the importance of, developing abilities and experiences in children as they approached and experienced their faith.

In the 1840s Bushnell also argued for the importance of fitting religious training to the emerging abilities of the child. In 1849 he wrote regarding the religious training of children by parents:

> Rather should they begin with a kind of teaching suited to the age of the child. First of all, they should rather seek to teach a feeling than a doctrine, to both the child in their own feeling of love to God, and dependence on him, and contrition for wrong before him, bearing up the child's heart in their own, not fearing to encourage every good motive they can call to exercise; to make what is good, happy and attractive; what is wrong, odious and hateful. Then as the understanding advances, give it food suited to its capacity, opening upon it, gradually, the more difficult views of Christian doctrine and experience.[4]

Bushnell's assessment is remarkable because his approach is first affective and later cognitive. He advocated first nurturing children on an emotional level and then as they develop cognitively adding theological content. This is quite compatible with current cognitive and faith-development theory.

Contemporary faith-development theory attempts to describe the *structures of faith* and argues that *all people have faith* in that all must in some way make meaning out of their life experiences. Regardless of the content of the faith, the fact of faith is believed to be a human phenomenon. James Fowler describes it this way:

> In speaking of faith as a generic feature of human lives—as a universal quality of human meaning making—I make the claim that God has prepotentiated us for faith. That is, as human beings we

It is critical to understand that having faith and putting our faith in Christ are not the same thing.

have evolved with capacities and the need for faith from the beginning. Whether or not we are explicitly nurtured in faith in religious or Christian ways, we are engaged in forming relations of trust and loyalty to others. We shape commitments to causes and centers of value. We form allegiances and alliances with images and realities of power. And we form and shape our lives in relation to master stories. In these ways we join with others in the finding and making of meaning.[5]

Fowler argues that all people believe in something, and in this sense all people have faith. We have already established that what people believe (the content of their faith) matters. Scripture affirms that we are to believe that certain facts are true. But faith development considers *how* people believe, examining the *deep structures* of human faith, exploring the ways people hold the content of their faith.

It is at points such as this that the meeting of the natural with the supernatural becomes evident. The supernatural element is the acceptance of the content of the Christian faith (1 Cor. 12:3). The natural element is in the way that content is believed. If it is true that God has designed (prepotentiated) humans to have faith and that the structure of faith develops through particular stages, then it could also follow that even the way our *faith in Christ* is held will follow these same developmental patterns.

It is critical to understand that *having faith* and *putting our faith in Christ* are not the same thing. Saying that faith is a human phenomenon does not imply that all people have faith in Christ. Everyone believes in something, but only those who believe in Christ are saved (1 John 5:12). Conversion is a change in the *content* (what we believe), not necessarily in the *structure* (how we believe) of our faith. Christian faith is unique in its content, but because it is exercised by human beings, its structures will follow the patterns of human faith development.

Rather than positing a conflict between developmental patterns and the work of God, those who follow this approach seek to establish a compatibility between developmental theory and the work of God in bringing people to faith. I am trying to respect both the research regarding faith development and the theological foundations for faith. I do not think that it is unreasonable to think that even Christian faith, because it is exercised by human beings, will follow the normal patterns of faith development. If it is true that God has created us to develop according to predictable patterns, could it not be true that faith also is subject to development? Because developmental stages allow for a great deal of flexibility within them, it is possible for God to work with each of us individually and yet to see predictable stages of faith designed by his hand.

FOWLER'S STAGES OF FAITH

James W. Fowler (1940—) is widely regarded as the seminal researcher in the psychology of religion, and his is the dominant theory of faith development. Trained at Harvard, he taught at Boston College and Harvard University before taking his current position as the director of the Center for Research in Faith and Moral Development at Emory University.[6]

While at Harvard, Fowler was introduced to the developmental research of Lawrence Kohlberg, who later became his colleague and close personal friend. Fowler was working to understand the psychological aspects of how people make meaning in their lives, and Kohlberg introduced him to the possibility of stages of this development. He settled on the term *faith* to describe the aspect of human experience he was researching.

Fowler describes himself as a "classical liberal protestant."[7] Influenced strongly by the theologies of Paul Tillich and H. Richard Niebuhr, and the a priori epistemological categories of Immanuel Kant, Fowler has developed a construct of faith that brings together a variety of issues. He offers the following brief definition of faith and explains it:

> Faith is a composing, a dynamic and holistic construction of relations that include self to others, self to world, and self to self, construed as all related to an ultimate environment. This view has been scorned by some critics for not providing a more unitary and precise definition of faith. . . . It tries to evoke an awareness of faith as a multidimensional, central form of human action and construction. Faith involves both conscious and unconscious processes and holds together both rational and passional dynamics. Faith holds together both religious and nonreligious directions and forms.[8]

When this definition is applied to faith in Christ, God is the *ultimate environment*, and relationship to him and to others is transformed. Life and life issues may now be understood through the lens of the Gospel, with the assurance that the sovereign God loves us and controls both our ultimate destiny and our current situation. We now see ourselves as "simultaneously justified and yet sinners" (Luther) and other people as having great dignity and worth but in peril as sinners before a holy God. Fowler's definition is rational in its cognitive acceptance of the biblical perspective and passional in its love for God and neighbor.

Fowler has suggested *six stages of faith* through which human faith may progress. Because structural developmental stages are not controlled exclusively by chronological growth, not all people progress to the later stages. The stages are as follows:

Primal Faith (Infancy)

Prior to the development of faith, the infant's predisposition to trust is formed through relationships with parents and others as a way of offsetting the anxiety that results from separations that normally occur during infant development.[9] Fowler calls this a "pre-stage" because it is not accessible to the normal modes of empirical inquiry used for faith-development research.

Stage One—
Intuitive/Projective Faith
(Early Childhood)

In this highly imaginative stage, the young child is strongly influenced by images, stories, and symbols and is not yet controlled by logical thinking. Perceptions and feelings are powerful teachers regarding those parts of life that are both protective and threatening. Images of faith are shaped by the significant adults in the world of young children.

Children raised in Christian homes learn by the attitudes of their parents that church is a good place to be. Prayer, a joy-ful spirit, and personal contentment by the parents will help form in the child an attitude that emotionally proclaims, "This

> *Children raised in Christian homes learn by the attitude of their parents that church is a good place to be.*

is my Father's world." While not yet able to provide logical descriptions, intuitive/projective faith knows certain realities about its environment.

Stage Two—
Mythic/Literal Faith
(Childhood and Beyond)

Emerging concrete operations (Piaget) allow this person to think logically and order the world by means of categories of causality, space, and time. It is *mythic* in the sense that it can now capture life's meaning in stories, but literal in that it is generally limited to concrete thinking. There is still a relatively undeveloped interiority of the person, with limited self-awareness. As a result, it is difficult for a person in this stage to take the perspective of another person.

In stage two a person tends to understand God in terms of moral reciprocity, keeping score of who must be forgiven and who must be punished. As a result, people in this stage must either ignore or deny various segments of their life experience.

The child in stage two understands Christian faith in rigidly literal terms, believing that heaven consists of an amazing housing development ("In my Father's house are many rooms" [John 14:2]) and the streets of the city are paved with gold (Rev. 21:21). At this stage the child is unable to see spiritual realities apart from the literal constructs and is therefore limited in the way she can think about and respond to biblical truth. An important task of mythic/literal faith is to sort out reality from make-believe.

Mythic/literal faith is highly appropriate for young children but should be set aside in later years. Jesus' approval of childlike faith (Matt. 18:2–3) affirms *humility and trust*, not childlike ways of thinking. Unfortunately, some congregations tend to "lock in" at this stage. Probably growing out of a desire to take Scripture literally, these groups are so rigidly literal in their thinking that the deeper teachings of Scripture elude them. Such faith is not appropriate for adults. Literalism should be a stop along the way, not a destination.

An interesting phenomenon in mythic/literal faith is what Fowler describes as "eleven-year-old atheism." As the new modes of thinking emerge, children are not quite able to reconcile their understanding of the world with their concept of God. Their literalness cannot yet accommodate the idea of an invisible God who is sovereign over the created order. Such cognitive conflict may result in a temporary crises of faith as they try to bring their worlds of ideas and experiences together.

Stage Three— Synthetic/Conventional Faith (Adolescence and Beyond)

A strong relational component to faith emerges in stage three, as adolescents see themselves in relationship with others. This stage is *synthetic* in that the beliefs and values of the previous stages are synthesized into some sort of coherent perspective. It is *conventional* in that it tends to adopt the belief systems and forms of a larger community. An emerging sense of selfhood develops, and self-identity is constituted by roles and relationships.

Stage-three people tend to be highly committed to the church, and for them the church becomes an idealized extended family. Their social and political activities, as well as religious and educational ones, are more often than not rooted in the context of the church. Because of their extreme identification with the church, conflict and controversy within the body tend to be highly threatening to them. Moreover, dissonance will occur when authority figures are in conflict.

God is perceived as an extension of interpersonal relationships and can be counted on as a close personal friend. In stage three people have no problem believing that *God has a perfect parking spot for them right in front of the store* because he deeply loves them and is interested in their best interests. God loves not only the individual but also the whole group with whom this person has identified. Those with synthetic/conventional faith are quite sure regarding who are the true people of God and who are not.

A limitation of this stage is an overdependence on significant people within the community of faith. Pastors, youth leaders, or other significant persons are depended on both for judgments regarding truth ("What do we believe about...?") and self-worth. A "third-person perspective" is lacking, and one fails to see himself and his group as others might see him. In addition, in stage three one is highly susceptible *to the tyranny of "they,"* allowing external control to become all important.

There can be great comfort in synthetic/conventional faith because there is a sense of community and belonging that is missing in much of contemporary society. Also categories tend to be sure, with clear delineations being made between truth and error and "the good guys" (us) and "the bad guys" (them). An ecclesiastical theology that stresses community and relationships and strong leaders can create and hold people in stage-three faith.

Stage Four—
Individuative/Reflective Faith
(Young Adulthood)

Stage four is marked by a double development of self and of religious thinking. There is an experience of selfhood that stands in contrast to the community self of stage three. Self-authorization emerges with the possibility of making choices based solely on the self, apart from the dictates and expectations of the group. It is now possible for one to take a third-person perspective and to see self and the larger community of faith in relation to society as a whole.

Self is now separated from the group, and the individual stands over against the group asking why the group believes and acts as it does. The eager "fitting in" of stage three is replaced with a conscious criticism (not necessarily negative) of stage four. It is *individuative* in the sense that the person now establishes his or her own identity (individuates), and *reflective* in that it is marked by a conscious thinking about (reflection on) the assumptions and practices of the group.

Individuative/reflective faith is usually marked by a sense of guilt and loss as the comfort of stage three is left behind. The faith community that has nurtured and supported the person is now the object of separation and critique. Especially those communities that foster synthetic/con-

ventional faith will not tolerate these changes easily, creating more guilt and sense of loss.

My own movement out of the more rigid fundamentalism of my youth was especially painful. As I began to question some of the more extreme beliefs of my group (such as "wearing a beard violates biblical standards") I felt that I was growing in my understanding of what it meant to be Christian. But my faith community told me I was "going liberal" (the worst charge to be leveled against a fundamentalist). It was a lonely time for me as I tried to determine if I was growing in faith as I thought I was, or losing my faith as my friends believed I was.

The primary limitation of individuative/reflective faith is its overreliance on its own perspective. There is a certain arrogance that allows one to set oneself over against a group and critique it. Out of this can emerge such a privatized faith that no external judgment is tolerated. Church becomes totally pragmatic at this stage, existing only to serve the needs of the individual. Stage-four faith will demythologize religious rituals, asking for the meaning behind the rituals. Such seeking can be important to the integrity of the group, but it can also be indicative of failure at any level to submit oneself to the authority of the group, God, or the Gospel.

Stage Five—
Conjunctive Faith
(Mid-life and Beyond)

With conjunctive faith one becomes aware of the limitations of self and is less sure of the judgments and assessments made in stage four. There is a deeper self-awareness by which one understands better the relativity of his perspective and has a greater awareness of the grandeur of God. Both divine immanence and transcendence are appreciated, with the theology of incarnation and holiness being held in a new, more paradoxical relationship. It becomes axiomatic that truth is multidimensional, and it becomes reasonable to assume that other people have insights we do not have. Significant encounters with other people and groups are sought and valued, as a new quest for understanding is begun.

Those who achieve conjunctive faith are increasingly aware of the possibility of idolatry within even their own doctrinal statements, so they are marked by greater tolerance to outside perspectives.[10] People "earn" this stage by the hard work of living reflectively through the earlier stages.

There is a new sense of humility in conjunctive faith that lessens the self-assurance of stage four. The new openness allows for and seeks dialogue with groups outside of one's own community, and this openness can be essential to cooperative efforts among a variety of groups. When coupled with proper biblical constraints, stage five can be profoundly helpful in allowing persons to see the multiple facets of truth and the limitations of any human perspective.

Stage Six—
Universalizing Faith
(Mid-life and Beyond)

Stage six requires a radical decentralization of the self and a radical new quality of participation with God. All matters of paradox and polarities are set aside for a new identification with the work of God and his kingdom. A new quality of freedom emerges in which matters of self are now identified with the "ground of being."

There is a new expectation of life focused on matters of love and justice, with divisions and oppression set aside. There is "a disciplined activist incarnation—making real and tangible—of the imperatives of absolute love and justice of which stage 5 has partial apprehensions. The self at stage 6 engages in spending and being spent for the transformation of present reality in the direction of transcendent actuality."[11]

An Evangelical Assessment

When Fowler discusses *faith*, he is referring to a common human attempt to make sense out of life. For him, faith is in a sense a hermeneutical grid through which persons interpret life and attempt to find meaning. He has attempted to separate out content from structure in the process of *faithing* (his word for exercising faith), examining the *how* of faith rather than the *what*.

When evangelicals discuss faith, they usually mean something specific—acceptance of a specific content in ways that involve their minds, emotions, and wills. They speak of "the faith," referring to a specific content held in a specific way. Are these two conceptions of faith compatible?

I believe that it is both reasonable and helpful to assume the validity of faith-development theory. The possibility of stages of faith can be rather difficult for the American individualist to accept, but it does not necessarily do injustice to the mystical work of the Spirit in the lives of people. Faith stages are broad categories and descriptions, not rigid, confining boxes. Part of the orderliness of God's creation could easily be that human beings develop in their patterns of faith in orderly ways.

But has Fowler successfully separated content from structure, allowing for any content of faith to be held? Just as Kohlberg's theory requires the emergence of *justice* as a primary content of the later stages, so Fowler requires the emergence of a content of faith strongly similar to the advanced theology of Paul Tillich. Fowler recognizes this fact and explains it as follows:

> Despite the growing empirical verification, however, its theoretical framework and grounding indisputably rest on theological foundations and reasoning. These foundations have convictional status and finally rest on the faith commitments of the theorist and of the faith tradition of which he or she is a part. They can be rationally explicated, however, and are subject to statement in largely formal and functional terms. To a degree not yet fully tested, they seem capable of being stated in terms derived from other traditions and cultures not Christian or Western. It is a principle thesis of this chapter that the acknowledgment and rational explication of these broadly theological foundations do not jeopardize the theory's claim to scientific integrity. In this regard there are parallels with the conviction-laden philosophical rationales for normative and descriptive theories of cognitive development and for developmental theories of moral and religious reasoning.[12]

It is difficult to be totally correct, just as it is difficult to be totally incorrect. Fowler has done excellent work in bringing together a variety of issues and weaving them into a description of the construct of *faith*. Moreover, he has come a long way in clarifying the research and scoring procedures for determining a person's faith stage. He is offering descriptions of the stages that allow for a variety of contents and has listened attentively to his critics, evaluating and responding to their concerns in reasonable ways. Also, he is aware of the determinant role his own theology is playing in his theoretical constructs.

It is precisely at this point that we must part company with Fowler. His use of Tillich and Niebuhr, with their assumptions about the nature of God, the role of human experience, and the substance of the Gospel, lead him, in the higher stages, to constructs that are not compatible with God's self-revelation in Scripture. Ultimately, we are not called to identification with the Ground of Being, but to a profound thankfulness for the grace of a holy God who both sought and enabled our redemption. We are called to *know him* (John 17:3) and *serve him* (Rom. 12:1) out of grateful hearts.

Fowler rightly recognizes, as we must also, that a theory of faith development cannot be totally scientific and value free. Rather, it must of necessity begin with a description of the end point of faith, that normative state toward which all faith must lead. He acknowledges that "any developmental theory involving an accounting of qualitative transformations in human knowing, valuing, committing and acting, must derive its *Tendenz* and normative direction from some faith vision of the excellence to which humans are called and for which we are potentiated."[13]

Ultimately evangelicals must offer an amended version of his stage descriptions *and validate them empirically* to make this theory compatible with a distinctively biblical perspective. A more biblically derived vision of the ultimate stages of faith would yield a theory more useful for our purposes but one that is exclusivistic in its orientation. That does not mean that we have nothing to gain from Fowler's theory as it currently exists. It does mean, however, that more work needs to be done from an evangelical perspective.

INSIGHTS FOR CHRISTIAN EDUCATION

Even though there are some theological problems with the faith-development theory as it currently exists, there is much good to be drawn from this work. If we remain mindful of the weaknesses and keep our own theological moorings firmly in place, the work of James Fowler and his associates yields some important insights for Christian education and the process of spiritual growth.

Faith as a Universal Phenomenon

Faith-development theorists present a "high" view of humankind, arguing that everyone has faith in something. Faith is not something only "religious" people have; everyone is engaged in a quest for meaning that is mediated through faith. All people make a leap of faith when they attempt to find meaning in their existence.

Since all people have faith, Christians need not feel inferior because they are people of faith. The distinction between the Christian and the secularist is the

better content for faith than people who are without Christ?

I am not thinking about winning religious or philosophical debates. I am thinking about speaking to a very real life need, which Fowler has described. God has designed us as thinking/feeling/believing creatures; we all must believe in something. The Gospel speaks to that need for transcendence, offering a content for the human propensity for faith to embrace. Fowler has done a great service in helping us to see that all people have faith.

A Description of Faith as Different From Religion and Belief

Influenced by Wilford Cantwell Smith,[14] Fowler offers a critical distinction between *faith* and *creed* that is especially needed by the evangelical church. Concern for doctrinal purity has so consumed us that we

---

Faith is not something only "religious" people have; everyone is engaged in a quest for meaning that is mediated through faith. All people make a leap of faith when they attempt to find meaning in their existence.

---

content of faith, not the *fact of faith*. A careful probing of another person's perspective will yield an ultimate core of beliefs and relationships that make up that person's faith.

There is grist for the apologetic mill here as the reasonableness of one's faith content is examined. Is the Gospel a more adequate faith content than the stock market? Does it make better sense to put one's trust in and give one's loyalty to Jesus of Nazareth than to any other center of value and power? Can we offer a

have tended to reduce the concept of faith to a creedal statement, which we refer to as a Statement of Faith. Such statements list the specific content to be believed by persons associated with its community of origin. It is assumed that if one signs the statement, one has faith, *because one concurs with this doctrinal position.*

But Fowler reminds us that faith is dynamic, evolving, and relational—an integral part of our life. It shapes the way we see and make meaning of our lives, controlling our values and perceptions and exercise of power. He reminds us that faith is not static, but dynamic, influencing the way we see and relate to the world around us. He offers a corrective to those who would reduce faith to a cognitive list of beliefs by which, if one asserts them to be true, one would be saved.

Fowler is much closer to the historical concept of *belief* than the modern perspective is. Contemporary usage has reduced belief to a purely cognitive construct (*notitia*) without its subsequent affective and volitional components. But historically belief meant *by-life*, meaning that what one believed was what one lived by. It was unthinkable to claim that one's belief did not shape one's life. Fowler is reminding us again of the true nature of faith and belief.

A More Complete View of Faith

Fowler's research can help Christian educators view people more completely. He shows us that faith is tied closely to self-image and to worldview. Psychologists have long understood the importance of self-image for the development of the person, but Christian educators have tended to leave that concern to the domain of the therapist. Fowler helps us realize that one's emerging self-perceptions will influence how one shapes and experiences his or her faith.

People who understand and view themselves primarily as roles and relationships (I'm a Sunday school teacher; I'm a mother; I'm a member of First Church) will find it very difficult to progress beyond a stage-three faith. The higher stages require an ego-strength not all people can exercise. Because faith is partly a human phenomenon (that is, a gift from God but exercised by human beings), a whole-person perspective is needed to understand how people may be experiencing their faith.

Responsible Christian educators try to understand the whole person, not being limited only to spiritual concerns. Because faith involves the whole person, it must be understood in the total context of development. Faith is not an isolated aspect of the human personality but is the outcome of various aspects of the personality being integrated into a unified perspective. Such understanding can guard us against superficial understandings of this complex theological/psychological phenomenon.

Listening to Faith With Sensitivity

Christian educators must learn to listen sensitively as people discuss their faith. Historically evangelicals have attended to content but have ignored structure. We have been so concerned with guarding what people believe that we have failed to listen to how they believe. We have ignored the possibility of stages of faith, striving only to make faith *stronger* without being concerned with making faith *more mature*. We have tended to police its content and tried to strengthen its power, but we have neglected its maturity.

Fowler helps us identify the maturity of faith. Becoming conversant with his stages can help us listen with greater sensitivity to the way people describe their faith. It can help us hear with deeper insight the way people understand and experience their faith.

There is always the danger of abusing developmental stages, quickly categorizing people as to their stages and then attempting to manipulate them into a higher and more adequate stage. Besides being disrespectful of persons, such an attitude betrays ignorance of the nature of developmental psychology. If Fowler's stages offer new ways to put people in "pigeonholes" and a new hierarchy of spirituality, then there will be more harm than good to the church.

But the point of developmental stages of faith is to help us understand better the ways people experience and exercise faith. If we can hear with greater sensitivity the structure of faith reported by people, we can understand better both those ideas and experiences that can bring comfort as well as those that might stimulate growth.

Describing Mature Faith

In addition, Fowler's stages can help Christian educators understand the maturity of faith of their people. Instead of focusing only on strength, they can also assess maturity.

Lower stages of faith are not inappropriate for young persons. A young adolescent in stage-two faith can have a *strong* faith (a deep commitment to God), which is perfectly appropriate for his or her age. But if this same person continues in a stage-two structure well into adolescence or adulthood, the faith can be said to be strong, but immature. That is, it is not developmentally appropriate for the person's age and place in life.

The young child who believes God will protect her from all harm has a strong belief in the sovereignty of God and specific childlike perceptions of what God's love for her entails. Such a belief may be appropriate for a child. But when she becomes an adult, if she still believes that nothing "bad" can happen to her because of her faith, she is both misguided and immature. A more mature faith can differentiate between God's redemptive involvement in life situations (Rom. 8:28) and an iron-clad guarantee that believers are exempt from life's trials.

As Christian educators become sensitive to the stages of faith they will be able to hear structure as well as content, and

maturity as well as strength. They will understand people more deeply and have a more realistic perspective on the health of their congregations. Moreover, they will have better possibilities for designing educational approaches fit to the level of maturity of their people. Fowler has offered a way of determining the relative maturity of faith, describing the stages through which a maturing faith will progress. His descriptions are not without error and theological bias, but they are helpful for describing how people grow in faith.

Being attuned to faith stages will help us recognize some of the characteristics of growth. When a person who has been highly conventional in his faith becomes more individualized and remote, this may be an indication that he is growing, rather than regressing, as is often feared.

A student recently came to me and expressed her confusion over her experiences as a Christian. She had been highly committed to her local congregation, enthusiastic over what was transpiring in the services. But now in her early twenties, away from home, she was finding herself increasingly discontent with her local church. In addition, she no longer "saw eye to eye" with her mother regarding spiritual matters. "My mother thinks I'm going liberal" was her cynical observation. When I asked her what *she* thought, she told me she felt that she was growing.

"My faith means more to me now than it ever did before," she explained. She felt that she was reading Scripture with new enthusiasm, praying with greater integrity, and becoming aware of sin in ways she never had before. "I feel like I'm growing, but because I can't support our church the way I used to, my mother thinks I'm falling away" was her sad commentary.

I explained to her briefly a little about the stage theory and told her that what she was describing was quite typical for young adults and was, in my estimation, an indication of growth. Rather than trying to "bring her back into the fold," I encouraged her on her quest for a more personal faith, urging her to use her time at seminary to learn to own her faith in more personal ways. Faith-development theory gave me the categories through which to listen and discern that indeed she was growing in her faith.

There are a variety of ways to discuss spiritual maturity. Most tend to be either highly mystical or highly individualistic. James Fowler has offered a reasonable way to view faith developmentally, with appropriate controls for how the stages are to be discerned. His theory is not perfect, but it does provide some helpful categories and important insights for Christian education.

Notes

1. Bernard of Clairvaux, *The Love of God and Spiritual Friendship*, abridged ed. (Portland, Ore.: Multnomah Press, 1983), 9.
2. Sharon Parks and Craig Dykstra have argued that a stage theory of faith may just be yet another fad, reflective more of our contemporary society than of sound research. (See Craig Dykstra and Sharon Parks, eds., *Faith Development and Fowler* [Birmingham, Ala.: Religious Education Press, 1986].) But they have not looked back adequately to historical precedents.
3. For a helpful discussion of historical precedents to current faith-development theory see Friedrich Schweitzer, "Developmental Views of the Religion of the Child: Historical Antecedents" in Fowler, Nipkow, and Schweitzer, eds., *Stages of Faith and Religious Development* (New York: Crossroad, 1991), 67–81.
4. Horace Bushnell, *Views of Christian Nurture and Subjects Adjacent Thereto* (Hartford: E. Hunt, 1849), 17.
5. James Fowler, "The Vocation of Faith Development Theory" in Fowler, Nipkow, and Schweitzer, *Stages of Faith*, 22.
6. As of this writing, Fowler's books include *To See the Kingdom: The Theological Vision of H. Richard Niebuhr* (Nashville: Abingdon, 1974); *Stages of Faith: The Psychology of Human Development and the Quest for Meaning* (San Francisco: Harper & Row, 1981); *Becoming Adult, Becoming Christian: Adult Development and Christian Faith* (San Francisco: Harper & Row, 1984); *Faith Development and Pastoral Care* (Philadelphia: Fortress, 1987); *Weaving the New Creation: Stages of Faith and the Public Church* (San Francisco: Harper & Row, 1991).
7. This description and following specifics are taken from Fowler's presentation to the National Association of Professors of Christian Education (now known as the North American Association of Professors of Christian Education) on October 22–25, 1987, Danvers, Mass.
8. Fowler, Nipkow, and Schweitzer, *Stages of Faith*, 21.
9. This understanding of infancy is strongly influenced by Erik Erikson's concepts of psychosocial development and its concerns for basic trust vs. basic mistrust and Margaret Mahler's conception of the psychological birth of the human infant.
10. A critical question remains regarding the extent of tolerance necessary to be clearly within the boundaries of stage five. Fowler's own theological content allows him greater leniency in this regard than would more conservative theological positions. He insists, however, that it is possible to hold to evangelical theology and still have conjunctive faith.

11. Fowler, *Stages of Faith*, 200.
12. Fowler, Nipkow, and Schweitzer, *Stages of Faith*, 33.
13. Ibid., 36.
14. Wilford Cantwell Smith, *The Meaning and End of Religion* (New York: Macmillan, 1962).

PART III

Learning and Spiritual Growth

10

Learning and Spiritual Growth

Nobody can really know theology for sure" is a senti-ment that is all too prevalent in some of today's churches. "Besides, God doesn't care what we think; he just wants to love us the way we are" is the justification offered for a nonthinking faith. This attitude conveys the idea that thinking is somehow irrelevant and not related to spiritual growth. Even though Scripture clearly affirms the importance of the content of our belief, some Christians maintain that content and learning are unimportant for spiritual growth. Why does this idea persist?

THE CONTEMPORARY CONTEXT

An outgrowth of the 1960s is the application of relativistic thinking to virtually all aspects of life. The cry of the sixties, "Do your own thing," was rooted in a sense of individualism that was extended to all areas of life. Besides the more obvi-ous trappings of dress styles and haircuts (or lack thereof), the relativity of the sixties also influenced morality, ethics, and ultimately metaphysics.

People were taught not only to do their own thing, but also to think their own thing. The relativity of the age was extended to morals, with "values clarification" assuring people that all moral values are relative and therefore equal. But perhaps even more destructive was the fact that epistemological relativity (people can only "know" from their own perspective) was extended to make all truth relative. No longer could we talk about *Truth*; now

life. Moral absolutes dictated that sexual intercourse outside of marriage was wrong. Moral relativity says people should decide for themselves how they want to live. Moral absolutes dictated that the practice of homosexual behavior was wrong. Moral relativity says that all people should be free to decide how they want to live their lives.

The loss of moral absolutes (ethics) has created divisions and confusion within

---

The loss of moral absolutes (ethics) has created divisions and confusion within our society, leading not only to the breakdown of social structures but also to great confusion on the personal level.

---

we must talk about *what is true for you* versus *what is true for me*. Truth (with a capital T, denoting absolute truth) was reduced to truths (with a small t, designating relative truth).

Moral relativity has resulted in ethical chaos, with our society now fighting over how right and wrong are to be decided. This battle is the loudest over the issue of abortion. So-called pro-life advocates argue that the right to life of the unborn child is the greatest good. So-called pro-choice advocates argue that the right of the woman to choose whether or not to continue her pregnancy is the greatest good. But in the absence of any agreement as to how to sort out values in an absolute way, there is no possibility of resolving the debate.

Moral relativity has created a wide variety of conflicting lifestyles. If there are no absolutes for right and wrong behavior, people can choose virtually any manner of

our society, leading not only to the breakdown of social structures but also to great confusion on the personal level. Without absolutes, how does one determine right from wrong? How is one to know if a behavior is acceptable or not?

The only absolute that is being maintained at this time is *tolerance*. That is, the only value society is sure about is that we should not have any absolutes. "Politically correct" thought is that which in no way offends, confronts, or limits the freedoms of another person or group. Other persons' *feelings* are to be protected at all costs, even to the cost of their minds. Tolerance, it is argued, is the pathway to freedom and happiness for all.

Tolerance is to be exercised not only in reference to lifestyle but also in the arena of ideas. Just as all *values* are relative and equal, the current climate argues that all *ideas* are relative and therefore equal. We should be free to do our own thing, and we should be free to believe our own thing.

Tolerance regarding ideas is fine if truth is relative. If there is no such thing as right and wrong or truth and error, then allowing all persons to think what they will is proper. But if there is absolute truth, and if it is knowable, the most loving thing to do is to correct ideas so they are congruent with truth.[1]

The contemporary climate of tolerance and relativity has crept into the church, so that wide diversity of theological stances is accepted. "All persons must decide for themselves what they believe" has become a norm, in the name of Christian tolerance. It would be unkind, it is assumed, to correct other people's beliefs, especially if the Lord revealed it to them. We must be tolerant and not "put God in a box."

The key is to determine when tolerance is called for, and when we should be intolerant. J. Gresham Machen left Princeton Seminary to form Westminster Seminary over issues of intolerance. Machen believed in civil freedom, and the need for religious tolerance. But he also believed that regarding doctrine, the church should be intolerant. D. G. Hart explains:

> Of course, Machen himself believed that the church should be intolerant. But the kind of intolerance he advocated was theological, not political. He believed that the church's primary task was to proclaim the Gospel, and that task required careful attention to theology. In fact, the Presbyterian Church's witness was circumscribed by the Westminster Confession. A Presbyterian minister's ordination vows prohibited him from preaching anything contrary to the confession. But when it came to public matters, Machen recommended the course of civil liberty.[2]

Conservatives have developed a reputation for intolerance. We have sometimes tried to force our views and practices in ways we should not. But to be sucked up into the climate of theological tolerance, which argues that the content of our faith does not matter, will cripple the church collectively and her people individually. Jesus taught that true freedom was attained by means of engagement with truth.

THE TRUTH SHALL SET YOU FREE

In the prologue to his gospel John observes that Jesus was "full of grace and truth" (John 1:14) and that "grace and truth came through Jesus Christ" (v. 17). He established a linkage between God's grace and truth that is sustained throughout the gospel.

Jesus taught Nicodemus that "whoever lives by the truth comes into the light" (John 3:21). Moreover, he taught the Samaritan woman that "God is spirit, and his worshipers must worship in spirit and in truth" (John 4:24). Truth for our Lord was both possible and functional; it is what we live by, and it is to control our worship.

In a most startling assertion, Jesus promised the Jews who believed in him and followed him: "Then you will know the truth, and the truth will set you free" (John 8:32). He went on to contrast his teaching with the devil's lies: "There is no truth in him" (John 8:44). The truth that sets one free is the truth of Jesus as the Son of God who sets people free from the wrath of God toward sin and from the power of sin in our lives.

In perhaps the best known statement regarding truth, Jesus affirms that he embodies the truth about God, as well as being the way to God and to life in relation to God (John 14:6). He then promises the ministry of the Holy Spirit, who is "the Spirit of truth" (14:17; 15:26; 16:13), to guide his disciples into all truth (16:12). Clearly Jesus saw truth as both a liberating and empowering force in the life of his disciples.

Christian education must approach and treat Scripture as truth if it is to produce spiritual growth.

In his high priestly prayer recorded in John 17, Jesus prayed for us saying, "Sanctify them by the truth; your word is truth" (v. 17). In reference to this verse, Carson observes,

> This can only mean that the means Jesus expects his Father to use as he sanctifies his Son's followers is *the truth.* The Father will immerse Jesus' followers in the revelation of himself in his Son; he will sanctify them by sending the Paraclete to guide them into all Truth (16:13). Jesus' followers will be 'set apart' from the world, reserved for God's service, insofar as they think and live in conformity with the truth, the 'word' of revelation (v.6) supremely mediated through Christ (himself the truth, 14:6, and the Word incarnate, 1:1, 14)—the revelation now embodied in the pages of this book. In practical terms, no one can be 'sanctified' or set apart for the Lord's use without learning to think God's thoughts after him, without learning to live in conformity with the 'word' he has graciously given. By contrast, the heart of 'worldliness,' of what makes the world the world (1:9), is fundamental suppression or denial of the truth, profound rejection of God's gracious 'word,' his self-disclosure in Christ.[3]

Finally, when he was brought before Pilate, Jesus stated, "For this reason I was born, and for this I came into the world, to testify to the truth. Everyone on the side of truth listens to me" (John 18:37).

John's gospel makes clear the central role of truth in the life of the believer. We are to live by the truth, worship in truth, be led by the Spirit of truth, and know the truth. In turn, engagement with the truth both sets us free and is used by the Father to sanctify us. Truth is embodied ultimately in the Lord Jesus Christ and in God's written Word.

The implications for Christian education are profound. There is no freedom and no spiritual growth apart from truth. Both salvation and sanctification come through the proclamation of and obedience to the truth. The Word of God is truth. Christian education *must approach and treat Scripture as truth* if it is to produce spiritual growth.

Learning means, for the Christian, engagement with and submission to God's truth. Christian education will part company with modern education in its passionate quest for truth. Current educational approaches have abandoned the possibility of truth, leaving education without a foundation. In the opening chapter of his book, *The Closing of the American Mind*, which critiques American education, Allan Bloom observed,

> There is one thing a professor can be absolutely certain of: almost every student entering the university believes, or says he believes, that truth is relative. If this belief is put to the test, one can count on the students' reaction: they will be uncomprehending. That anyone should regard the proposition as not self-evident astonishes them, as though he were calling into question 2 + 2 = 4. These are things you don't think about.

The students' backgrounds are as various as America can provide. Some are religious, some atheists; some are to the Left, some to the Right; some intend to be scientists, some humanists or professionals or businessmen; some are poor, some rich. They are unified only in their relativism and in their allegiance to equality. And the two are related in moral intention. The relativity of truth is not a theoretical insight but a moral postulate, the condition of a free society, or so they see it. . . . The danger they have been taught to fear from absolutism is not error but intolerance. Relativism is necessary to openness; and this is the virtue, the only virtue, which all primary education for more than fifty years has dedicated itself to inculcating.[4]

While I disagree with much of Bloom's solutions, I think his assessment of the situation is correct. Such thinking is prevalent in the church also, crippling people both morally and spiritually, inhibiting their growth in Christ. The kind of learning needed is learning that engages truth, shaping how people worship and live, used by God to set people free and sanctify them for his kingdom.

A VISION FOR CHRISTIAN EDUCATION

One of the most remarkable examples of a sustained teaching ministry in a local church was carried out in the seventeenth century by the Episcopalian Richard Baxter (1615–1691). Baxter was forced to resign from the Episcopal church because he could not tolerate the church's position that Episcopal ordination was essential for the practice of Christian ministry. He became one of the leading pastors of the English dissenters. But during his years as an Episcopal pastor at Kidderminster, he personally taught all of the families involved in his church.

Baxter was a prolific and wordy writer, often repeating himself and going off into long and somewhat unrelated essays. But the heart of what he wrote was excellent, both for his century and for ours. His most widely received book, *The Reformed Pastor* (1656), offers a timely vision for what educational ministry can and should be. The book is not sectarian: his term "Reformed" does not mean Calvinist, or even Protestant, but rather refers to one who is revitalized and renewed in his own heart.[5]

Baxter wrote to fellow pastors, encouraging them to take their teaching ministry seriously. He advocated personally and systematically catechizing the entire congregation, keeping careful records of what each family had been taught. Using this method, he systematically taught the eight hundred families in his congregation each year.

Baxter's approach is not appropriate for today's culture. Work weeks, family schedules, economic realities, travel distances, and a host of other factors would make his program impossible for most present-day church leaders. But his concern for systematically teaching God's truth for the health of the congregation and nation is not only relevant but critical for the church in any age.

Baxter's concern was that pastoral ministry must be carried out on a personal as well as a public level. He acknowledged the validity of preaching to large groups, but contended that people's individual questions, concerns, and doubts are addressed best on the personal level. People can be taught best to know doctrine and think in biblical categories when they are instructed individually or in small groups.

Baxter offered twenty reasons why a personal, systematic approach to teaching the congregation should be implemented.

133

He made little distinction between evangelization and edification, properly seeing the first as leading naturally into the second. He argued,

> Personal ministry, when it is well managed, will also build up those being established in the faith. How can you build without laying a good foundation? How can people advance in the truth when they are not first taught the essentials? The fundamental we need to lead men to is further truth.[6]

Baxter was concerned for clarity in his preaching. His concern for his people could be written with equal conviction for today's congregations. He stated,

> For my part, I study to speak as plainly and effectively as I can. Next to my private study, this is my first priority. Yet I frequently meet some of my hearers who have listened to me for eight or ten years and still do not know whether Christ be

people. He saw a direct correlation between spiritual maturity and learning biblical and theological truths. Rather than berating the people for their lack of knowledge, he challenged the pastors to take their responsibility as educators more seriously. He valued the pulpit ministry but also understood the weaknesses of preaching as the primary mode of educating his congregation theologically. His vision was for both a strong preaching ministry and an equally strong instructional ministry, because both were essential to the life of the church.

PREACHING AND TEACHING

Many congregations understand the importance of teaching, and so they seek a pastor who can teach. But their expectation is that the teaching should be done from the pulpit to the entire congregation. The result is that preaching is lost, and

---

Both preaching and teaching are critical for a healthy and growing body, which is the church. Choosing between preaching and teaching is like choosing between the right and left wing of an airplane.

God or man. They wonder when I tell them of His birth, life and death. They still do not know that infants have original sin. Nor do they know the nature of repentance, faith, or the holiness required of them. Most of them have only a vague belief in Christ, hoping that He will pardon, justify, and save them. And the world still holds their hearts.[7]

Baxter traced the spiritual weakness of seventeenth-century England to the theological and biblical ignorance of the

teaching is limited to a one-way monologue from the pastor to the congregation. From an educational perspective, this is hardly ideal.

A teaching pastor may carefully explain each verse but ends up sounding like a commentary wired for sound. He or she will "stand alongside the text," offering explanations regarding its meaning, but sacrificing the ability of the text to sing and sting as it speaks to the hearts and lives of the congregation.

Preaching focuses on proclamation of the truth, with calls for response. Sound preaching explores both the biblical text and the contemporary context of the people, applying biblical and theological insights to the life experiences of the people. Its emphasis is on proclamation and application. As an art, it is sadly absent in many of our evangelical churches.

Teaching focuses on explanation and understanding of the biblical text. Its methods lead learners to discover and understand truth in increasingly deeper ways, ultimately enabling people to think in biblical categories. Its emphasis is on explanation, discovery, and understanding.

Of course, preaching is concerned with explanation and understanding, and, conversely, teaching is concerned with proclamation and application. The difference lies in emphasis and in the methods used. Preaching is normally more limited methodologically than is teaching, with the emphasis placed more on proclamation and application than on understanding. But both preaching and teaching are critical for a healthy and growing body, which is the church.

Choosing between preaching and teaching is like choosing between the right and left wing of an airplane. As both wings are critical to flight, both ministries are critical to spiritual growth. When either is ignored, the outcome can be disastrous.

When the two are blended together, emphasizing a teaching ministry from the pulpit, there are two negative results—the ministry of preaching is ignored, and teaching is conducted in one of the most ineffective modes, one-way communication to a large group. A better approach is to value both the preaching and teaching ministries, allowing the preaching to be distinctly exhortative and the teaching to be distinctly educative. There will be an overlap in the ministries because the distinctions between teaching and preaching are not rigid, but there will also be equal emphasis on understanding and responding.

EDUCATIONAL IMPLICATIONS

Since spiritual growth requires engagement with the truth, and teaching is most efficient when done personally or in small groups, what educational implications can be drawn for the church?

Christian education must focus on teaching Scripture.

Because it is truth that sanctifies and sets us free, and because God's Word is truth, effective education must teach the Word of God. Interaction with Scripture is essential to the spiritual health of the congregation, and without it spiritual growth is impossible.

There is an increasing deemphasis on Bible teaching in the educational programs of our churches, with growing emphasis on meeting felt needs. Courses on managing money, communication in marriage, breaking patterns of codependency, and a host of other "need oriented" studies are replacing more biblically and theologically oriented studies. The underlying assumption seems to be that Bible and theology are irrelevant to modern life.

The theological liberals of a generation ago held the same assumption, discarding traditional biblical teachings for more modern concerns. Their shift was rooted in a fundamental mistrust of the reliability of Scripture. The modern challenges of both lower and higher criticism left them with an errant and fallible Bible. They were driven to find the Word of God in their experience, rather than in the written Word of Scripture. But they were consistent with their belief regarding the nature of divine inspiration.

Modern evangelicals are characterized by a high degree of confidence in the authority, infallibility, and inerrancy of Scripture. We are known primarily as "people of the book." Yet, our practice is not consistent with our belief. We argue the theological importance of Scripture but increasingly treat it as peripheral to our faith.

Learning the Word means living the Word. Only knowledge that is being translated into action is acceptable.

If it is true that God has inspired the biblical authors and that Scripture contains the very words God has intended, then it follows that we must teach the Scriptures to our people. We, of all people, must be those who not only claim to value the Bible but also in fact *teach the Bible* to our people.

Scripture is not irrelevant to modern experience. Its timeless truths are as relevant and essential today as they were when they were first written. The central themes of Scripture—holiness, election, propitiation, sin, redemption, providence, and a host of others—are critical for us if we are to live as the people of God. If our people are to have their minds renewed, our educational programs must teach them the Bible.

Karl Barth, the brilliant Swiss theologian, did not share the same view of Scripture as modern evangelicals, but he

did value the Bible. When he could not swear allegiance to Adolph Hitler, he was forced to resign his teaching position at Bonn University. His final words to his students were these: "And now the end has come. So listen to my last piece of advice: exegesis, exegesis, and yet more exegesis! Keep to the Word, to the Scripture that has been given us."[8]

Karl Barth understood that Christianity is first a religion of the text, whose identity and authority are rooted in the doctrine of inspiration. Our educational programs must reflect this conviction if we are to nurture spiritually mature believers.

Education must focus on God's Word as Truth.

The Bible must be taught by those who have deep confidence in it. While doubt is not a sin in itself, it cripples the effectiveness of a Bible teacher. A person who wonders whether Scripture is truth or one of a variety of options for belief will hardly be able to lead others into growing faith. But those who are convinced of the infallibility of Scripture will be able to lead others into fruitful engagement with God's Word.

There seems to be a creeping distrust of Scripture among some evangelicals. Some are worried about declaring the inerrancy of Scripture because of certain abuses of that position. But a reasonable view of inerrancy contends that the Bible is without error in all that it affirms. It recognizes that there are figures of speech that are not to be taken literally, and that there are even grammatical errors in the text, reflective of the humanity and personality of the human authors. But it also affirms that God does not lie, and that his Word is trustworthy in all that it declares. We must take a foundational stance on the inerrant (without error) and infallible (incapable of failing) Word of God.

Such conviction causes the teacher to proclaim with confidence the principles and message of Scripture. When teachers are convinced that the Bible is truth, they will teach students with confidence and authority. The apostle Paul urged Titus to appoint elders in every town. Part of the qualifications of an elder was that "he must hold firmly to the trustworthy message as it has been taught, so that he can encourage others by sound doctrine and refute those who oppose it" (Titus 1:9). The twofold responsibility to encourage and refute is rooted in conviction regarding the trustworthiness of the message. Without this conviction, teaching can hardly be encouraging.[9]

Learning implies a deep engagement with the Truth.

Since the goal of our education is righteousness, we must help students engage the truth in ways that cause them to grow. Learning involves the whole personality—intellect, emotion, and volition. Learning that promotes spiritual maturity is not only cognitive. The monasteries of the Middle Ages promoted learning that was cognitive only, and they had little effect on their culture. Rather, learning the Word means living the Word. Only knowledge that is being translated into action is acceptable.

Paul warned the Ephesians about their way of life, and he tied it directly to their thinking. He wrote, "So I tell you this, and insist on it in the Lord, that you must no longer live as the Gentiles do, in the futility of their thinking. They are darkened in their understanding and separated from the life of God because of the ignorance that is in them" (Eph. 4:17–18). His solu-

tion was that they must "be made new in the attitude of [their] minds" (Eph. 4:23).

Learning God's Word is more than mastery of its content. It includes that but moves on to changed attitudes and actions that are governed by the concerns of Scripture. It is engaging the truth and letting the truth shape and form our thoughts, feelings, and actions. It is hard cognitive, emotional, and volitional work, but it is also the pathway to righteous living.

Education must be carried out on as personal a level as possible.

Because the focus of educational ministry is understanding so that response is possible, educational settings must allow for interaction, clarification, and exploration. Contexts must be designed to allow for personal interaction between teacher and learner and to allow for questions, discussion, and exploration of ideas.

Educational ministries must avoid the "sit and soak" approach to learning, for this allows and even encourages people to function passively in educational contexts. Richard Baxter discovered that his people could sit under his preaching for years and still not understand the elementary truths of the faith. It was not until he taught them in small groups that he was able to ascertain what they actually understood and move them to deeper levels of learning.

The nature of learning necessary for spiritual growth is highly personal. Persons must individually engage the truth and examine their lives in light of the truth. Just as our Lord spoke with Nicodemus personally, so we must be available to help people think through issues on a personal level. This does not imply that we must tutor people personally; but it does mean that smaller, more personal groups are to be preferred over larger ones.

At Trinity Evangelical Divinity School, where I teach, some of the classes are quite large. It is not unusual for me to teach an introductory-level course to eighty students at once. I am painfully aware that I am reduced to a primary reliance on lecture and that I hardly even know the students. It is possible that over the ten weeks of the course I may not say one personal word to half of the students in the class.

Other classes have limited enrollments or draw fewer students. In these classes I can use a greater variety of teaching methods and can engage the thinking of the students in much more effective ways. The possibility of shaping a life is greater in the small classes than in the large. Any teacher who is sensitive to effective learning understands this principle.

Christian education must be viewed as part of the ministry of the church, not as its total ministry.

God has ordained both teaching and preaching as means of building people in the faith. A dominantly cognitive educational ministry that is not balanced with a more affective preaching ministry will not provide an adequate context for spiritual growth. Conversely, a dominantly affective preaching ministry not coupled with a more cognitive teaching ministry cannot by itself produce spiritual growth. Both preaching and teaching must be valued, and both must be provided.

Scripture values the roles of both pastors and teachers, and both ministries must be present. Clearly pastors teach, and teachers pastor; there is not a specific line of demarcation. But both emphases need to be present for the people of God to mature.

Christian education is most effective when it is carried out in systematic ways.

Richard Baxter kept careful records on what each person had learned, so that his or her knowledge might develop in systematic ways. Certainly there is a place for psychological curriculum planning that is geared to the immediate interests

There is plenty of room for creativity in determining how and when content will be studied. But there must be the discipline of teaching all of Scripture faithfully.

and needs of the people. But there is also a need for logical curriculum development geared to the logical unfolding of the content being learned.

Because Scripture contains logical argumentation and because theology is a highly logical discipline, it makes sense to offer a teaching ministry that develops logically. Some people claim that logic is Western in orientation because it is linear and that the Bible is Eastern and therefore more circular in its reasoning. Such a distinction between Eastern and Western logic is both false and deceptive.

It is false because both Eastern and Western minds use both sorts of logic. An Eastern mind, for example, does not do mathematics or electronics differently from a Western mind. Both worldviews and mindsets reason in these disciplines in the same way. Moreover, a Western mind can appreciate narrative as well as an Eastern mind. While there is a preference for linear thinking in the West and circular in the East, both kinds of logic are used in both cultures.

The distinction is deceptive in that it tends to force people to choose how they want to think. Some people reject theology as Western, and therefore flawed, as if God does not communicate in logical, linear thought. Others view narrative as somehow second-class and not as important as pure doctrine. Such thinking will cause persons to miss whole sections of Scripture that do not comply with their preferred way of thinking.

But a proper view of inspiration causes us to value all of Scripture equally and to strive to learn from the differing kinds of literature and logic found within it. Because it is the Word of God, we will listen to and learn from all of the Bible.

The design of the educational program must produce a systematic study of the themes and sections of Scripture. There is plenty of room for creativity in determining how and when content will be studied. But there must be the discipline of teaching all of Scripture faithfully. Because learning is necessary for spiritual growth, we must teach in ways that allow people to engage the full truth of Scripture.

Notes

1. Of course, another order of question is whether or not any individual or group actually knows the truth. In a properly pluralistic society, it is assumed that all people know only part of the truth. The point of pluralism, properly understood, is not tolerance of competing views, but rather allowing competing views to contend with each other so that truth may be discovered. But pluralism should rest on the possibility of both the existence and knowability of truth. Pluralism built on relativity is doomed to fail.
2. D. G. Hart, "J. Gresham Machen: The Politically Incorrect Fundamentalist," *Tabletalk* 17, no. 3 (March 1992): 14–15.
3. D. A. Carson, *The Gospel According to John* (Grand Rapids: Eerdmans, 1991), 566.
4. Allan Bloom, *The Closing of the American Mind* (New York: Simon and Schuster, 1987), 25–26.
5. Richard Baxter, *The Reformed Pastor*, abridged and ed. by James M. Houston (Portland, Ore.: Multnomah Press, 1982), xiii.
6. Ibid., 106.
7. Ibid., 114.
8. Eberhard Busch, *Karl Barth: His Life from Letters and Autobiographical Texts* (Philadelphia: Westminster, 1976), 259.
9. I write as one who has wrestled long and hard with the question of the reliability of Scripture. I urge people to face such questions head on and determine for themselves the truthfulness of Scripture. But I also urge that they not teach the Bible publicly until these matters have been settled. It is no favor to pass our doubts on to others.

11

Learning and Early Childhood Influences

Responsible Christian education requires that from their earliest days children should be raised in the faith. That is, we are to "raise [our] children in the training and instruction of the Lord" (Eph. 6:4). This is both a mandate and a privilege for Christian parents.

How is faith formed in the child? What does the process look like, and how can we enable faith to grow in our children? How can we obey the biblical mandate in ways that are compatible with how children learn? What do theology and psychology tell us about how we may best teach our children?

The theological answer to how faith is formed is that it is first a gift from God. The reason we pray for the salvation of others, children and adults alike, is that we instinctively realize that God must draw them to himself and give them faith. And the reason we give thanks to God for our salvation and for the salvation of others is that we understand that salvation is his gift. Indeed, any thinking Christian realizes that faith is first and foremost a gift from God.[1]

But the truth of God's sovereignty over faith and salvation does not remove the necessity of human responsibility. Parents are still responsible for raising their children in the faith, and the church is responsible for teaching the children so that they may believe. Divine sovereignty does not eliminate human responsibility. Both concepts are taught in Scripture, and these truths are not incompatible.[2]

Theology tells us that faith is God's gift, and psychology helps us understand how children learn. As we saw in chapter 2, the Bible teaches that we are responsible to train our children to be Christians, and psychology helps us understand some of the early influences on children's thinking.

EARLY PATTERNS OF REINFORCEMENT

As we saw in chapter 6, behaviorists understand human behavior in terms of environmental stimuli, primarily rewards. They believe that the best explanation for human actions and learning is that people are "reinforced" (rewarded) for behaving in specific ways. Some behaviorists go so far as to claim that rewards and punishments explain all of human behavior.

As people who value human worth and dignity and who see human beings as more than an amalgamation of predetermined responses, most Christians reject behaviorism as a dominant explanation of learning and as an acceptable mode of teaching.

But just as it is difficult to be totally right, so it is difficult to be totally wrong. There is a certain element of truth in behaviorism that should not be denied. While its assertions regarding human nature are wrong and its theories are inadequate to explain all of human behaviors, there are some aspects of learning that can be explained in terms of rewards and punishments. At least we can say

that there is an influence from the patterns of reinforcement, especially from early childhood, that affect us throughout our life. Mark Cosgrove observed,

> The Christian has no quarrel with Skinner's data. Skinner has uncovered some of God's laws governing certain animal and human behaviors. The problem arises only when Skinner generalizes from his data and makes broad assumptions about the nature of reality that are insupportable by his data and in conflict with biblical revelation.[3]

The most sophisticated form of behaviorism is B. F. Skinner's *operant conditioning*. Operant conditioning differs from the more historic and primitive classical conditioning (most usually associated with Pavlov and later with J. B. Watson) in its emphasis on *operant* behaviors. Operant behavior is emitted by the organism at its own initiative. Operant conditioning argues that those behaviors (operants) that are positively reinforced (conditioned) are more likely to be repeated. In other words, reward a behavior, and it will probably be repeated. Conversely, ignore or punish a behavior, and it is less likely to be repeated.

Even though this is not an adequate explanation for all learning, it does help us understand something about how young children learn some of their behaviors. They tend to imitate adults, adults are pleased and compliment (reward) the child, and the child repeats the behavior. Much of our early learning can be explained in these terms. B. F. Skinner explained it this way:

> A behavioristic analysis rests on the following assumptions: A person is first of all an organism, a member of a species and a subspecies. . . . The organism becomes a person as it acquires a repertoire of behavior under the contingencies

> *Christian maturity is more than a matter of outward behavior. It is possible to train people to do the right things, but they may do them for the wrong reasons.*

of reinforcement to which it is exposed during its lifetime. . . . It is able to acquire such a repertoire under such control because of processes of conditioning.[4]

Skinner's assessment that an organism *becomes a person* as it learns certain behaviors is abhorrent to Christian theology. But his contention that behaviors are acquired due to patterns of reinforcement is probably correct. Much of the early learning of children is a result of rewards and punishments.

Can faith be learned in this way? If we reward our children for behaving like Christians, will that make them Christians? Obviously the answer to this question is no. But there is an aspect of faith that can be taught in this way.

Part of our faith is volitional, dealing with the choices we make and how we behave. God is concerned with behavior, and an aspect of faith deals with how we behave. Belief is not divorced from the rest of life, and obedience is an important aspect of being a Christian.

Part of our responsibility as parents and teachers is to teach children to behave in appropriate ways, ways that are pleasing to God. Patterns of reinforcement

are one of the more powerful ways to teach appropriate behavior.

Christian maturity is more than a matter of outward behavior. It is possible to train people to do the right things, but they may do them for the wrong reasons. The limitation of a purely behavioristic approach to learning is that it is concerned only with the external aspect of the person, ignoring inward motivations.

But patterns of reinforcement do shape attitudes. Because children are whole beings, the shaping of behaviors will also shape attitudes. The practice of prayer before meals, prayer before trips, and prayer before bedtime shapes not only the actions of children, but also their attitudes. In this regard, prayer is more caught than taught.

Lawrence Kohlberg has demonstrated that the lower levels of moral development are influenced by external contingencies. Morality is first acquired in relationship to self-interests. That which is seen to be rewarding is followed, and that which is punished is avoided. This is how children first gain moral reasoning. God instills within each of us a conscience, and that conscience is molded by external influences.

REINFORCEMENT IN SCRIPTURE

The validity of using reinforcement as a means of shaping behavior is demonstrated in Scripture. God promised blessings for obedience and pronounced cursings for disobedience. It seems that he began the training of his people by appealing to outcomes—rewards and punishments. He does not leave his people at this level, but there are numerous examples of motivation by outcomes in Scripture.

As the nation of Israel prepared to enter the Promised Land, Moses taught them what God had promised:

So if you faithfully obey the commands I am giving you today—to love the LORD your God and to serve him with all your heart and with all your soul—then I will send the rain on your land in its season, both autumn and spring rains, so that you may gather in your grain, new wine and oil. I will provide grass in the fields for your cattle, and you will eat and be satisfied.

Be careful, or you will be enticed to turn away and worship other gods and bow down to them. Then the LORD's anger will burn against you, and he will shut the heavens so that it will not rain and the ground will yield no produce, and you will soon perish from the good land the LORD is giving you. (Deut. 11:13–17)

The motivation for Israel was clear. If they wanted God's blessing, they were to love and obey him. If they failed to do so and prostituted themselves to other gods, they would be cursed. It is a rather basic appeal to obey God because of the consequences.

Lest they miss the point, Moses summarized the issue a few verses later:

See, I am setting before you today a blessing and a curse—the blessing if you obey the commands of the LORD your God that I am giving you today; the curse if you disobey the commands of the LORD your God and turn from the way that I command you today by following other gods, which you have not known. (Deut. 11:26–28)

The New Testament also demonstrates the importance of external rewards. Even the apostle Paul observed, "I have fought the good fight, I have finished the race, I have kept the faith. Now there is in store for me the crown of righteousness, which the Lord, the righteous Judge, will award me on that day—and not only to me, but also to all who have longed for his appearing" (2 Tim. 4:7–8).

If this were the only motivation to obey God and serve him, it would be inappropriate. However, Paul also delighted in serving God because he was grateful for his salvation. Christians ultimately are to be motivated by gratitude, not by the rewards they may receive. Yet there is an aspect of the human heart that is concerned with outcomes. To ignore this is to ignore an important aspect of how God has created us. Indeed, God seems to appeal to this characteristic of the human heart to motivate his people toward righteousness.

If this is the only motivation for adults to serve God, their faith is immature. But especially for children, the early motivations and influences can be understood best in terms of rewards and punishments. This is how God has designed them to learn. It is natural and normal for children to be concerned with rewards and punishments. This is a part of human psyche that is always present.

EARLY CHILDHOOD LEARNING

My wife and I have fostered twenty-seven children. Most of them have been with us in their early years, normally beginning at infancy and progressing through early childhood. Perhaps one of the most consistent observations we have made is the importance of these early years. Each child comes with his or her own personality and characteristics (nature) but each is also profoundly influenced by environment (nurture). Our task in nurturing these little ones is to provide an environment that allows their unique personalities to emerge and to teach them right from wrong.

The easy task is letting their personalities emerge. Much like a flower emerges from a bud, so a wonderful personality emerges as these little ones develop. It is always with a degree of wonderment that we watch these fascinating people emerge from the somewhat predictable sameness of infancy.

The more difficult task is to teach them right from wrong. Shaping values and behaviors of children is a complex task, one that requires wisdom and prayer. But there are certain principles that always seem to be applicable to training children.

Early-childhood learning always begins with human relationships. Our first task when we bring a child home from the hospital (beyond the obvious feeding and clothing) is to establish an emotional bond. Infants need to feel safe and loved. Cuddling, holding, talking, and eye contact all serve to help the child feel secure.

As children mature, there is a continued development in their human relations.[5] They learn to trust others besides their parents and learn to function as social beings. These learnings come from imitating the behavior of others and from the rewards and punishments brought on by their own behavior. Parents learn to praise and reward their children when they behave properly and to punish them for inappropriate behavior. Through these relational experiences the child learns to function in relation to others and to give and receive love.

It is sad that some children are born into settings that cannot provide appropriate loving environments. Such a situation can be so devastating that children fail to thrive. Some of the children who have come to us have almost given up their will to live. This condition is usually the result of neglect. Our job with these little ones is literally to love them back into the desire to live. This is accomplished through the very physical means of holding, talking, cuddling, and responding when they cry.

As children mature, they must learn appropriate social behaviors. Learning to function properly in relation to others is a vital aspect of functioning as human beings. Social behaviors are also taught through imitation and rewards and punishments. "Say thank you" followed by "Good girl" are common phrases for teaching correct social behavior. There is both instruction and rewards for the

> *Early-childhood learning always begins with human relationships. Our first task is to establish an emotional bond.*

child. In this case the reward is verbal.

Children are taught to obey parents, play nicely with other children, respect other people, and treat others appropriately. We do not bite, hit, pinch, or physically hurt others. We are to help, be kind, be respectful, and be gentle with others. Proper social relationships are modeled by the parents and rewarded when practiced by the child. For improper social relationships the child is punished appropriately.

Children must also be taught basic living skills. As they become physically able, they are taught to dress themselves, practice the skills of basic personal hygiene, and feed themselves. The goal is to produce persons who are capable of functioning independently, able to carry on basic living skills on their own. These skills too are taught through modeling and patterns of reinforcement. "When you can put your jacket on, we can go to the store" provides the promise of a reward for appropriate behavior. The goal is to train a child for basic living skills necessary for later developmental tasks.

Beyond human relations, social behaviors, and basic living skills, children must also learn effective patterns of communication. Children first learn language, imitating the sounds they hear their parents make. Mom and Dad respond with appropriate rewards—"Listen, I'm sure he just said 'propitiation'!"—and the child continues to gain language abilities.

> *A proper use of the methods of behaviorism is not incompatible with Christian education. It can even be effective for teaching children Christian living.*

Simple language acquisition matures into appropriate patterns of communication. Again, through rewards and punishments, parents train their children to communicate in appropriate ways. "I can't understand you when you whine" is a means of punishment designed to help the child learn to communicate in appropriate ways. "I will give it to you when you ask properly" promises a reward for appropriate patterns of communication.

Clearly, not all children's learning nor all parenting skills can be reduced to a system of rewards and punishments. Skinner's error is that of reductionism; reducing all of human behavior to a matter of rewards and punishments. But neither must we ignore the truth of behaviorism.

I have already expressed my concerns about the philosophy of behaviorism and have indicated why I believe it is inappropriate as a dominant paradigm for Christian education. But now I must also admit the validity of the mechanics of behaviorism as a part of understanding human learning and education. There is a place for rewards and punishments to shape behavior as an aspect of parenting and training young children; however, Christian education is more than rewarding and punishing. Behaviorism is an inadequate philosophy of education, but the mechanics of behaviorism are powerful, especially for teaching children. A proper use of the methods of behaviorism is not incompatible with Christian education. It can even be effective for teaching children Christian living.

LEARNING TO BE CHRISTIANS

In a very real sense, one cannot *learn* to be a Christian. Being a Christian requires God's supernatural work of regeneration and his gracious gift of faith for salvation. But in another sense we must teach our children to follow the Lord and in that sense to be Christians. As we saw earlier, Christian education is both a natural and a supernatural enterprise.

Christianity has a content to be believed and a worldview to be acquired. Part of teaching children is to provide them with a Christian perspective on life and the realities in which we all live. For the Christian parent and church, there are several foundational realities that should be learned through the example and direct teaching of adults. Included in these realities are critical concerns about God, our relation to him, and our relation with other Christians. The following realities should be included in the training of our children.

146

God is present and real.

Children cannot see God, but they can see their parents live in the reality of God's presence. Prayer, humility, reverence for God, and lifestyles that honor him are all means of instructing the child regarding the reality and nearness of God. As parents practice the presence of God, children learn the reality of God.

Children will imitate the behavior and attitudes of the parents. They too will begin to practice God's presence, not from a logical base, but from the base of environmental example. The Old Testament's stress on feasts and rituals was specifically an educative device for the children. The action of the parents (who had experienced the reality of God's works in their lives) was designed to teach the children (who had not experienced God's miraculous interventions firsthand).

Therefore, the Jewish feasts and rituals were designed to give the children an experience that could teach them of the baptism and communion, along with our celebrations of Advent, Christmas, and Easter, are powerful teachers of our children of the reality and presence of God.

The many informal practices of Christian living are even more powerful teachers of God's presence. Our daily attitudes and actions do much to teach our children about God. Teaching them to pray, to be thankful for God's provisions, and to be aware of God are the daily lessons of God's existence, even if we cannot see him.

God is to be feared and loved.

A proper attitude toward God is to fear him and to love him. His holiness teaches us to fear him, because he is unlike all else; and his mercy teaches us to love him, because he deals with us in grace. Parents must teach their children to fear and to love God.

An unbalanced emphasis on either attitude will create an unbalanced faith. If

---

The attitudes and practices of our services of worship shape how a child thinks about God. Theology is worked out in the practices of the church, both formally in the worship services and informally in the life of the family.

---

reality and presence of God. They had not experienced the Passover event, but they could now experience the Passover feast. Through this practice, the children could be taught the reality of God, and the experiences that showed his love for his people.

We do not practice the feasts and rituals of the Old Testament, but we do follow the ordinances of the New. The rituals of children only fear God, they will serve him from improper motivation, striving only to avoid his punishment. But if there is only love, without any sense of fear, their relationship with God may become too casual and trivial. With a proper attitude, one will understand that this terrible, holy God is a God of mercy and grace. Love for God must be rooted properly in the soil of the fear of God.

How parents talk about God will shape the child's attitude. If God is discussed only in the most casual terms ("God is so neat!") without proper reverence, the child will never learn to fear him. Conversely, if God is presented only in the most stern terms ("God will send you to hell if you do that!") the child will never learn to love him. A proper theology of God should shape how we talk about him.

Early childhood influences do much to shape how children feel and think about God. Our worship services also speak volumes about how we approach God and how we think about him. The attitudes and practices of our services of worship also shape how a child thinks about God. Theology is worked out in the practices of the church, both formally in the worship services and informally in the life of the family.

God is to be obeyed.

The ultimate expression of our faith is in our obedience. When faith is translated into active obedience, we can be sure the faith is real. Our Lord asked, "Why do you call me, 'Lord, Lord,' and do not do what I say?" (Luke 6:46). The ultimate act of worship is to live a life of obedience to God.

Early on, children can be taught that God is to be obeyed. This is taught, not by forcing the child to obey, but by living a life of obedience ourselves, modeling for our children what obedience to God looks like. If our attitude is that God is to be obeyed, our children will learn to obey him themselves.

Obedience to God is taught first by example. The consistency of the parent's lifestyle will be the primary influence. Seeing parents working with glad hearts to obey God will serve as a living demonstration of what it means to be Christians. True Christians obey God out of a thankful heart, striving to please him in every way.

Obedience to God can be a tricky thing in that it must be obedience to that which God has actually said. Sometimes obedience to an inner voice or private revelation can lead to more problems than benefits. The notion "I think God wants me to . . ." can be confusing both to the child and to the parent. But obedience to his Word as recorded in Scripture is direct. Striving to live in proper obedience to what God has said in the Bible is the most appropriate expression of our faith.

An important part of nurturing children in the faith is helping them find ways to obey God in their lives. Teaching them that God's Word has implications for the way they are to live their lives will serve to lay the early foundation for a life of obedience.

Young children need to be taught obedience in very direct ways. "God wants you to obey Mommy and Daddy" is very appropriate to teach them. Later, as children become more mature cognitively, they can be asked to reason out their own expressions of obedience.

Early childhood can be a fertile ground for instilling the attitude that part of being a Christian is to live a life of obedience. At times, obedience is costly. Rather than teaching children that following the Lord is always easy and fun, steps of actual obedience will teach the reality that sometimes obedience hurts. But we obey God, not because it is fun, but because we love him and it is right. Such training will serve to lay the foundation for a mature faith in adulthood.

God is to be served.

We are not only to obey God but also to serve him. Going beyond what is commanded, a grateful heart serves the Lord with gladness. A true doxological lifestyle (Rom. 12:1–2) serves God as an act of worship. Again, this is an attitude to be modeled by the parents and hopefully instilled in the child.

It is unrealistic and unwise to ask more of children than they can deliver. It used to be not too unusual to hear well-meaning speakers asking children to dedicate their lives to service for God. Children who were only eight or ten years old were making commitments to be missionaries. I once counseled a student who was preparing for missionary service because when she was a child she promised God she would serve in this way. As an adult, she did not want to do this but felt bound by her childhood commitment. Asking children for such a commitment does them a great disservice.

But it is not a disservice to teach children to serve God in an immediate way. Giving them tasks they can do in service to the Lord is appropriate. Instilling an attitude that we are to serve God, rather than that he is here to serve us, will be a basis for later theological development.

An attitude for service is shaped at a young age. Asking children to help and requiring them to do so can be important lessons for later life. Parents must always be cautious not to bully children into doing what they truly do not want to do; but they should encourage their children to develop an attitude of service.

Rewarding young children for serving God is appropriate. Rather than undermining the proper motive (to express our love for God), rewards will reinforce in language they understand that they have done a good thing. It is inappropriate to use rewards with teenagers, but it is highly appropriate to use them with children. This is characteristic of the way they learn.

Service need not always be rewarded. Behaviorists speak of *intermittent reinforcement*, which means that appropriate behaviors need to be rewarded only periodically. But when children do acts of service, verbal or other sorts of rewards help them understand that they have done right.

The key here is not to promise the reward prior to the service but to offer it after the act has been done. Rather than telling children, "If you do this, I will give you . . . ," we can respond by telling them, "Because you did this, you may have. . . ." When we respond with praise such as "I am proud of you when you help like that," we can instill an attitude of service in our children.

Involvement in church is important.

No Christian can become mature alone. God has given us one another and has given us gifts for service for one another, so that the whole body may become mature. Therefore, involvement in the body of Christ is not optional, but imperative. We must be actively involved with our local congregation if we are to grow spiritually. This is true also for children. Church attendance is one of God's primary means of bringing us to maturity. Children must be taught to value involvement in the body.

For most children this is not a problem. If the parents attend church with joy, the children will usually do the same. An adult woman told me that one of her dominant childhood memories was of her father quoting, "I was glad when they said unto me, let us go unto the house of the Lord." Her memory was of the family all packed into the family car, and joy radiating from her father's faith. The man truly loved to go to church.

Of course, church is not where we go, but who we are. The church is people, not

No Christian can become mature alone. Therefore, involvement in the body of Christ is not optional, but imperative.

a building. But we must value being with the people of God, his called-out ones, and we must value the activities of the church. Worship, instruction, fellowship, and outreach should be important activities in the life of the believer.

Children should be brought to church with expectations that they will be involved in positive ways. It is not just the teacher's responsibility to engage the children and make them like the experience; parents are also responsible to send children with expectations regarding behavior and involvement. Discipline of children is one of the dominant concerns in today's churches. Parents must take the lead in setting standards for their children's behavior and rewarding or punishing as is needed.

Obviously, very young children should have little expectations placed on them, other than to play nicely and to obey the teacher. Two- and three-year-olds are primarily having attitudes shaped to learn that church is a good place to be. But as the children get older, parents should expect them to learn in Sunday school and to do the work assigned to them. Rewards for work well done can be a positive factor in showing the children that we value what they are doing and learning.

Jesus loves us.

The final reality to be taught to children—that Jesus loves us—is set against the backdrop of the previous five. They should learn not only that God the Father is to be feared and loved, obeyed and served but also that his Son Jesus loves us. The great truth

Jesus loves me, this I know,
For the bible tells me so

is at the heart of the Gospel and is a truth children can understand. Even though they cannot see God, children can know the love of God through Christ.

The reality of Christian experience is Sabbath—resting in God's care for his own. We can stop working to attain salvation and rest in the fact that we are saved by grace, apart from the deeds of the law. This truth should penetrate deep into the heart of believers, shaping how they live and think and feel in relation to God. It is this truth that sets us free to serve him out of thankful hearts.

Children have a great need to be loved and to know that they are loved. God has designed them in just this way. Teaching a child about God's love, expressed through Jesus, is one of the great joys of raising children. Tender hearts respond to the truth of the love of God.

God's love is taught in both attitudes and actions. Parents should take time to point out God's gracious provisions to their children. It is because of God's mercy that we have food to eat, warm homes, friends, families, and church. Even in the difficult times, the goodness of God's love for his own can be seen. But it is the responsibility of parents to point it out to their children.

One of the wonderful things about children is their ability to point God's love out to us. More than once my own daughters have been the vehicles of God's instruction to help me gain proper perspective. As we train our children to see God's hand of love, they also through the eyes of childhood help us to see.

It seems that it is a lifelong struggle to rest in God's love. Perhaps it is our own sinfulness, or the strategy of the evil one, but at times we all find ourselves wondering if God really loves us. The truth that he does love us must be deeply rooted in the hearts of the parents and must be taught to the children.

As parents learn to live in the reality of God's love and to show the love of God to their children, the children will learn to accept his love for themselves. The humility of children allows them to accept God's love easier than adults. While we may struggle with the concept, children believe it. Later, as their lives become more complicated, the question will become more relevant to them. The devotional book for teens *If God Loves Me, Why Can't I Get My Locker Open?*[6] is an expression of the later complexities that can cause confusion in adolescence.

There are other realities that can and should be taught to children. But these serve to illustrate how, through modeling and instruction, coupled with appropriate rewards, children can have early childhood influences that shape their faith. Even in periods of economic stress, with both parents working outside the home, and even with the reality of broken marriages and single-parent families, these realities can and must be taught to the children.

Parents will sometimes fail at these tasks. The truth is that we all will have times when we do not do well in modeling or instruction. It is the long view that we must keep in mind. If, overall, we do well at these tasks, we can do much to teach our children to be Christians.

PATTERNS OF REINFORCEMENT

There are a variety of ways that young children can be trained in their growth as Christians. The following suggestions are some of the most obvious applications of the use of reinforcement to help build Christian faith in our children.

Parental Approval

By far the most powerful influence in the lives of children is the approval of their parents. Children greatly desire to please their parents and want to know that their parents approve. Praise from a parent is a powerful reinforcement for good behavior.

We were having dinner with friends when five-year-old Kurt spilled his milk. His father, with utter sincerity, praised him, saying, "Oh Kurt, you only spilled half a glass tonight!" What my wife and I observed was that this was a dad who was in the habit of praising his kids.

Too much praise can be ineffective. After a while the child ceases to hear it. But genuine, heartfelt praise, especially in matters of faith, can do much to train a child to be Christian. Hugs, pats, and words expressing approval from parents are the language that children understand and the rewards they seek the most.

Approval From Other Adults

Children can also be reinforced for good behavior by other adults. Teachers especially become very important in the lives of children. When a grandparent, relative, friend, or teacher praises children, they respond almost as strongly as they do to their parents.

As children mature, they need to be exposed to more adults and to authority figures outside the home. Usually, one of the first people to become influential beyond immediate family is the Sunday school teacher. Approval from the teacher can be an important source of reward for a growing faith.

Those who work with children need to develop the habit of praising children for appropriate behaviors. I do not agree with the teaching of behavior modification that negative behavior is to be ignored, but I do believe that it is infinitely more powerful to praise good behavior than it is to punish bad behavior. In the long run, we all grow more from positive experiences than from negative ones. "Catching" children doing right and praising them for it will reinforce right attitudes and actions.

Punishing Wrong Behavior

There is a place for punishment in nurturing children. Even the heavenly Father punishes his children, and this is a sign of his love (Prov. 3:11–12). So too, we must love our children enough to discipline them.

The point of punishment is not to inflict pain or to exact justice but rather to train. To emphasize the importance of what is being taught, it may be necessary to discipline the child. Discipline may be in the form of a verbal rebuke, a withholding of a privilege, or, in rare instances, a spanking.

Only a child's parents should administer a spanking and never in anger and never in ways that can cause bodily harm. But there may be times when a child needs to know that he or she has done wrong and that part of the consequences may be a spanking. "He who spares the rod hates his son, but he who loves him is careful to discipline him" (Prov. 13:24).

Those who work with children in the church must also be willing to discipline. Verbal rebukes, withholding of privileges,

and removal from class if necessary can all be means to train the child. There should be more praise than rebuke, but because depravity extends to children, there will be times when discipline is needed.

Churches should establish agreed-upon disciplinary procedures and agreed-upon standards of conduct for children. Parents should be made aware of these policies and agree to them before their children are enrolled in church activities. In this way consistency can be achieved, and the child will know and understand the limits of acceptable behavior.

God does not ignore negative behavior, and neither should we. If we are to be models of the Father for our children, we need to teach them that there are consequences to negative behavior and that we will love them enough to discipline them. Disciplining children is hard work, but is also worth the effort.

Rewards in Christian Education

Children understand the language of rewards and punishments, and rewards can have a place in Christian education. Rewards are prone to abuse, but they also can be used effectively. Rewards for attendance, good behavior, and even memory verses, if not made the primary focus, can be effective.

The value of behavior-modification techniques is that they can be effective in shaping good behavior. If the reward itself becomes the focus ("The one who memorizes the most verses will win a new bike!"), the emphasis is wrong. But if it is an added benefit to good behavior, a reward can be a helpful means of reinforcing proper behavior and good attitudes in children. "If you all sit quietly during the story, we can have a special treat" is not inappropriate in the Sunday school.

Influences on faith in early childhood are primarily environmental and can be explained in terms of operant conditioning. But these are the means God uses to instill faith in the children of believing parents. At the end of the day, we are still dependent on God to use these efforts to bring our children to faith. It is not simply a mechanistic process. It is rather a matter of parental responsibility coupled with dependence on the mercy of God to regenerate children and bring them to faith. Our task is nurture, and his task is regeneration.

Notes

1. Both Calvinists and Arminians alike agree on this point. The differences arise regarding whether God works with all people equally and whether it is possible to resist or refuse his gift of salvation. But all Christians agree that faith and its resultant salvation is a gift from God.
2. For very readable discussions of these topics, see D. A. Carson, *Divine Sovereignty and Human Responsibility* (Atlanta: John Knox, 1981); and J. I. Packer, *Evangelism and the Sovereignty of God* (Downers Grove, Ill.: InterVarsity Press, 1961).
3. Mark P. Cosgrove, *B. F. Skinner's Behaviorism: An Analysis* (Grand Rapids: Zondervan, 1982), 108.
4. B. F. Skinner, *About Behaviorism* (New York: Knopf, 1974), 207.
5. Much more than simple patterns of reinforcement are at stake. Margaret Mahler has provided important insight into the psychological birth of the infant as symbiosis and individuation take place. For a superb explanation see Margaret Mahler, Fred Pine, and Anni Bergman, *The Psychological Birth of the Human Infant* (New York: Basic Books, 1975).
6. Lorraine Peterson, *If God Loves Me, Why Can't I Get My Locker Open?* (Minneapolis: Bethany House, 1980).

12

Learning by Interaction and Observation

THE WORD

I open my mouth to speak and the word is there, formed by the lips, the tongue, the organ of voice. Formed by the brain, transmitting the word by breath. I open my mouth to speak and the word is there, traveling between us, caught by the organ of hearing, the ear, transmitting the thought to the brain through the word.

Just so do we communicate . . . you and I: the thought from one mind leaping to another, given shape and substance, so that we know and are known through the word.

But let me speak to my very small daughter and the words mean nothing, for she does not know my language. And so I show her: "This is your foot," I say; "and it is meant for walking." I help her up; "Here is the way to walk." And one day "walking" shapes in her brain with the word.

God had something to say to Man, but the words meant nothing, for we did not know his language. And so we were shown. "Behold the man," He said. "This is the image, the thought in my mind. . . . Man as I mean him, loving and serving. I have put him in flesh."

Now the word has shape and form and substance to travel between us. Let Him show forth love till one day "loving" shapes in your brain with the Word. (author unknown)

This writing expresses the inadequacy of words alone to express thoughts and ideas. After God had given a revelation of himself through creation and through words, he

---

The central question in Christian education is, How do we best teach the faith?

---

revealed himself incarnate in his Son. He showed us his intention for humankind through the example of Jesus.

God has designed people to learn in a variety of ways, and it would be foolish to limit our teaching only to words. Education that is effective uses other means besides language to teach for spiritual growth.

The central question in Christian education is, How do we best teach the faith? Historically, the dominant answer has been "Through instruction." Therefore, we have established schools in our churches, with classrooms, teachers, formal curriculum, yearly promotions to higher grades, and all sorts of other trappings of formal education. The formal *structuralist* approach to Christian nurture has been effective in communicating truth, but many have argued that such a structured approach is ultimately ineffective for bringing about changed lives.

The two most responsible critics of formalized Christian nurture have been Lawrence Richards and John Westerhoff.

Both have offered alternative approaches to educating for faith based on social-learning theory. Richards' approach is rooted more in individual relationships, whereas Westerhoff's is rooted in the faith community.[1]

The basic assumption of the socialization approach is that faith is learned more like culture and is best passed on through relationships and modeling. Just as a child is informally socialized into a given culture, so children can be socialized into Christian faith. God will use the relationships and examples of the Christian family and community to communicate the content and substance of faith to children, and he will regenerate and then bring them to faith through the process of socialization. This approach is based on the belief that faith is learned more like culture than like mathematics.

SOCIAL-LEARNING THEORY

Social-learning theorists ask, "How does a child learn socially acceptable behavior?" We do not set up formal classes or schools for learning the social mores of a culture, and yet we generally train children effectively to behave in socially acceptable ways. How is this accomplished?

Albert Bandura believes that much of human behavior is a function of observing and imitating the behavior of others.[2] Children watch how their parents behave and then imitate that behavior. Many toys are designed specifically to enhance imitative behavior. Children are given replicas of adult tools so that they may imitate the adult world through play.

The motive that prompts imitative behavior is reinforcement. We learn to imitate by being reinforced for doing so, and continued reinforcement maintains imitative behavior. Parents are normally pleased when children imitate their behavior, and their praise will prompt the child to continue the process of imitation. Other adults also will normally praise the imitative behavior of children.

Social learning is ultimately explained in terms of operant conditioning. If the person can imagine both reinforcement and the behavior of the models they are imitating, all imitative behavior can be explained in terms of operant conditioning.

I once visited a church where I talked with a boy about nine years old. "You should have been here last night," he informed me. "God blessed in a marvelous way."

How did he learn to express himself in such a way? Most nine-year-olds do not make this sort of observation. Obviously he was imitating the enthusiasm and language of the adults in his congregation; and no doubt he was reinforced for doing so. He was being very effectively socialized into his religious community.

Social-learning theory recognizes two different kinds of models, both of which will elicit imitative behavior. *Symbolic models* are people in books, films, television, entertainment, or sports. Rather than actual living persons with whom the person has a relationship, symbolic models are ideal representations of persons. When advertisements appeal to a sports figure to sell their product (such as Gatorade's campaign slogan, "I want to be like Mike," referring to basketball star Michael Jordan), they are using a symbolic model.

Biblical appeals to historical figures, such as the examples of faith in Hebrews 11, are the elevation of symbolic models. These were real people, but as historic figures they had no actual relationship with the readers of the epistle. Moreover, when we hold up Jesus as an example, he is being extolled as a symbolic model.

Exemplary models are actual living persons with whom the student has a rela-

tionship. Pastors, youth leaders, parents, and peers can all serve as exemplary models. These are living examples of the behaviors being taught. When the apostle Paul urged the Corinthians, "Follow my example, as I follow the example of Christ" (1 Cor. 11:1), he was using himself as an exemplary model.

Reinforcement for imitating the model may come in one of three ways. First, there may be direct reinforcement by the model. Parents who praise children for imitating them are using this technique. Second, the direct consequences of the behavior being imitated can serve as a reinforcement. If the behavior works, accomplishing what is desired, the consequences are the reward. Finally, the person can be reinforced vicariously by seeing the model reinforced. If a person sees behavior working for the person being imitated, that in itself will serve as reinforcement for imitation.

I knew some foster children, twin boys, who had not been given much training in their first two years of life. When they came to their foster family, they were almost completely out of control. One of the first problems that needed correction was their tendency to bite each other. The mother used a puppet with large teeth. Whenever the puppet bit, he was spanked and told, "We don't bite in this family!"

The boys saw the puppet being punished for his behavior and soon learned that biting was not appropriate. Then when one brother bit, the other responded, "We don't bite in this family!" Vicarious reinforcements can be positive (a reward), or aversive (a punishment). Thus social-learning theory explains both the acquisition of behaviors and the extinguishing of behaviors.

Imitation is more than the simple replication of the behavior of others. The theory and the fact is more complex than that.

Bandura demonstrated three different categories of behaviors that can be explained through social-learning theory.

The *modeling effect* is the child's imitating new behaviors seen in others. For example, if a child is exposed to overtly aggressive behavior and then begins to

has now chosen to be a social worker. Her behavior is similar but not identical to ours. But clearly this choice was influenced by the example of her parents.

Examples of social learning are prevalent. Because of the powerful informal forces of relationships and examples,

---

Because of the powerful informal forces of relationships and examples, much of human behavior is learned through imitation. The power of modeling and imitation can also be effective for nurturing persons in the faith.

---

act out aggressively herself, the modeling effect is being exhibited. Exposure to models, especially for younger children, can produce startling new behaviors in the child. When parents wonder, "Where did he learn that?" they will instinctively think about who might have modeled the behavior in question to their child.

The *inhibitory effect* was described above regarding the biting puppet. Seeing the puppet punished for biting inhibited the same behavior in the twins. This approach is used by therapists to inhibit deviant behavior in clients. The opposite can also happen, by what is termed the *disinhibitory effect*. Exposure to models doing behavior that a person normally would not do will disinhibit the person's tendency to avoid the behavior. For example, if a child normally would not use profanity, but is exposed to enough bad language, he or she will finally be disinhibited and will begin to use foul language also.

The *eliciting effect* acknowledges that people sometimes exhibit similar, if not exactly the same, behavior as has been modeled. My wife and I have chosen to be foster parents, while our oldest daughter

much of human behavior is learned through imitation. And the power of modeling and imitation can also be effective for nurturing persons in the faith.

OBSERVATIONAL LEARNING IN SCRIPTURE

The Bible is filled with examples of observational learning, presenting models of what God desires, and calls us to imitate these examples. Perhaps the dominant example is our Lord. John tells us, "The Word became flesh and lived for a while among us. We have seen his glory, the glory of the one and only Son, who came from the Father, full of grace and truth" (John 1:14).

John reminds us in his epistle that "whoever claims to live in him must walk as Jesus did" (1 John 2:6). Here, an assurance that our salvation is real will be that we are imitators of Christ. If we are not living as Jesus did, we cannot claim to be in him.

Jesus himself called for imitation. After the last supper with the apostles, he modeled servanthood in a most remarkable way. When they had finished eating, he got up, removed his outer garment, wrapped himself in a towel and washed their feet. When he finished, Jesus explained:

> You call me "Teacher" and "Lord," and rightly so, for that is what I am. Now that I, your Lord and Teacher, have washed your feet, you also should wash one another's feet. I have set you an example that you should do as I have done for you. I tell you the truth, no servant is greater than his master, nor is a messenger greater than the one who sent him. Now that you know these things, you will be blessed if you do them. (John 13:13–17)

Part of Jesus' ministry was to be an example. Not that we are to live exactly as he did, but that we are to adopt his values and perspectives, living our lives in a way similar to the way he lived his.

The apostle Paul made numerous appeals to his life as an example, expecting his followers to imitate his behavior. To the church at Philippi he wrote, "Join with others in following my example, brothers, and take note of those who live according to the pattern we gave you" (Phil. 3:17). Again he said, "Whatever you have learned or received or heard from me, or seen in me—put it into practice. And the God of peace will be with you" (Phil. 4:9).

Paul clearly saw his responsibility to be an example to the church, and he desired that he be imitated. This can be seen as either highly arrogant or as a proper realization that imitation is an important aspect of learning to be Christian. His plea "Follow my example, as I follow the example of Christ" (1 Cor. 11:1) is a critical reminder of the responsibility of modeling for all who are in ministry.

Scripture raises both exemplary and symbolic models to be imitated. Church leaders are to be examples to the flock (1 Peter 5:3), and all are to follow the example of the prophets who went before. Imitation of models is a biblical concept for bringing people to maturity.

OBSERVATIONAL LEARNING AND CHRISTIAN EDUCATION THEORY

The concept of observation and imitation has long been an aspect of sound Christian education theory. Writers from a variety of theological perspectives have all agreed that modeling and imitation are powerful means of inculcating faith in others. This is not a new and innovative idea; rather, it has been an accepted component of the theory of nurture for some time.

The first of the current religious educators to build his theory solidly on a socialization model was C. Ellis Nelson. In his book *Where Faith Begins*, Nelson argued that the origin of faith resides in the community of faith and is modeled for new members.[3] Nelson believed that models are the *ideals* toward which believers can strive, but not necessarily actual people. "Love your enemies" is an ideal of the kingdom of God, which Jesus presented, and serves as a model for kingdom people. It is not an actual person, but an ideal that serves as the model.

Earlier Harry C. Munro wrote that teachers are important models for their students. In his book *Protestant Nurture* Munro argued that the character and personality of the teacher have a more dominant effect on the lives of the student than the content of the lesson.[4] It is always hard to assess such a claim as this, because there is no clear way to measure the actual power of an influence. But what we do know is that the life of the teacher can have a powerful impact on students.

> *The combination of sound Christian character and Scripture is the key to a teacher's influence.*

I regularly ask people to identify factors they perceive to have had a strong impact on their spiritual growth. Almost always some people will name a teacher, pastor, youth leader, or some other leader as having had a powerful influence on them. When I probe further, I generally find that it is not the content of the lessons that is remembered, but rather the force of the personality. It is indeed the character and personality of the teacher that is identified.

I believe that the combination of sound Christian character and Scripture is the key to a teacher's influence. Character alone, apart from the Word of God, will not produce righteousness. Conversely, the Word of God, if it is not communicated by a righteous teacher, will be less likely to have a powerful influence on the student.

Randolph Crump Miller, having been influenced by Horace Bushnell, wrote that parents are the dominant models for their children. In his classic *Biblical Theology and Christian Education* he argued that what the parents are makes a primary difference in the nurture of children. He placed a strong emphasis on the context of family relationships as critical for nurturing faith in the Christian home.[5] This theme is also carried on by Richards and Westerhoff.

John H. Westerhoff also argued that the corporate life of the church, its liturgy, and its practices model faith for the children. Observation of and inclusion in the life of the worshiping community are critical means of passing on the faith to the children.[6] He believes that the contours of the faith community will shape its educational method and serve as a demonstration of what it means to be Christian for the children of the congregation. In this way, each local church will model the faith in slightly different ways as it lives out its own theology in its particular expressions.

If Westerhoff is correct, and I think he is, then this has powerful implications for how congregations behave. What must children learn about faith if they grow up in a church that is always arguing, fighting, or even splitting? What is being modeled for them regarding the truth of the Gospel and what it means to be a Christian?

Because of abuses of instructional models of nurture, some Christian educators want to conduct Christian education almost totally from a socialization approach. Lawrence Richards has argued passionately for a socialization model, because he believes that instructional approaches are unable to communicate *life*, which he sees as the unique mark of true Christianity.[7] Regarding the applicability of a formal instructional model, Richards states, "Formal education may be effective in dealing with symbols and concepts abstracted from life. But when change and development in the total personality are desired, non-formal education has all the advantages."[8]

Given the long history of socialization as a mode of nurture and the obvious biblical emphasis on modeling and following the example of others, is it appropriate, as Richards suggests, to make socialization our primary emphasis in Christian education? What are the advantages and disadvantages of socialization as the primary mode of Christian education?

POSITIVE ASPECTS

There are four primary positive aspects to socialization that must be maintained for effective Christian education.

This is a clear function of the church.

The obvious emphasis on socialization in Scripture cannot be denied. The church is to function as a community, with its primary testimony to be in the quality of its relationships. How the disciples loved each other was to be their testimony to the world around them (John 13:35). The church as a redeemed community is the context in which Christian nurture is to take place, and observational learning is always a part of community relationships. Wherever there are people gathered in a society, there will be observational learning. Because the church is a community, observational learning will be part of it.

The biblical focus is on models of faith.

The Bible speaks often of people as models of faith, and this emphasis seems to assume the fact of observational learning. Why would God raise up models for us if it were not that we were to imitate them? Our Lord said, "A student is not above his teacher, but everyone who is fully trained will be like his teacher" (Luke 6:40).

The biblical focus on modeling and imitation make it clear that this is part of God's plan for educating in faith. Because modeling and imitation constitute a natural way to learn, God uses them to help his people grow in faith.

The process of modeling does not permit academic detachment.

A purely formal, cognitive approach to education can allow the teacher to teach in a detached way, not allowing the truth to penetrate his or her life. The possibility of "academic objectivity" can cause truth to be taught in impersonal, sterile ways. But when the teacher must be a model of what is being taught, there must be a deeper involvement with the truth. Content can no longer be taught in abstract, detached ways.

A purely instructional mode of education tends to proceed from the teacher to others. The focus of the teacher will normally be outward. But a socialization approach also forces the teacher to look inward, because hypocrisy cannot be tolerated. An enculturation form of teaching is dependent on the teacher's living the truth as well as discussing the truth. Socialization does not permit dry academics removed from life.

Emphasis is on the faith as a lived reality.

Christian growth includes the acquisition of knowledge, but it is more than that. Christian maturity is living out the truth in the arena of life. It is the doing of the truth and not merely the hearing or understanding the truth. "Faith by itself, if it is not accompanied by action, is dead" (James 2:17).

Socialization emphasizes that there must be something to be observed in the life of the believer. The teacher must be modeling maturity, and the student must be imitating it. An observational mode of teaching and learning absolutely requires that something be happening in the lives of teachers and students alike. The possibility of a faith divorced from life is eliminated. Abstract discussion of truth devoid of obedience is not possible in a proper socialization model. Talk and walk must be integrated.

ing the right behaviors. It is a matter of right relationship with God. The danger is to confuse the external with the internal, to confuse social custom with regeneration and true faith.

The teacher must be modeling maturity, and the student must be imitating it. An observational mode of teaching and learning absolutely requires that something be happening in the lives of teachers and students alike.

NEGATIVE ASPECTS

While there are obvious advantages to a socialization model of nurture, to abandon totally an instructional mode is dangerous. There are some inherent weaknesses to socialization as an exclusive model for nurture that must also be considered.

People can imitate behavior and not know God.

There is the very real potential for persons to be socialized into a Christian subculture and never truly know the Father. A person can learn the language, behaviors, attitudes, and values of Christianity, but never be saved. An early advocate of a social approach to Christian education was the classic liberal George Albert Coe, who observed,

> Just as children readily accept our instruction, so they willingly imitate our religious acts. The evening prayer, grace before meals, participation in public worship—these, under favorable conditions, are well liked; they require no compulsion. But they cannot, without further evidence, be regarded as clear signs of piety.[9]

Coe is correct in his assessment. Christian faith is more than a matter of learn-

I attended college with a woman who was a strong leader in our school. She had been raised in a Christian home, had attended Christian elementary and secondary schools, and was now training for professional ministry. Her life and testimony were exemplary. She returned to the college for a visit about a year after graduation. I was then on faculty and we talked. She told me that while she was studying in graduate school she realized that she was not a Christian! When I protested, telling her I saw her faith in her life, she stopped me. "I knew the language and the lifestyle, but I didn't know God" was her simple reply.

There can be a real danger of getting people to "live like Christians," but never introduce them to the Lord. Salvation is a matter of faith, and faith includes relationship to God. Socialization may teach a person to fit into the Christian community without having a living relationship with God.

This criticism is not unique to socialization. This can happen in any mode of nurture, because we cannot measure, or know for sure, someone else's relationship to God. But there is a specific inherent danger in confusing fitting into a subculture, such as Christian subculture, with having a redemptive relationship with God. Advocates of a purely socialization model of Christian nurture must recognize this danger.

We must remember the prophet Malachi's message to Israel. He told them that God did not want their feasts, sacrifices, and offerings. Through the prophet God said, "Oh, that one of you would shut the temple doors, so that you would not light useless fires on my altar! I am not pleased with you . . . and I will accept no offerings from your hands" (Mal. 1:10).

Even though God had ordained the feasts and sacrifices, he now refused them, because they were being offered devoid of commitment. The people were practicing empty rituals, devoid of meaning, and were therefore an abomination to the Lord. They had been socialized into their *religion*, but had no true *faith*, no true relationship with God.

Socialization is weak in communicating propositional truth.

Observational learning is strong in communicating values, behavior, and attitudes. Those aspects of a social orientation that are more immediate and existential are communicated well. But the systematic truth of Scripture is not clearly communicated in a purely socialization mode. The content of Scripture may be lost as the forms of the faith are being passed on.

A pure social learning approach to Christian nurture could lead to heresy being taught and believed, without anyone realizing it. It is the propositional truth of God's revelation that provides the safeguards and norms for our faith. If the propositional truth is lost, the foundation is lost.

Richards rightly asserts that the church's mission is to pass on life to its members. It is life, given by the regenerative power of the Holy Spirit, that sets the believer apart. But we must remember that life is mediated to us through God's words, and his words must be valued and maintained. Peter said to Jesus, "Lord, to whom shall we go? You have the words of eternal life" (John 6:68).

Paul encouraged the Philippians, "shine like stars in the universe as you hold out the word of life" (Phil. 2:15–16). He acknowledged the importance of modeling and imitation, but he also maintained the critical need for the Word of God to be proclaimed.

Teaching of the Word can be done through the example, rituals, and liturgy of the congregation, but it must also be done through systematic, intentional instruction. A socialization approach to nurture is essential; but it must be coupled with an instructional approach that proclaims the propositional truth of Scripture. It is not an "either/or" but a "both/and" situation. Both modeling and instruction are required for effective Christian education.

Maturity requires knowing both how to live in obedience to God and why our lifestyle is an expression of obedience. Learning forms without underlying reasons cannot produce maturity.

The musician Mason Williams tells the story of how he learned to cook a ham roast. His mother instructed him that first the bone must be removed from the roast, and then it could be cooked. When he asked why, she explained that this was how her mother did it. When he asked his grandmother why the bone must be removed from a ham roast, she explained that this is what her mother did. He asked his great-grandmother, and she explained that she never had a pot large enough to cook a roast with the bone still in it!

If we pass on rituals and lifestyles without proper reasons for them, people can fall into the trap the prophet Malachi condemned. When the church becomes only forms, without a theological and experiential base supporting the forms, institutionalism and deadness will result. A purely socialization model can lead to heresy and empty forms, just as a purely instructional model can lead to a dead orthodoxy.

Socialization focuses on experience, not on absolute truth.

Christian living must be an experienced reality, or it is no reality at all. Words, apart from experience, are dead. But equally dangerous would be experience that is not based on truth. These are false and deceitful, and serve only to lead people away.

If experiences drift away from their truth base, they become pure relativism. One person has one experience, another a different one, and without truth there is no basis from which to judge the experience. It becomes relative in that one experience is equal to any other.

Many people argue their theology on the basis of their experience. They will explain what God did in their lives, failing to understand that they may be wrong in their interpretation of their experience. We can draw incorrect conclusions about the nature and character of God, or about his works if we base our conclusions only on our experience.

Christian experience must be filtered through the grid of biblical and theological understandings. Our experiences must be interpreted and evaluated on the basis of Scripture because our experiences can and do lie, or are prone to misinterpretation. Experiences are not unimportant, but neither are they normative. Experience must be judged by the standard of the Word of God.

IMPLICATIONS FOR EDUCATIONAL MINISTRY

A theory of Christian education must include a strong component of modeling and imitation, because these are biblical methods of instruction and are in agreement with how God has designed people to learn. But our model of how to pass on the faith and life must not be exclusively sociological, because such an approach leads to the danger of losing, or at least reducing, the content of the faith. Both instructional and socialization approaches should be used. Given the strengths and weaknesses of a social learning approach, the following implications can be drawn.

The quality of life of the teacher is critical.

When choosing teachers for Christian education, both what they know and how they live must be considered. Younger people especially will learn by imitation, and the life of the teacher must be worthy of emulation. The teacher must model what he or she is teaching.

The need to model what we are teaching can be very bad news if we are teaching perfection. If we must always model perfection and faith and maturity, none of us are worthy to be considered teachers. But God has called us, not to model perfection, but to model redemption. We are to be living demonstrations, not of how good we are, but of how good God is. We are to be models of the Gospel, of God's

164

redemptive acts in sinful humanity. Being a model of the truth means being a model of what it means to be a sinner growing in Christ. We are, as Martin Luther taught, *simul justus et pecatores*, simultaneously justified and sinners. We model how God takes sinners, such as ourselves, and through his grace turns us into saints.

The quality of life desired in a teacher is authenticity and true faith. If persons are authentic, allowing students to see the process of redemption taking place within them, and if their faith is real, they have the makings of good teachers.

Opportunities to see into the life of the teacher must be available.

Teachers must be willing to risk the vulnerability of allowing students to see them as they really are. If the process of redemption is to be modeled, teachers must be sufficiently open to allow the process to be seen. Teachers who are extremely private, closed persons do not share themselves with their students. They teach the "content," but do not give of themselves.

Teaching that is truly Christian proceeds from a heart of love for God and love for the student. Part of loving students is being willing to share oneself with them. In fact, I believe there is no real gift of love without the gift of oneself. Teachers must be willing to share themselves with their students.

Teachers can share themselves by talking at deeper levels rather than simply sharing their ideas and judgments. They must also be willing to share their *feelings*, because it is at the feeling level that the true self is shared. It is at the feeling level that we are the most vulnerable, but it is also at the level of feeling that we are being the most honest.

> *If persons are authentic, allowing students to see the process of redemption taking place within them, and if their faith is real, they have the makings of good teachers.*

It is a scary thing for us to share our feelings with others, because this makes us the most vulnerable. It is like taking our clothes off in public. Even if we get dressed again, everyone will remember what we looked like in our underwear!

In my teaching at Trinity, I often share with my classes on the feeling level. I tell them how I *feel* about being a seminary professor, or a foster parent, or an author. This is deeper than what I think about it, because when I share my feelings, I share my true self. But it is also at the feeling level that the work of God can be seen the most clearly.

It is embarrassing to admit that sometimes I am scared about teaching, or frustrated with foster parenting, or insecure as a writer. But in telling my class who I really am, I am letting them see who God has chosen to use. They discover that I am not perfect, but a sinner trying to do the work of God. Such admissions are hard to make, but necessary if I am to be authentic.

Beyond talking about their lives, teachers must also allow students to see them in real life. Relationships with students means having them in our homes, taking them with us when we minister, and letting them see us function in settings not restricted by the confines of formal education. Part of modeling the truth means letting the truth be seen as it is being worked out in the arena of our own lives. It requires that students see their teachers in real life situations.

Provide exposure to a variety of models.

Because people learn from both exemplary and symbolic models, both kinds should be used in Christian education. Beyond the teacher, youth leader, pastor, and parent, symbolic models should also be used. There is a place for Christian biographies, both as books and as films and plays, to help people see examples of authentic Christian living. The examples of women and men of the faith living out their beliefs in a variety of life contexts can do much to teach others about Christian living.

Beyond biographies, speakers who have a clear Christian testimony serve well to inspire especially teenagers to Christian living. Sports figures can be particularly influential in helping teens see what real Christian living looks like. Conscious exposure to models of Christian living is a good use of the power of social learning theory.

Stress relationships in educational contexts.

People will imitate most those with whom they have a relationship. Education that is powerful stresses both content and relationships. Teachers must love their students and enter into a relationship with them. Through the power of the relationship, students will imitate their teachers. Paul could urge the church at Corinth to imitate him because he had a relationship with them. At the writing of the second epistle the relationship was not good, but even then he appealed to the example he had been in their midst.

If imitation is to take place, it must be preceded by relationship. If students know they are loved by their teacher, they will quite naturally imitate their teacher. But students will not imitate those they do not like. Therefore, relationship is the foundation for effective socialization. As Christians, our relational basis is our love for God and our love for his people.

Notes

1. Lawrence O. Richards, *Christian Education: Seeking to Be Like Jesus Christ* (Grand Rapids: Zondervan, 1988); John Westerhoff III, *Values for Tomorrow's Children* (Philadelphia: Pilgrim Press, 1970); *idem, Will Our Children Have Faith?* (New York: Seabury, 1976).
2. Albert Bandura, *Social Learning Theory* (Morristown, N. J.: General Learning Press, 1977). See also A. Bandura and R. Walters, *Social Learning and Personality Development* (New York: Holt, Rinehart and Winston, 1963).
3. C. Ellis Nelson, *Where Faith Begins* (Louisville: John Knox, 1967).
4. Harry C. Munro, *Protestant Nurture* (New York: Prentice Hall, 1956).
5. Randolph C. Miller, *Biblical Theology and Christian Education* (New York: Scribner, 1956).
6. Westerhoff, *Values for Tomorrow's Children.*
7. Lawrence O. Richards, *A Theology of Christian Education* (Grand Rapids: Zondervan, 1975), 13.
8. Ibid., 64.
9. George Albert Coe, *A Social Theory of Religious Education* (New York: Scribners, 1929), 140.

13 Learning by Logical Development

At first glance it seems that the world is divided into two sorts of persons—those who process things logically, and those who process things psychologically. The logical types think things out in a clear, orderly way, coming to conclusions on the basis of evidence, and then acting accordingly. The psychological types process things more according to feelings and intuitions, acting on hunches, intuitive insights, or simply the raw emotion of the moment. The logical types say, "I think," and the psychological types say, "I feel." Neither seems to understand the other, and both feel superior to the other.

Of course, the dichotomy presented is false. No one is purely logical, and no one is purely psychological. We are all mixtures of both, having tendencies in one direction or another, but we are never purely one or the other. But does it even matter?

HEAD AND HEART IN BIBLICAL PERSPECTIVE

The Bible emphasizes both the importance of the mind and the importance of the heart. In fact, the Bible stresses

169

that both mind and heart are primary! But the primacy ascribed to each is different in kind. The mind is primary in order, and the heart is primary in importance.

For Jesus, there was to be no disjunction between heart and mind.

We live in what is perhaps the most anti-intellectual age in the history of the church. We value science and technology but tend to despise the intellectual. Even our language betrays this bias. We ask people, "How do you feel about . . .?" rather than, "What do you think about . . .?" We are more interested in emotional judgments than in intellectual ones.

But as we have seen, the Bible puts a strong emphasis on the mind. God is concerned about how we think about issues and has revealed to us truth to be known and understood. God never asks us to love and affirm that which we do not understand. The route to loving God is first knowing something about him. In order of sequence, the Bible first appeals to the mind, asking us to make rational judgments from which to shape our lives.

The Bible does not, however, stop at the level of the mind. It is perfectly possible to understand something but not have it grip us and control us. It is possible to have a faith that is all intellectual, involving none of the heart.

The heart is primary in importance because it is through the heart that we respond to and obey God. The mind is taught so that the heart can love. Jesus taught, "Love the Lord your God with all your heart and with all your soul and with all your mind" (Matt. 22:37). For him, there was to be no disjunction between heart and mind.

But for some reason that I cannot fully decipher, the modern climate dismisses the mind as somehow unimportant to the faith. People proudly proclaim that they do not want to study, because they want to love the Lord with a childlike faith. They seem to think that childlike and childish are the same. They fail to remember Paul's observation to the church at Corinth: "When I was a child, I talked like a child, I thought like a child, I reasoned like a child. When I became a man, I put childish ways behind me" (1 Cor. 13:11).

Later, in the same epistle, the apostle rebuked them, writing, "Brothers, stop thinking like children. In regard to evil be infants, but in your thinking be adults" (1 Cor. 14:20). Clearly God's idea of a childlike faith is not a faith that is uninformed or unsophisticated. His desire is that we reason and think like adults.

The Bible presents a direct connection between how we think and how we behave. Paul describes the enemies of the Cross as those whose "mind[s] [are] on earthly things" (Phil. 3:19), as opposed to believers, who are to set their "minds on things above, not on earthly things" (Col. 3:2). The focus of the mind (what we think about) and the attitude of the mind (how we think about things) are to be different for the believer.

Paul makes this point most forcefully to the church at Rome:

> Those who live according to the sinful nature have their minds set on what that nature desires; but those who live in accordance with the Spirit have their minds set on what the Spirit desires. The mind of sinful man is death, but the mind controlled by the Spirit is life and peace, because the sinful mind is hostile to God.

It does not submit to God's law, nor can it do so. Those controlled by the sinful nature cannot please God. (Rom. 8:5–8)

The apostle draws a direct connection between how we think and how we behave, urging the Roman church to think correctly. It is in this context that he later urges them to have their minds renewed (Rom. 12:2). The connections between thinking and behaving are demonstrated further in the next verse when he writes, "For by the grace given me I say to every one of you: Do not think of yourself more highly than you ought, but rather think of yourself with sober judgment, in accordance with the measure of faith God has given you" (Rom. 12:3). His contention is that how we think about ourselves will shape how we behave.

Since Christian maturity is shaped partly by how we think, it is incumbent upon the responsible Christian educator to understand how God has designed us to think. If teaching includes the shaping of minds so that right thinking may lead to right living, how do persons think in rational ways?

HIGHER COGNITIVE PROCESS

We have seen that the way children think develops through predictable stages. Their thinking matures from a simple sensorimotor stage to the complex stage of formal operations, from which they can form and test hypotheses. Adult thinking exhibits increased expressions of the capacity for formal operations. But what does this mode of thinking require of the educator?

Jerome Bruner has done much to help our understanding of the higher cognitive processes in the human mind. Born in New York City in 1915, Bruner was educated at Duke University (B.A.) and Harvard Graduate School (Ph.D.). He is the past president of the American Psychological Association and was the first American to be given a major chair at England's Oxford University, where he held the Watts Chair of Experimental Psychology.[1]

Bruner is most widely recognized for his work in cognitive studies, which focused on a wide variety of issues, but with primary emphasis on children. His widely quoted assertion "Any subject can be taught effectively in some intellectually honest form to any child at any stage of development"[2] is perhaps his most well-known and most radical idea. The root of this idea is his understanding of perception and models for education. Rising and falling with Piaget, Bruner contends that if a concept is presented in an appropriate way, it can be grasped at any level of cognitive development.

In his work on perception, "he helped to show that how a stimulus is identified depends on the needs and desires of the perceiver. . . . He maintained that perception was a process of categorization."[3] It is the process of categorization that helps us understand the way people think about ideas.

Bruner was concerned with *conceptualization*, which is to be aware of concepts. It is through conceptualization that a person thinks. A *concept* is an abstraction we make in our minds that represents objects or events that we perceive to have similar properties.

Categorization is Bruner's term for conceptualization. When we think, we fit concepts into categories that we form in our minds. In order to fit into a category, a concept must have similar attributes and values as those concepts already included in the category. So, for example, the category "farm animal" will include those animals normally found on a farm, such as cows, horses, pigs, and chickens.

New experiences or insights cause us to shift how we categorize concepts. Perhaps our concept of "llama" fits into our category of "weird South American animals." But then we discover through reading or direct observation that some people raise llamas on their farms. Now we might shift llama into our category of "farm animals." (Or we might shift the farmer into our category of "weird people to be avoided"!) Our thinking is partly a matter of perceptions and categorization.

Categorization, according to Bruner, is absolutely necessary for thinking and functioning cognitively. It achieves at least five critical functions for us.[4] First, it serves to reduce the complexity of the environment. If we can think in categories rather than specifics, the environment becomes much less complex. Parents can tell their children, "Don't pet strange dogs," using the category of "dog," rather than having to use the names of specific breeds of dogs. It is easier to think and talk in more broad categories than in specifics.

Second, categorization allows us to recognize objects or ideas we have never previously encountered. While I was in junior high, my next door neighbor collected and traded sports cars. In the several years we were neighbors, he brought home dozens of exotic automobiles. Even though I had never seen a Masserati or a Ferrari before, I was able to recognize the object as a car because it fit the characteristics of my category of "car."

Third, categorization reduces the necessity for constant learning. We can, through categorization, recognize new objects without having to go through any actual new learning, and we are able to draw inferences about the new idea or event from the basis of our previous knowledge.

One day I stopped in at a store with my daughters to look at bicycles with them.

In the store was the biggest dog I had ever seen, a mastiff. I had never seen a mastiff before, but because of my cognitive category of "large dogs" I was able to draw certain inferences about this animal before me. After he had knocked me to the ground in his friendly greeting, I added a few more inferences to my category.

The encounter with the mastiff illustrates the fourth result of categorization also, namely that categorization serves to direct behavior. No one had to tell me to be nice to the dog, because my category of "large dog" (and my category of "self-preservation") served to instruct me regarding my behavior. Even though I had never been in that exact situation before, my cognitive categories instructed me on how to behave.

Finally, categorization reduces the complexity of the environment by allowing us to relate objects or classes of events together. The process of relating ideas together is accomplished through *coding systems*. Coding systems are either broad and generic in nature or are more exclusive and hence narrow. So, for example, the broad generic code of *mammals* will include the more specific code of *small annoying dogs*. It is through coding systems that retention and discovery, among other tasks, are achieved.

For example, I may come home to my wife who excitedly announces, "We are having artichokes for dinner." At this point I'm not sure if she is describing the meal or some guests she has invited. But I see that the table is set for only the immediate family and that there is some sort of strange vegetable being set before me. The use of the code "vegetable" helps me understand that this *may* be edible, may be good for me, and may become a regular part of my diet. Even if we never eat artichokes again, I can now retain the concept that an artichoke is a vegetable.

It is the cognitive coding systems that make perception possible. As we encounter ideas, events, or experiences, our mental response is to conceptualize them through the process of categorization, which is perception. For Bruner, to perceive is to categorize.

Higher learning involves the formation of categories and coding systems. These categories and coding systems permit accurate perception, promote discovery, facilitate in the transfer of learning, and aid in memory. Our minds function cognitively through the process of categorization.

Teaching involves helping people establish more accurate and more meaningful cognitive categories. If we take a young child to a farm and show her a cow, she might very well exclaim, "Doggie!" The reason for this is that the animal before her fits her very unsophisticated category of "dog." It is big and hairy and has four feet—it has to be a dog. But we correct her, telling her, "No, that is a cow." "Cow," she repeats, eager to establish a new category.

Later she sees a horse. "Cow!" she exclaims, with obvious delight. This new animal fits the category she has established because it is very big, hairy, lives on a farm, and smells nasty. Any fool can see this is a cow. But again we help her with her categories, explaining that this is a horse, showing her the differences. And so her learning progresses, maturing through more and more complex and sophisticated categories.

CATEGORIZATION AND CHRISTIAN EDUCATION

Since Christian education is partly about the renewal of the mind, and since part of how we learn is to develop better and more sophisticated categories, a task of Christian education is to help people establish biblical and theological categories and use them in thinking. The categories of holiness, sin, redemption, justice, sanctification, and a host of others must become the grid through which people think about and decide upon their life experiences. I have been stressing that we need to teach people the Bible so that they may live biblically. The connection between knowing the Bible and thinking biblically is rooted in the process of categorization.

I was once asked if I would perform the marriage ceremony of a Christian couple who had "gotten into trouble." The woman was five months pregnant, but they loved each other and wanted to be married. In the midst of the premarital counseling I asked them, "If you had it to do over again, what would you do differently?" They thought for a few moments and then responded thoughtfully, "Use birth control." After a while I asked them about that answer, telling them I was surprised that they, as Christians, were not repentant and that they did not say that they wished they had not sinned by their sexual conduct. The woman looked at me rather surprised and said, "But I never thought of it as sin!"

Here was a couple, both claiming to be Christians, who simply did not think in biblical categories. They had violated the seventh commandment and were being rushed into a marriage for which they were not ready, but it never dawned on them to see themselves as sinners and their behavior as sinful. I do not blame them for their lack of understanding, but I wonder about the Christian education that caused them to think this way.

A systematic Christian education, such as the one practiced by Richard Baxter, will lead people into increasingly more biblical ways of thinking. It will begin with broad theological categories and help people develop increasingly more adequate ways of thinking about their world and their lives. "More adequate" implies more careful use of biblical and theological insights.

Our society teaches us how to think, but the categories it uses are far from those of the Word of God. Society in the United States thinks primarily in psychological and economic categories. People are trained to think in terms of self-fulfillment and "the bottom line." These categories are psychological and economic, respectively.

When people seek a career, they ask, "What will be fulfilling and what will make money?" Even some Christians assume that God wants them fulfilled and God wants them to have money. Their operative categories and ways of thinking are from the world. They are then baptized into a pseudo-Christian perspective. It is sad to realize that this may be a result of our educational programs, because this is how we train people to think.

Of course, Jesus had a different perspective, calling for self-denial, a willingness to suffer, and obedience to him (Matt. 16:24–26). Believers are to make career decisions around the issues of God's glory and service to him and to others. Jesus' promise is that it is through this path that we will find our lives.

Those who dislike systematic theology do so because they have not found theology to be helpful, experiencing it as irrelevant to their daily lives. If theology is approached and taught as a series of propositions to be learned and rearranged into more sophisticated patterns, I would have to agree. That kind of theology is indeed both irrelevant and a waste of time.

But theology, properly understood, is a way of thinking and a way of seeing. The categories of theology should allow us to see the world in different ways and to think about life from a biblical perspective. Taught properly, theology offers categories through which the mind can be renewed.

The central theme and integrating center of theology for John Calvin was the glory of God. His theology centered around this

---

A systematic Christian education will lead people into increasingly more biblical ways of thinking.

---

issue and everything was seen, ultimately, as a means of magnifying God's glory. This was the generic category that shaped and influenced his theology.

In his presentation regarding human ability to know God, he argued that "the attributes of God according to Scripture agree with those known in his creatures."[5] He maintained that there are three verities necessary for us to know, namely, *mercy* (because that is the basis for our salvation), *judgment* (because that is what is exercised against wrongdoers), and *justice* (because through justice believers are preserved and nurtured).

The problem is that few Christians these days think in such categories. We think in certain biblical categories (such as God's power and Satan's power) but rarely think in relation to mercy, judgment, and justice. Because we fail to think in these ways, we fail to see God's mercy, trust in his judgment, or seek his justice. The way we think influences the way we behave.

As Christian educators we need to think in biblical and theological categories ourselves. If we are not having our minds renewed, we will never be able to teach others to do that. But learning new categories in functional ways is hard work. Retraining our minds, and the minds of others, is a difficult task. How should we teach so that we may help people establish new conceptual categories?

THE ROLE OF THE TEACHER

Broadly, there are two approaches to teaching people to think. One approach, generally the more common, is for the teacher to function as an expert establishing new categories for the student. The teacher will lecture, or use some other transmissive approach, telling the student what categories to use and how to assign information to the various categories. Most systematic theology is taught in this way. The teacher introduces students to the field, explains the broad subdivisions of the study, and then systematically leads the student through a vast array of information. The reasoning is highly deductive, moving from broad general ideas to the more specific.

The alternative mode of teaching is an inductive approach. In this process the teacher questions students, prompting them to discover truth for themselves. This approach normally starts with a specific biblical text and leads students through a discovery mode to establish categories for themselves. Generally a more creative and less structured approach, this mode is more student-centered than the former.

Either mode can be effective in helping people to think, and either can help people establish biblical categories. It is really a matter of style and of relative strengths and weaknesses of each approach.

Expository Teaching

David Ausubel is the leading exponent of the first approach, which he calls expository teaching. He summarizes his position as follows:

> Beginning in the junior high school period, students acquire most new concepts and learn most new propositions by directly grasping higher-order relationships between abstractions. To do so meaningfully, they need no longer depend on current or recently prior concrete-empirical experience and hence are able to bypass completely the intuitive type of understanding reflective of such dependence. Through proper expository teaching they can proceed directly to a level of abstract understanding that is qualitatively superior to the intuitive level in terms of generality, clarity, precision, and explicitness. At this state of development therefore, it seems pointless to enhance intuitive understanding by using discovery techniques.[6]

Ausubel believes that meaning is related to cognitive structure. The only way we can make meaning of something is by relating it to something already in place in our cognitive structure. So, when Jesus said, "I am the good shepherd," the statement had meaning to the hearers because the concept of "shepherd" was already in their minds. To a person who has no idea of shepherd, the statement has no meaning.

Ausubel believes, moreover, that our cognitive structure is organized from the most inclusive downward to the most specific, like an inverted pyramid. Therefore our best teaching should be deductive, moving from the general (the most inclusive) to the specific.

Learning is identified as *subsumption*, which is the process of incorporating meaningful material into existing cognitive structures. If there are no cognitive structures into which the material can be placed, there can be no learning. If, when we hear someone lecture, we cannot make any sense of what is being said, this indicates that we had no existing cognitive structure to accommodate those ideas. To us the lecture is only meaningless words.

Forgetting, according to Ausubel, is *obliterative subsumption.* When we forget, we lose the distinctiveness of the information, and it is lost. It becomes blended in with other, similar information, can no longer be discriminated as a discrete idea, and is therefore "forgotten."

The distinction between holiness and righteousness, made earlier in this book, is a rather fine line. People tend to lose the distinctiveness between the two concepts, and they become blended into one. When this happens, people are no longer capable of differentiating between them, and as a result, the different meanings of holiness and righteousness are forgotten.

Ausubel identifies three variables that will serve to make receptive learning meaningful. First, there must be an *organizer.* The organizer serves to provide categories into which the new information should be placed. When a person listens to someone talk but does not understand what is being discussed, it is because there has not been an organizer provided. When we say, "Wait a minute; I don't know what you are talking about!" we are asking for an organizer from which to make sense of the information.

Second, there must be *discriminability* in the information being presented. Students must be able to see how this information is different from what they already know so that the new material can be retained. Differentiation between ideas is essential to understanding and retaining new information.

Third, Ausubel believes that students must be in a state of *readiness* to receive

new information. That is, existing cognitive structures must be in place, and the student must be developmentally ready to receive the new information. If, for example, students have no existing cognitive structures of *Jesus,* they will hardly be ready for a discussion of his preincarnate state.

The role of the teacher for Ausubel is to present information in logical ways, moving from the known to the unknown, helping students develop and refine their categories. This is exactly what good lecturers do. They provide the student with an orientation to the information they will receive (in Ausubel's terms an "*advanced organizer*"), move them from familiar to new ideas, helping them to organize the information in meaningful ways. An effective lecture is well organized and presented in ways that are relevant to the students' experience and ways of thinking.

Discovery Learning

The alternative approach, generally known as *discovery learning* is advocated by Jerome Bruner. He contends that learners should not be presented with the material in its final form but rather should be encouraged to discover relationships of information for themselves. Students should organize material themselves, putting it into their own categories. It is up to the student to discover relationships among concepts.

Discovery learning implies less directive teaching methods. Rather than explaining, teachers ask. Bruner believes that students must acquire skills in problem solving, and this takes place best as students work out issues for themselves. The motivation will be intrinsic, coming from the student's desire to "find an answer."

Necessary to this kind of learning are four factors. First, students must be trained to think in terms of relationships

Discovery learning implies less directive teaching methods. Rather than explaining, teachers ask. The motivation will be intrinsic, coming from the student's desire to "find an answer."

of ideas. Rather than learning concepts in isolation from one another, students must always be prompted to think in integrative ways, relating ideas to ideas.

Second, there must be an adequate need state in the learner. Students will not want to learn unless there is a moderate arousal within them to learn. Therefore, a task of the teacher is to arouse in the student an internal interest in the material at hand.

Third, discovery learning requires some degree of mastery of specific information relative to what is being learned. If, for example, we ask people to do theology with no understanding of biblical data, the discoveries they make will probably be heretical. They will achieve only a pooling of ignorance rather than sound theology. But if people are knowledgeable of biblical data, they will be ready to reason to more sound theological conclusions.

Finally, diversity of background information allows for better integrative thinking. The more broadly defined categories there are in place, the more effective the integration. People with no awareness of, say, political science, will be hard pressed to make political judgments regarding political process. Perhaps what is more important, people without theological categories cannot make theological judgments on political issues.

Bruner's approach works best with students who are predisposed to thinking about relationship of ideas. Background in

problem solving and thinking for oneself allows students to function well in a discovery context. But students trained to be receptors of information from the teacher find themselves waiting for the teacher to give the "right answer." They see teachers as experts who know their way around the information and will explain it properly to them. To them, student discussions of ideas are not terribly meaningful or may even be a waste of time.

The outworking of Bruner's approach requires what he calls a *spiral curriculum*, which repeats key ideas at successively higher levels. Intentional repetition of ideas allows students to develop generic codes for information and to process it at higher and higher levels. Thus it is perfectly appropriate to study the same books of the Bible repeatedly, because each successive repetition allows for new understandings and insights.

TEACHER-CENTERED AND STUDENT-CENTERED LEARNING

Both Ausubel and Bruner believe that students learn by categorization. Both believe that the role of the teacher is to help students develop and maintain categories for thinking and for organizing information. The debate resides over who should develop the categories. Ausubel advocates a more teacher-centered approach, whereas Bruner advocates a student-centered approach. There are strengths and weaknesses for both.

The strength of Ausubel's approach is its efficiency. Especially when teaching such a broad and complicated field as theology, helping students with categories seems appropriate. Rather than ignoring two thousand years of Christian thinking, we can lead students through the doctrines, helping them see how the great minds of the church have thought about issues. Instead of making them sort through data and ideas that may take years to discover, we can show them the logic and the conclusions, literally saving them years of work.

Also, in almost all fields of study there are accepted categories in place. It is the use of these accepted categories that makes communication possible. Part of any systematic inquiry is the use of common terminology and common categories. If people all develop their own terms and categories, meaningful communication is hindered.

I once had a student offer a long dissertation on hermeneutics in which he discussed at length how a sermon is best constructed. When I pointed out that he was discussing homiletics, his retort was, "I guess we have different definitions of hermeneutics." Until we could agree on what our terms meant, we could not have any meaningful dialogue.

The weakness of expository teaching is that it does not teach students to think on their own. The term *receptive learning* implies that the student is primarily a receptor. Reception is not a bad place to start. Recognizing that others know more than we do and that we need to be quiet and listen can be the start of important growth. It can also save a great deal of time and effort.

But as learners progress, they must also become independent thinkers, no

longer dependent on others for information. I once watched a group of college professors, all with earned doctorates, call their former teacher to find out how to answer a rather basic question. What struck me most was that their education had not led them to be independent thinkers. They were still dependent on their professor!

At Trinity I teach both master's and doctoral students. If the training I provide for the doctoral students were simply more lectures, I would be robbing them of what they rightly deserve. They do not need me to give them more information; they need me to help them think better. Thinking can be modeled in an effective lecture, but the students must also be able to practice the process through dialogue and class projects.

The strength of Bruner's approach is that it teaches students to think. By involving them in the learning process and stimulating them to establish and work with their own categories, his technique serves to create independent thinkers. Discovery learning teaches people to discover ideas and the relationship of one idea to another. It teaches people to use their minds for more than filing cabinets of other people's ideas.

A second strength is that it makes people more responsible for their own education. Rather than merely receiving information from others, students must think for themselves and draw their own conclusions. Students must take responsibility for their positions on issues, because they have had to come to them on their own.

Trinity Divinity School is built partly on the realization that within orthodox Christianity are a variety of beliefs. The faculty is theologically diverse, with a variety of orthodox positions represented. As a result, students are not trained in one theological position. Rather, they are exposed to several options, with the responsibility for the position they take left up to them. As a result, our students graduate holding a variety of theological positions, but they also graduate knowing how to think. I think that is a strength of the education we offer.

But Bruner's approach also has several weaknesses. Some students do not come to clear conclusions before they graduate from Trinity. It takes them longer to sort things out for themselves, and discovery learning is a slower process. Especially when it is used in the church, we must be aware that people are in and out of our educational programs. As a result, they may never come to any firm conclusions, because they are not there long enough to do so. They may enjoy the process but never find the meaning.

A second weakness is that the discovery process is dependent on a regular ongoing inquiry. It cannot be accomplished well in a short amount of time. If persons are in and out, they may not ever gain the "big picture" of what is being studied. Discovering and organizing categories requires long, regular learning experiences to be accomplished well.

A fact regarding both approaches is that they are dependent upon good teachers. Not every teacher is a gifted lecturer,[7] and therefore not every teacher can do expository teaching well. It takes certain skills and personality traits to lecture well, and not all teachers possess them.

Conversely, not every teacher is able to lead students to discovery. It requires patience, insight, and not a small degree of creativity to come up with effective means to prompt students to discover and find meaning. Some teachers do not have the ability nor the inclination to teach in this way.

Without being flippant, I would suggest that what teachers do is teach, and what

students do is learn.[8] By that I mean that sometimes we as teachers establish the categories for the students, and sometimes they do it for themselves. We do not always even know exactly what is going on. We teach, and they learn, and the process is very complex.

IMPLICATIONS FOR CHRISTIAN EDUCATION

Given the Bible's emphasis on the way that we think and the rather intricate ideas involved in a mature faith, and given the insights regarding the higher cognitive process of categorization, the following implications can be drawn.

Students must acquire biblical and theological categories for thinking Christianly.

The major themes of the Bible must become functional categories in the mind of the believer. If we do not think the way God does about life and the reality around us, in what sense can we consider ourselves Christian? The renewal of the mind calls for the establishment and use of the themes of the Bible to guide our thinking.

I was teaching on the West Side of Chicago the night the Los Angeles riots over the first Rodney King verdict broke out. My class of predominantly African-American students were rightly upset about both the verdict and the response by the Black community. As they talked that night about the situation, I asked them how they made sense out of it theologically. I urged them to think about the situation in biblical and theological categories. My goal was that theology be functional for them, and not just academic. The resulting discussion was powerful, as we used theology as a means of understanding and shaping our response.

I believe that this is an important part of being a Christian. It is not just doing the right thing but also thinking in the right ways. The right ways of thinking are rooted in the categories of the Bible.

Each subgroup in Christendom will emphasize slightly different issues. The biblical themes we see and emphasize varies from group to group. But there remains a core set of beliefs, common to all Christians, that should shape our thinking and living. These core beliefs must become functional cognitive categories in the minds of believers.

Teachers must listen to how their students think.

We cannot be satisfied only with the content of our students' thoughts; we must also be concerned with how they think. Listening to the categories they use and the information placed within those categories helps us understand how they think. Even the expository teacher must listen to the students as they use the information they are gaining. If the cate-

We cannot be satisfied only with the content of our students' thoughts; we must also be concerned with how they think.

gories of thinking used by students is no different from the categories of the world around them, we are not doing an effective job educationally.

Problem solving is an effective means of hearing students think. By asking them to reflect on a situation or event, the teacher can listen for the categories they use, and the concepts included in those categories. If Bible and theology never come up in their thinking, we have not helped them to use these categories. They may have memorized them, but that is not the same as using them.

Information must be presented in ways that help students categorize it properly.

Many teachers use the lecture method, but not all do it well. A good lecture proceeds in logical order, beginning with the known, to activate existing categories, and then proceeding to the unknown, to provide new information. An effective lecture will lead students in logical steps to organize and thus make the new ideas useful.

The use of an *advanced organizer* does much to help students organize material well. An advanced organizer is simply a way of orienting students to what is going to be learned so that they know how to make sense of it as they receive it. If I am going to lecture in a class, I will often write on the corner of the board a brief outline of the main points I intend to cover. This serves to let the students know where the lecture is headed and what point I am in at any given time. This, in turn, serves to keep them oriented and able to follow the logical development of what I am discussing.

Teachers should work to organize materials well and to communicate that organization to the students. Better learning is achieved when the material is presented in a logical way. One of my colleagues tells of a notoriously unorganized professor at Harvard Divinity School. The professor dropped his lecture notes as he entered the room. A student jumped up to help the professor pick up and reorganize his material. The student handed the professor the first pages he had retrieved, and the professor simply began lecturing at that point. The fact that the notes were in random sequence made no difference to the professor. However, this event was not lost on the students! They had no idea what he was discussing.

Because logical thinking requires the organization and reorganization of categories, it is incumbent upon teachers to present material clearly. The Word of God proceeds logically, and our presentation of it should be logical also.

Teaching people to think theologically requires both expository teaching and discovery learning.

One of the most remarkable teachers of theology is John Gerstner. He is a renowned expert on Jonathan Edwards and a formidable scholar. As a teacher, he is one of the most powerful and frightening instructors ever to visit a classroom.

His mode of teaching is highly Socratic. He has students read extensively prior to class, a classic expository approach. But when the students come to class, his method is almost exclusively the discovery mode. He questions the students on their understanding of the material and the implications of the content to other areas

Effective education shapes students to know the truth and to think with the truth, so that their behavior is shaped by the truth.

of life and thought. The approach is frightening because it is highly logical, and each student has to depend on his or her own ability to think.

The power of Gerstner's approach is that he teaches students to think theologically; they must know the material, but they must be able to think with the material. He is not satisfied until his students think clearly regarding the implications of what they have learned.

If it is true that mind does shape heart and will, then it is imperative that Christians learn to think about the truth. Effective education shapes students to know the truth and to think with the truth, so that their behavior is shaped by the truth.

Notes

1. *Academic American Encyclopedia* (Princeton, N.J.: Arete, 1980), 525.
2. Jerome S. Bruner, *The Process of Education* (New York: Random House, 1960), 33.
3. *Academic American Encyclopedia*, 525.
4. J. S. Bruner; J. J. Goodnow; and G. A. Austin, *A Study of Thinking* (New York: John Wiley, 1956).
5. John Calvin, *Institutes of the Christian Religion*, 2 vols., ed. John T. McNeill (Philadelphia: Westminster, 1960), 1:97.
6. David P. Ausubel, *Educational Psychology: A Cognitive View* (New York: Holt, Rinehart and Winston, 1968), 19.
7. How's that for an understatement?
8. This painfully obvious observation was pointed out to me in the textbook by Guy R. Lefrancois, *Psychology for Teaching*, 4th ed. (Belmont, Calif.: Wadsworth, 1982), 121.

14

Learning by Experience

"Experience is the best teacher" is an often-quoted proverb, emphasizing the truth that experience is an important source of learning. It is difficult to offer a logical argument to contradict a person's life experience. If we try to do so, the person will normally respond, "But I know it's true. It happened to me." Teenagers especially believe their experience above almost any other source of truth.

However, we do not always interpret our experience correctly. We are hardly objective observers of our own life experience, and therefore our interpretations may be less than objective.

The story is told about a farmer who was working in his field one hot spring day. He looked up and saw the letters *PC* clearly visible in the cloudless sky. The man was a believer, and he felt sure that this was a sign from God that he was to leave the farm and enter the ministry. He was sure that *PC* stood for "Preach Christ." He left the farm and began a long and unfruitful ministry. Even though he was a terrible preacher, he felt he must be true to the sign God gave him. One Sunday as he was boring a congregation nearly to tears with an uninspired sermon, he told them of his vision. An old farmer in the back row called out, "I think it stood for 'Plant corn'!"

The problem, of course, is that there are no objective standards by which one can judge such an experience. Without objective standards, we are lost in a sea of relativity, with each person having to find his or her own meaning.

The philosophy of existentialism raises the role of experience to preeminence, arguing that truth itself resides in experience. The only thing we can trust, and the only thing we can believe in, existentialists argue, is our own experience. For the existentialist, experience is the only meaningful source of truth and is the only valid means of knowledge. If existentialism is true, then we must each find truth for ourselves, and each person indeed will have his or her own truth, unlike the truth of anyone else.

Existentialism ultimately leads to despair. If all that exists is our own experience, in the ultimate sense everything is meaningless. If all we can trust and all we can know is our own experience, then, like the historic French existentialist Jean-Paul Sartre, we will be reduced to absolute relativity and absolute despair.

But as Christians, we know that reality and truth exist outside of our own experience. Because God exists, reality is measured against him, and truth comes from him. There is more to life than that which is limited to our experience, and truth exists outside the limitations of our experience. Truth exists in relation to God, not in relation to ourselves.

As educators, however, we must also recognize and use the power of experience in shaping belief and in aiding learning. Our task is to use experience to help people learn about life and to live life as mature believers.

WHY DO WE BELIEVE?

From a theological perspective, we know that belief of the Gospel is a gift from God (Eph. 2:8–9). But from a human perspective, what is it that shapes us to believe the things we believe? From where do beliefs emerge? What causes us to believe the things we believe? What sorts of things does God use to develop belief in us?

Most of us like to think that our beliefs are all quite rational. We consider the evidence and draw logical conclusions that serve to shape the way we believe. That sounds good, but in reality beliefs are shaped by a variety of factors. Sociologists conclude that a combination of at least four different factors shape our beliefs.

First, beliefs tend to follow the patterns of early childhood reinforcement. That is, we tend to believe in accordance with how we were raised as young children. Parents praise their children for certain beliefs and rebuke them for others, and so they shape the beliefs of their children.

Most people raised in the United States believe that capitalism and a free market economy constitute the best possible economic system. Even without the benefit of instruction in basic economic theory, we accept this as true because that is how we were raised.

There are many beliefs imbedded deep in the minds of adults that are the product of early childhood training. We believe them because we were taught to believe them. We are hardly conscious of their existence unless they are challenged by someone around us. These sorts of beliefs are held uncritically and deeply influence our lives.

Attitudes toward other races are usually shaped first by early childhood patterns

We all can look back to certain teachers who had a strong influence on us and shaped our beliefs. For all of us, our beliefs are somewhat a function of our commitments to people.

of reinforcement. If our parents were open and accepting of people of other races, we will be also. But if our parents believed that people of different races are inferior, or to be feared, we will have these racist perspectives imbedded in us, until they are challenged.

Second, beliefs tend to follow our commitments to people. As we become committed to a person, we tend to adopt that person's beliefs. Children believe the way their parents do because they are committed to their parents. A young child will ask, "Mom, are we Democrats or Republicans?" Whichever way the mother responds is fine with the child. "Whatever mom and dad believe is what I believe" is the child's motto.

During adolescence commitments tend to shift off of parents and onto peers. As a result, the beliefs of the adolescent tend to shift also. No longer do teenagers believe just as their parents do. They now begin to adopt the belief system of their peers.

The power of a Christian youth group is rooted in this truth. Youth groups work by getting kids committed to the youth leader and to each other. If the group holds to Christian beliefs, teens coming into the group will tend to adopt Christian beliefs also. Youth ministry functions most effectively through relationships because it is through relationships that teens' beliefs will be shaped.

When students go off to college, it is not unusual to see them become commit-

ted to specific professors. When they do, their beliefs will again shift to those held by the favorite professor. We all can look back to certain teachers who had a strong influence on us and shaped our beliefs. For all of us, our beliefs are somewhat a function of our commitments to people.

Parents are correct in being concerned about who their kids choose as friends. Friends will influence beliefs because beliefs tend to follow commitments to people. The apostle Paul reminds us of this truth when he warns, "Do not be misled: 'Bad company corrupts good character'" (1 Cor. 15:33).

When my wife and I were first married, many of our beliefs were quite diverse. Her background was more Christian and more conservative than mine. But because of our commitment to each other, our beliefs moved closer together, and now in most regards they are virtually identical.

Third, beliefs tend to follow the lines of logical thinking. That is, we will believe only what makes sense to us. If our beliefs seem totally illogical, we usually will abandon them.

For the Christian, because we believe in the existence of God, it is not illogical for us to believe in miracles. Logical thinking does not discredit the miraculous. It does, however, require that belief in the miraculous have a logical basis.

For this reason, teens become concerned with the appropriateness of belief in God. "Does it make sense to believe in God?" they ask, because they want to believe only what is logical. Apologetics is crucial for persons who are trying to sort out beliefs according to logic.

Especially for adults, beliefs must make logical sense. It becomes impossible to believe what is absurd and easier to believe what is reasonable. Beliefs can be strengthened when they are shown to be logical and consistent.

There is a place for careful, logical discourse in Christian education. The reasonableness of the faith can be an important factor in shaping belief, especially in adults. We can never argue someone into the kingdom, because acceptance of the Gospel comes as a gift from God. But God may use the force of the logic to shape a person's belief.

Finally, beliefs tend to follow behavior. We have a greater tendency to believe what we do than to do what we believe. Because of the power of experiences to shape beliefs, we will order our beliefs according to our behavior. Much of our belief system tends to be a result of how we have lived.

There are times when we realize that our stated beliefs and behaviors do not match. When such cognitive dissonance happens, we usually will change our beliefs. "I don't really believe that any more" will be our explanation for why we are acting as we are.

The reason we tend to change beliefs easier than behavior is that behavior is public but beliefs are private. It is easier to say, "I don't believe that" than it is to say, "I am being hypocritical." Therefore we change our belief systems to match our behaviors.

Harvard College was founded on an orthodox statement of belief. But over the years it wandered far from its stated beliefs. Rather than changing practice

back into accord with the statement of belief, Harvard chose to change its stated beliefs. It was easier to rewrite the doctrinal statement than it was to bring behavior back in harmony with the original belief system.

People may do the same thing. They commit to a statement of beliefs, but later their practice may violate their beliefs. Rather than repenting of the behavior, they change their beliefs to conform to their new behavior. We tend to believe what we do rather than do what we believe.

For the Christian, another option exists. We can repent of inappropriate behavior, confess our sin, and bring our behavior back in line with our beliefs. Repentance and confession are powerful means to relieve the cognitive dissonance that results from behaving in ways that contradict our beliefs.

Unfortunately, some Christian educators get this principle backwards. They attempt to force people into right behaviors through manipulation and guilt. "If you really believe this you will . . ." goes the line of argument. Long discourses on why we should pray, witness, or practice other virtues are offered, but they serve to do little to change the behavior of the hearers. The problem is that the educators are coming at it backwards.

D. James Kennedy, author of *Evangelism Explosion*[1] and pastor of the Coral Ridge Presbyterian Church in Florida, illustrates this point well. He was conducting seminars on evangelization but was seeing little results. The problem was that his behavior was not matching his message. A pastor showed him how to do personal evangelism. He let him experience the excitement of actually leading another person to faith, and Jim Kennedy was hooked. The power of the Evangelism Explosion technique is that it gets people doing evangelism, and this behavior then shapes their belief in evangelism.

It is amazing to see how Jesus taught his disciples to pray. He never offered a "prayer seminar," never seemed to lay any kind of guilt on them regarding their prayer life. Rather, the picture that emerges in the gospels is that he modeled prayer for them. Repeatedly we are told that Jesus was praying by himself while the disciples were with him. Finally, they said to him, "Lord, teach us to pray" (Luke 11:1). His strategy was to provide an example and then to get them praying. Through the experience of prayer their commitment to prayer was shaped.

Prayer has been a difficult issue for me. I have always held to a theology that emphasizes God's sovereign control over all of life. This perspective had not been presented to me in a proper balance with the biblical emphasis on human responsibility and the Bible's emphasis on prayer. I had a difficult time understanding how prayer related to the sovereignty of God. As a result, my prayer life was not strong.

In his mercy, God allowed me to suffer through some difficult times. Every source I sought for help could do nothing. Finally, in utter desperation I turned regularly to God in prayer. I found relief, comfort, and finally the solution through those times of prayer. The experience of prayer has now shaped my belief in prayer in ways that logic alone never could. It was ultimately my behavior that shaped my belief.

USING LIFE EXPERIENCES

If it is true that behavior shapes belief, how can we as Christian educators shape the experiences of students to help them believe? How can we influence their lives in such a way as to provide experiences that will mold their beliefs?

Some Christian institutions try to have such a strong influence on their students that they actually control life experiences to influence belief. Through rigid rules and regulations they strive to regulate lives in an attempt to produce mature believers. Rigid control, however, fails to acknowledge human dignity adequately and is an expression of behaviorism in its effort to shape persons through environmental influences. A more acceptable approach is needed.

Learning contexts usually fall into one of three categories. *Formal learning* contexts are the most controlled, having the most structure. Formal learning is characterized by designated classes, a tightly organized curriculum, external accountability, clearly delineated outcomes, and regulated time constraints. Students come for a designated period of time, progress through a prescribed series of courses, attain a specified level of expertise, and are granted some sort of certificate of completion.

The strength of formal education is in its prescribed nature. There are very predictable time frames and usually specific sets of outcomes. Students know when instruction starts, when it ends, and what is expected. Accountability tends to be high, with the outcome being a diploma, a degree, or some other sort of recognized certification.

But formal education is weak because it can be carried out almost insulated from normal life experiences. The designation "ivory tower" calls attention to the fact that formal education is somehow different from "real life." It is, by design, removed from life experience and stresses theory and cognitive efforts. As a result, the experiences provided in formal education are limited in their ability to teach in the way that everyday life can teach. Formal education is powerful for lower levels of learning, but not as strong at moving people into the higher levels of application and adoption.

Larry Richards has been a critic of the trappings of formal education in the church. His concern regarding institutionalizing Christian education has caused him to decry the trappings of formal education as a mode of nurturing faith. He believes that formal educational techniques are virtually useless for shaping faith in people.[2]

The opposite of formal learning contexts is *informal learning*. Informal learning is the stuff of everyday life, the so-called college of hard knocks. Through the normal experiences of life, through the good and the bad, we learn a great deal. In completely unstructured contexts we learn about life, and through our experiences acquire all sorts of skills.

One of the most significant responsibilities many people ever face is that of raising children. Once in a while we may take a formal class on parenting, but for the most part we learn it through trial and error. Through the experience of being a parent and from the example of others, we develop our parenting skills. In almost totally informal ways we learn to do some of the most critical things we are ever required to do.

I particularly enjoy fishing. (I always try to maintain a distinction between *fishing* and *catching*, doing much more of the former than the latter.) My fishing skills are being honed in the context of informal learning, by trial and error. But I enjoy the process and the outcomes, because there is no real pressure, and the only person I have to please is myself.

The strength of informal learning is that it is ubiquitous and almost totally based on experience. It is through experiences that we learn, and the learning tends to be powerful. We hold tightly to

the beliefs that are shaped by experience. The lessons of life are held much more firmly than the lessons of formal education. Informal learning tends to be more influential for most people than formal learning.

The weakness of informal learning is that it can be wrong, or at least incomplete. Because we have to please no one but ourselves, there is virtually no accountability. Life can be misinterpreted,

> *We hold tightly to the beliefs that are shaped by experience. Informal learning tends to be more influential for most people than formal learning.*

and improper conclusions and inappropriate skills developed. I am sure I have developed some bad habits from fishing alone, and these weight the outcomes far more in favor of the bass than me.

This weakness is not too serious when it is related to fishing, but it becomes much more critical when it influences something like parenting. Parents can do great damage to their children if all they know is how they themselves were raised, or if all they do is follow their own instincts. I doubt that any of us would want to be treated by a physician who learned medicine in a totally informal way.

God can and does use life experiences to teach us. He brings us through many sorts of events, either easy and enjoyable or difficult and painful, and these are the "stuff" of growth. Many people fail to realize that we do not have to understand what God is teaching in order to grow. The Preacher reminds us,

As you do not know the path of the wind,
* or how the body is formed in a*
*   mother's womb,*
so you cannot understand the work of God,
* the Maker of all things (Eccl. 11:5).*

Even though we do not understand what God is doing, we can grow and learn through the life experiences he brings to us. We can say this with assurance because "we know that in all things God works for the good of those who love him, who have been called according to his purpose" (Rom. 8:28).

Our responsibility as Christian educators is to recognize that our students are continually learning through their life experiences and that God is at work teaching them through those experiences. We cannot shape their life experiences ourselves, but we can recognize the power and validity of the experiences as sources of learning for them. Our pastoral responsibility is to stand alongside and encourage people to see the hand of God and trust the hand of God, even when they cannot understand the hand of God. We are called to faith, by which we trust the character of God even when we do not understand the work of God.

Between formal and informal learning rests a third approach called *nonformal learning*. Nonformal learning is more difficult to define, but it can be described. It constitutes those modes of learning that have some of the structure and intentionality of formal contexts but also the spontaneity and freedom of informal learning. Perhaps the most familiar expression of a nonformal context is the Sunday school.

Sunday schools have structure, with set times and places for instruction, a planned curriculum, and designated teachers. But they do not have any rigid external controls, no accreditation standards, and no forms of formal recognition. They have the freedom to "go with the flow" (a formal educational term meaning they can be responsive to life context) and to stress relationships as well as content. Teachers can visit students outside of class, spend time informally with them, and use life experiences in ways teachers in a formal context cannot.

There is great power in nonformal learning. It has enough structure to keep it going in a systematic way but enough freedom to use life experiences for teaching. For years people have tried to announce the death of the Sunday school, but it just keeps going. I think this is because of the potency of nonformal learning.

Some of the power of nonformal learning is in its capacity to use life experiences for teaching. It has the freedom to be responsive to what is happening in the lives of students, using these experiences for teaching. It does not force the experience as the behaviorist does, but it uses the experience as a means of teaching. But how can teachers use the life experiences of students in their teaching?

EXPERIENTIAL CHRISTIAN EDUCATION

Educators who value experiential Christian education use the life experiences of students for teaching. Recognizing that students continually have experiences that are powerful for teaching, they attempt to use these for reflection and insight so that the student may grow.

Many times Jesus used the experiences of his students for instruction. He reflected on what they were doing, or on what had happened to them, as a means of teaching.

He did not manipulate their life experiences, but he used them for teaching.

Luke tells the story of Jesus' visit to the home of Martha and Mary, two women who were responsive to his teaching. Discord arose as Mary chose to sit at Jesus' feet, while Martha was "distracted by all the preparations that had to be made" (Luke 10:40). Martha became so upset she gently rebuked Jesus for not caring that the work was being divided unequally. Jesus used this time to teach her about choosing what is better versus what is merely important.

Luke continues to walk us through Jesus' ministry, showing the theological

---

If teachers do not know their students, they can hardly use their experiences for learning.

---

development in his teaching. But he also shows us Jesus' method of teaching, which was responding to the life experiences of his hearers. He reflected on life practices, social customs, prevalent religious logic, and a host of other issues, all in the context of the life experience of the learners.

Too often Bible and theology are taught in antiseptic formal ways, devoid of connections with real life. Teachers can become so controlled by the agenda they want to cover that they fail to use the actual events of the day. But there can be important outcomes from reflecting on the life experiences of students.

While teaching a class on moral and faith development in adolescence, I asked the students to tell their own life history of faith. One woman told how she had been raised in a very conservative context that had forced her to miss much of the normal experiences of adolescence. Her story was quite painful.

As she went on, she wondered aloud why she had maintained her faith and *held on to God* during those difficult years. I was able to reflect on that with her, pointing out that it had actually been God holding on to her. Her faithfulness through those difficult years was an expression of God's grace in her life.

She had never seen God's provision quite like that before. My simple reflection on her life experience opened a powerful new insight for her. But if I had failed to expect students to discuss their life experiences in class, I would not have been able to make that point for her.

The arena of life provides an important context in which to demonstrate the truthfulness of God's Word. Through both the negative and positive experiences of life we illustrate the validity of biblical perspective and values. But if the educator fails to use the life experiences of the students, a splendid opportunity is lost.

Experiential education requires that the teacher be aware of the life experiences of the students. If teachers do not know their students, they can hardly use their experiences for learning. The power of nonformal education is that it allows greater freedom to use the lives of the students for teaching.

There are certain rare times when I can use life experiences in my teaching at Trinity. Once in a while something happens in the community or in the nation that provides grist for the lesson. We are able to do theology regarding events and use this to learn the lesson of the day. But these times are somewhat rare, due to the nature of formal education.

But in the nonformal context of Sunday school, home Bible studies, youth groups, or my advisee groups at Trinity, I am free to use life experiences for teaching. I can ask students what is happening in their lives and then think with them theologically about their experiences. The context allows for this kind of freedom, a freedom rarely found in a formal setting.

Thomas Groome is the leading proponent of this kind of intentional reflection on life experiences.[3] His "shared praxis" approach to religious education leads students to intentional reflection on their lives in the context of a group and in light of the Gospel. There is great power in the approach he advocates, but there is also a critical weakness.

The power resides in the fact that he leads people into intentional thought about their own lives. He helps people tell their own life story and reflect on it critically in light of the Christian story. He helps people do theology on their own lives, asking if where they are in their lives is in keeping with where the Gospel calls them to be. This is powerful intentional teaching.

The weakness of his approach is in his use of a *dialectical hermeneutic* that places theology and experience as thesis and antithesis in dialectical relationship with each other. He wants theology to critique experience, but he also wants experience to critique theology. The synthesis is a new understanding of the Gospel, mediated through theology and experience.

Dialectical hermeneutics denies the absolute truthfulness of Scripture. There is only the tension between experience and theology and a continual reformation of "truth" based partly on experience. I believe it is important both to critique experience on the basis of theology and to reshape a theology that fails to reflect true experience, but we must never critique the Bible on the basis of our experience. Its truth is not subject to reformation on the basis of our experience. Our only option is to bow before its truth and accept its authority over us. It can and should critique us, but we do not critique it. How, then, can we capture the strength of experiential education without falling into the trap of sitting in judgment on Scripture? The following guidelines are helpful for capturing the life experiences of students without losing the authority of Scripture over them.

Be aware of the life experiences of your students.

Effective Christian education will use the experiences of the student. It is incumbent upon the teacher to know the students and to listen to what the students say about their lives. If teachers do not provide opportunities for students to

> *Teachers must create a climate of openness and honesty in the class. This is accomplished first through the example of the teacher.*

talk about their lives, they will not be able to use the experiences of the students. Nonformal educational settings allow students to talk more freely about life and allow teachers to use life experiences more directly.

Teachers must create a climate of openness and honesty in the class. This is accomplished first through the example of the teacher. If teachers will risk openness and honesty, reflecting before the class on their life experiences, the students will be more willing to share their lives. A climate of trust and honesty is needed for students to talk about their own lives.

Appropriate questions by the teacher can do much to enable a process of honest sharing. Even a generic question such as, "How are things going for you this week?" can set a tone for open communication. But when teachers ask this question, it must be with an intention of listening and responding. People will not risk sharing their lives if they are not being taken seriously.

Reflect theologically on life experiences.

The point of Christian education is to bring life experiences and Christian theology together so that life is influenced by theology. Effective teaching helps students discover that theology functions as an interpretive framework for understanding and responding to life experiences. Teaching for spiritual growth requires honest interaction with the life experiences of the student from a theological perspective.

Again, even a generic question such as "How do you make sense of that theologically?" helps a student learn to think about life from a biblical perspective. It has never dawned on many students to think about life through the lens of their theology.

If, for example, a student reports that she has prayed a great deal about an issue, and it seems that God has not answered, we have a great opportunity to think with her about her theology of prayer. "Can you tell me why God may not be answering?"

can be the lead-in to a significant discussion regarding prayer. The key will be that the discussion must be rooted in a proper biblical perspective on prayer.

Theology is not a discipline to be studied apart from real life experiences. It is the framework through which we interpret life and the content that causes our minds to be renewed. Teaching students to think Christianly requires that the categories and perspectives of the Bible become the categories of their thinking. The categories become functional as we help students think with them.

When Jim and Tammy Faye Bakker lost their ministry, much of the Christian community was upset. While teaching a class on theological foundations of Christian education, I asked the students to think theologically about what had transpired. Rather than allowing them to process the events only on an emotional level, I asked them to use their theology to understand the issues. Such intentional theological reflection caused the students to look at that tragedy in new ways. Such passages as Matthew 6:19–24 became the framework through which our analysis was made. I was teaching the students to reflect theologically on a current event, and this became the platform from which we could examine our life values.

Let life question you.

Too often, in our attempts to understand life we offer uninformed opinions on what God may or may not be doing in a given situation. The temptation is great to explain the work of God, even when we do not understand it ourselves. Through the prophet Isaiah, God reminds us:

"For my thoughts are not your thoughts,
   neither are your ways my ways,"
   declares the LORD.

*"As the heavens are higher than the earth,
so are my ways higher than your ways
and my thoughts than your thoughts."*
(Isa. 55:8–9)

standing of God?" and open the way for pivotal learning. To that question there are answers to be explored and measured against the teaching of Scripture.

Life experiences can and should force us to examine our understanding of God's character and work and drive us back into the Bible for insight. As life questions us, it helps us see where and how we need to grow.

If we only attempt to question life, asking, "Why has this happened?" we open the way for silly, unhelpful responses. We settle for speculation, attempting to explain the very things we do not understand.

We have all heard the type of explanation that tries to make what is bad sound good. "Maybe the Lord gave you a flat tire to protect you from an accident" is the kind of unfruitful speculation that should be avoided. We must come to peace with the fact that we cannot understand nor explain the works of God.

A better approach is to let life question you. By this I mean that we should explore how the life experience is affecting our faith. "What does that do to your understanding of God?" is a question worth exploring, and a question that can be answered. Life experiences can and should force us to examine our understanding of God's character and work and drive us back into the Bible for insight. As life questions us, it helps us see where and how we need to grow.

In the example above, if the teacher attempts to offer various explanations of "what God is doing" in not answering prayers, the potential for wrong answers is profound. But the teacher can ask, "What is this experience doing to your under-

Be willing to leave matters unresolved.

One of the greatest temptations in teaching is to "look good" by always having a great answer for any question. In addition to protecting our own pride, we can be tempted to "make God look good." We want to protect his reputation, so we offer answers even if we do not really understand. Enough bravado and high sounding language can usually convince students that an answer has been given, even if it has not.

In my earlier days as a teacher, I had a strong need to prove myself by offering answers to any question and any experience. I actually developed the ability to look knowledgeable, even when I did not have a clue as to what was going on. Such posturing and bluffing is sin and needs to be confessed as such.

Later in life, when I had experiences I could not understand, my uninformed theology and feigning insight did little to help me make sense of my life experiences. I found that I could only examine my own heart and see what my faith was like as I struggled with difficult life questions. As I grew in my theological understanding, some of my questions were answered, but not all.

Students do not need us to offer answers we do not possess. They need, rather, for us to listen empathetically and to model for them confidence in God in the face of unanswered questions. They need to know that our God cannot be reduced to simple pat answers and that part of walking with him is accepting the mysteries.

There are times when we must be willing to say, "I don't know." We cannot make theological sense out of all of life's experiences, but we can confront the experiences through the eyes of faith, trusting God even when we do not understand. Like Job, we must be willing to say, "Though he slay me, yet will I hope in him" (Job 13:15).

Use current events for teaching God's truth.

Not all of the experiences we use must come directly from the life of the students. Current news events can also provide powerful issues for theological discussion and insight. Events in our own local vicinity or events in the national or international news can and should be the subject of theological reflection. My colleague Bruce Fields tells his students that theology must be done with the Bible in one hand and the newspaper in the other.

We have all seen examples of poor theology done from current events. Those who are enamored with prophecy spend inordinate amounts of time trying to relate current events to their eschatological perspectives, usually determining that a certain political leader or another is the Antichrist.[4] That is not what I have in mind.

If our goal is to help people think biblically so that they may live biblically, one of the ways to do this is to reflect on the news from a theological perspective. Theology helps us make sense not only of our own lives but of the events of life around us as well.

Jesus did just this in Luke 13:1–5. He reflected on two different current events to help the disciples see their need of repentance. He used the news of the day to engage their minds and to make his point. They all knew about the construction accident and the slaughter of the Galileans. These events served as his point of reference to help them think about their standing before God.

Chuck Colson models this approach well. In his regular contributions to *Christianity Today* he takes current events and writes about them in theological perspective. His essays on the political process and on issues before Congress are models of how to think theologically about current events. These can be an excellent resource for learning to apply theology to the current scene and to make sense of contemporary issues from a biblical perspective.

Life experiences offer a constant illustration of the truthfulness of God's Word and of the dangers of ignoring his Word. Effective Christian educators who enable spiritual growth are those who confront life experiences head on, attempting to understand them in light of Scripture and seeking biblical responses to life events. This is the stuff of real life. It is the kind of teaching that helps people to have their minds renewed and their lives transformed.

Notes

1. D. James Kennedy, *Evangelism Explosion, 3rd ed.* (Wheaton, Ill.: Tyndale House, 1983).
2. Lawrence O. Richards, *Christian Education: Learning to be Like Jesus Christ* (Grand Rapids: Zondervan, 1988).
3. Thomas Groome, *Sharing Faith: A Comprehensive Approach to Religious Education and Pastoral Care* (New York: HarperCollins, 1991).
4. My colleague Scot McKnight preached part of a sermon at Trinity "proving" that Perry Downs is really the beast of Revelation 13:11–18. I think he was wrong.

Chapter

15

Teaching for Spiritual Growth

The focus of the educational ministry of the church must be the spiritual development of her people. The church is "a chosen people, a royal priesthood, a holy nation, a people belonging to God, that you may declare the praises of him who called you out of darkness into his wonderful light" (1 Peter 2:9). Our educational task is to help people understand and live in this reality. Teaching for spiritual growth requires helping people live righteously to the glory of God.

Curriculum theory speaks of the *organizing principle*, the core idea around which the curriculum is focused. The function of the organizing principle is to enable educational planners to have a basis for decisions. Whatever is to be included and whatever is to be excluded is determined on the basis of the organizing principle. In addition, educational methods must be chosen in relation to the central value expressed in the organizing principle.

Church leaders must have a basis from which to make educational decisions. The organizing principle of the educational ministry of the church should be the spiritual growth of her people. Her central task is to produce people who are spiritually mature. Paul said the goal of his ministry was to "proclaim him, admonishing and teaching everyone with all wisdom, so that we may present everyone perfect in Christ" (Col. 2:28).

Many times churches divert from this central task, becoming involved in activities that are good and helpful at a certain level but are not at the core of their responsibility. The best is sacrificed on the altar of the good. The result is that the people of God are ignorant of basic biblical truths and unable to walk in the fullness and power of the Holy Spirit. People leave the church, discouraged regarding the authenticity of the Gospel, and the church fails to be salt and light in a desperately needy world.

The church is experiencing remarkable growth in South America, Asia, and Africa, but is declining in North America. I believe the decline is due partly to the failure of Christian education to focus on the central task of teaching for spiritual growth. Some churches are experiencing numerical and financial growth, but this must not be confused with spiritual growth.

If I wanted to speak tongue in cheek I would say that the church in the United States is in good shape except for two issues: We do not believe the Bible, and we have never received Jesus. Other than that, we are doing quite well.

Of course this is overstatement, but it is not completely void of truth. The false gospel proclaiming that we can be Christians without obedience to the lordship of Christ indicates both a failure to believe the Bible and a refusal to receive him to whom all authority in heaven and earth has been given. Such thinking strikes me as a form of the drunkenness with which God afflicts his people in judgment (Jer. 13:12-27). How else can we explain teaching that denies the rightful authority of the Lord? The responsibility of Christian education is to teach God's people God's truth and to teach it in relation to life. The truth is to be lived, not simply understood.

The message of the prophet Malachi needs to be heard by the church in the United States at the end of the twentieth century. God declared, "I am not pleased with you" (Mal. 1:10). The reason for his displeasure is that Israel was maintaining religious practices without any true heart for God. God asked, "A son honors his father, and a servant his master. If I am a father, where is the honor due me? If I am a master, where is the respect due me?" (Mal. 1:6).

Through the prophet Malachi, God placed the blame on the religious leaders of the nation, because it was they who had led the people astray. Malachi proclaimed:

> "For the lips of a priest ought to preserve knowledge, and from his mouth men should seek instruction—because he is the messenger of the LORD Almighty. But you have turned from the way and by your teaching have caused many to stumble; you have violated the covenant with Levi," says the LORD Almighty. "So I have caused you to be despised and humiliated before all the people, because you have not followed my ways but have shown partiality in matters of the law" (Mal. 2:7-9).

We must be sure that our teaching produces growth, not stumbling. The teacher bears a grave responsibility (James 3:1). Because God holds us responsible for our educational ministries, we must take them seriously. The following priorities are issues that I have tried to stress throughout this book—ones that by God's grace can help us teach for spiritual growth.

First, the centrality of the Bible must be maintained. Moses taught that "man does not live on bread alone but on every word that comes from the mouth of the LORD" (Deut. 8:3). It is possible to know the Bible and not be spiritually mature, but it is impossible to be ignorant of God's Word and be spiritually mature. Spiritual maturity begins with a knowledge of the Bible.

In an age of increasing distrust of Scripture—even among those who might call themselves "evangelical"—we must teach the Bible as the only rule of faith and life. Focusing on "felt needs" as opposed to the real need for the Bible causes people to stumble in the long run. Education that enables spiritual growth must be profoundly biblical, because it is God's Word that gives life.

The Bible must be taught as truth to be lived, not simply as knowledge to be understood. It must be taught in relation to real life, not as academic information detached from the experiences of people. But the Bible must be taught, or the people will stumble like drunkards, not knowing which way to turn or how to make sense of their lives from a biblical perspective.

Second, the educational context must be community. The mark of the Christian is our love for one another (John 13:35). Education done in isolation is an anomaly if it claims to be Christian. Spiritual growth takes place in community as the body of Christ ministers to itself and builds itself up by means of the gifts of the Spirit.

We are not the people of God alone. We are called out from the world but into relationship with one another. We are a new creation, being fitted together by God and equipped to minister to one another. Our Lord has apportioned grace to each of us. Paul reminds us,

It was he who gave some to be apostles, some to be prophets, some to be evangelists, and some to be pastors and teachers, to prepare God's people for works of service, so that the body of Christ may be built up, until we all reach unity in the faith and in the knowledge of the Son of God and become mature, attaining to the whole measure of the fullness of Christ (Eph. 4:11–13).

We attain maturity in relationship to other believers as together we build up one another. Education that is truly Christian stresses community and relationships. We need one another if we are to fulfill our mandate to teach for spiritual growth. The doctrine of the body of Christ must be lived in reality, not in empty words.

Third, because God has spoken and his Word is truth, spiritual maturity involves how we think. Paul desired that the church at Colosse might have "the full riches of complete understanding" (Col. 2:2). His view of spiritual maturity clearly involved the shaping of people's thinking so that they might love God with their minds.

Education that leads to spiritual maturity engages the mind and shapes the way people think. Thinking in and of itself is not spiritual maturity, but correct thinking is critical to the health of the believer individually and the church corporately. In an age when many people resist even the possibility of truth, Christian education must contend for the truth, helping believers to have their minds renewed by the Word of God.

Fourth, teaching for spiritual growth requires that we take the developmental process in people seriously. Part of respecting persons is respecting the patterns of development that God has written into the fabric of humankind. Human beings are complex, but the complexity can be reduced if we understand the developmental process.

Even though the current state of developmental psychology is not perfect, it offers insights that help educators fashion both content and method to the abilities of the learner. The developmental process is a reality whether or not we choose to acknowledge it. Our teaching will be more effective and learning will be more powerful if we can understand and work with the developmental patterns of our students.

Fifth, spiritual maturity involves the whole person. Maturity has to do with how we think, where we place our affections, and how we behave. It is cognitive, affective, and volitional, involving mind, heart, and will. It requires a complete educational perspective.

Therefore teaching for spiritual growth entails methods that engage the whole person. It is not a matter of gimmicks, but a reasoned educational process that helps people think, feel, and act in accordance with God's Word. Trivializing the educational process by shallow content and silly methods is an ignominy to the privilege of teaching the people of God. We must take the task more seriously than we have in recent years.

Finally, teaching for spiritual growth can only be done when God is in the process. Just as we can never lead someone to the Lord on our own, so we can never bring anyone to maturity on our own. It is God who must give a new heart (Ezek. 36:24-32) and God who brings his own to maturity. Paul reminds us that

> For those God foreknew he also predestined to be conformed to the likeness of his Son, that he might be the firstborn among many brothers. And those he predestined, he also called; those he called, he also justified; those he justified, he also glorified (Rom. 8:29-30).

Human responsibility and dependence on the power of God go hand in hand. We are responsible to teach, and to teach well. We must work at the educational process and work hard to teach to the best of our ability. But we must also understand that we can never produce the fruits of righteousness in another person by our own will and effort. Only the Father can bring his children to maturity. Yet he chooses to use our efforts to accomplish his goals. He graciously allows us to feed his sheep. And we do so, not that we may be fulfilled or honored, but that he may be glorified.

The point of our ministry must always be the glory of God. He is the one who matters and the one who is to be glorified. He is the great shepherd of the sheep, and it is him whom we serve.

The Evangelization of Children

A traditional and critical concern in Christian education has been the salvation of children. "Leading the child to Christ" has been one of the primary objectives of Christian education, especially in the Sunday school. Child evangelization is an extremely important issue. Unfortunately some of the approaches to leading a child to Christ have been based on rather poor or incomplete theology. I do not impugn the motives of those who work with children when I say that if we are to conduct a ministry that is honoring to God and fruitful in the lives of children, we must consider carefully the theological and biblical foundations of our practice.

Evangelizing children is both an emotional and a theological issue. That is, we strongly desire to see children brought to the Lord early in their lives, and at the same time we want to take Scripture seriously, being guided by its insights into such a critical concern. We dare not approach this topic lightly but must consider carefully how the church has attempted to understand the issue and to practice bringing children into faith.

THE NATURE OF SAVING FAITH

The root cause of many of the shortcomings of current approaches to childhood salvation (and this points out a general weakness in the evangelical churches) is a foundational misrepresentation or misunderstanding of the true nature of saving faith. It is clear from Scripture that people are saved by faith alone. The message is always, "Believe in the Lord Jesus, and you will be saved" (Acts 16:31). The problem is that the message has been changed to "Receive Jesus as your personal Savior, and you will be saved," or

"Just ask Jesus into your heart, and you will be saved." While both of these messages have an element of truth, both fall short of the true biblical message.

The issue is the nature of saving faith. What does it mean to "receive" Jesus in the sense of John 1:12? It means not simply the reception of the benefits of his substitutionary death on our behalf, but rather the reception of him, the risen Lord and head of the church. Faith in the biblical sense can never be separated from obedience. As the apostle John wrote, a life not characterized by obedience can in no way be considered a redeemed life: "We know that we have come to know him if we obey his commands. The man who says 'I know him,' but does not do what he commands is a liar, and the truth is not in him" (1 John 2:3–4). If we are to take John at his word, we must realize that we cannot say that we have received Jesus if our lives are characterized by disobedience.

The implications for the presentation of the Gospel are obvious. As we proclaim the good news that Jesus has died for our sins according to the Scripture and that he has purchased our redemption with his blood, we must also proclaim that he is Lord. We must make clear that to receive him implies that we must accept not only his gift of redemption but also his rightful authority over our lives. A critical aspect of the Great Commission is that we are to teach the new disciples to obey all that Jesus has commanded (Matt. 28:20). Our faith must influence our attitudes, behavior, and values. If all of these areas of life are not brought under the lordship of Christ, then we have not truly "received" him. Rather than receive him as personal Savior (which is not biblical terminology), we must receive him as Lord, and he will then become our personal Savior.

The issue at stake is much more than terminology. There are no magic words that automatically result in salvation. Rather, there is an attitude, which may be expressed in a variety of phrases, that the Father considers as proper for salvation. Because attitudes are difficult, if not impossible, to study, Scripture describes for us the fruit of the faith that results in salvation. James tells us simply that "faith by itself, if it is not accompanied by action, is dead" (James 2:17). Our Lord put it in even stronger terms when he taught, "Not everyone who says to me, 'Lord, Lord,' will enter the kingdom of heaven, but only he who does the will of my Father who is in heaven" (Matt. 7:21).

Scripture presents faith as very serious business. There are no light and easy ways into the kingdom. It is true that people are saved by faith alone, but if that faith is not expressed in the life of the believer by deeds, it is not true saving faith.[1]

When this understanding of faith is considered in relationship to children, the issue becomes even more complex. Can a child even comprehend the issues at stake sufficiently to be capable of saving faith? Obviously the Scripture affirms that possibility when it instructs us to teach children the ways of God. But, as we will see, this is not quite as simple as some would have us believe.

ORIGINAL SIN

How we approach the evangelization of children depends largely on our understanding of original sin. Based primarily on the teachings of Romans 5, this doctrine states that the original sin of Adam as federal head of the human race has been passed on to all of humanity so that all people are born guilty before a holy God. This issue is most critical when considered in relation to an infant who has died. Because of the sin of Adam, does it now follow that this child must be condemned to hell?

Historically there have been two theological answers to this question. The first deals with infant baptism; the second, with the age of accountability. Infant baptism is

> *How we approach the evangelization of children depends largely on our understanding of original sin.*

understood in at least three different ways. The Roman Catholic perspective is that infant baptism cleanses the child from original sin. If children die without baptism, they will not be allowed directly into heaven. Therefore it is critical, from a Roman Catholic perspective, to baptize children as soon as possible.

The Lutheran perspective is somewhat different. Lutherans believe that when infants are baptized, God graciously "works faith" into their hearts so they may be saved. A Lutheran perspective is that faith is analogous to trust. Just as infants are capable of trusting their mothers, so God makes them capable of trusting him. For Lutherans, baptism is the means of grace through which God saves infants by instilling faith within them.

From a Reformed perspective, the rite is normally understood as analogous to the circumcision of the Jew and is the sign of a covenant between the parents and God that the children will be raised in the Christian faith. Later, when they are old enough to confirm that their faith is indeed real, they are brought into full membership of the church by means of a service of confirmation. It is believed that if these children die prior to confirmation, their sin will be forgiven because of the covenant established through baptism. Churches that hold the Reformed perspective believe that when parents raise their children in the faith, God will regenerate them and give them the gift of faith.

The second theological answer to the salvation of an infant concerns the matter of accountability. That is, some churches maintain that before children are able to exercise faith on their own behalf, God will not hold them accountable for their own sins or their own sinfulness, and if they die before being held accountable for their sinful condition, they will be forgiven by God. Adherents of this position reserve the rite of baptism for believers only.

If children will ultimately be held accountable for their sins, it is essential that they be brought to faith as early as possible. Those who reject infant baptism are faced with the difficult issue of how a child should be brought to faith. What is the best or most appropriate way to evangelize a child?

APPROACHES TO CHILD EVANGELIZATION

Within the last two centuries in the United States the question of how a young child is to be led to Christ has been answered in a variety of ways. Each approach has specific strengths and weaknesses inherent within it.

Revivalists

One of the more extreme positions was held by the eighteenth-century dissenters in England and some of the later revivalists who followed in their tradition. Growing out of an extreme Calvinism with a strong emphasis on total depravity, revivalism held that a child was not capable of having saving faith. Coupled with an emphasis on the sinfulness of children was a serious respect for the demands of faith on the life of the individual. As a result of this perspective, revivalists believed that the responsibility of the church to children was to convince them that they were terrible sinners and that when they were old enough to repent properly, they must then give their lives to Christ.

Perhaps this perspective is best represented by a poem Isaac Watts wrote as a child, formed as an acrostic of his first name:

> *I am a vile polluted lump of earth,*
> *So I've continued ever since my birth;*
> *Although Jehovah grace does daily give me,*
> *As sure this monster Satan will deceive me,*
> *Come, therefore, Lord, from Satan's claws relieve me.*[2]

The kind of nurture that resulted from this perspective was quite extreme. Christian parents believed that it was their task to show their children their sinfulness whenever possible, thus instilling in them an awareness of their terrible plight before a holy God. The parent would be careful to point out that a natural childish desire to play rather than to study was an example of the sinful nature of the child. Moreover, parents would teach their children that they were not able to pray or do any other such religious practice that would be pleasing to God. The message was simply that children are sinners condemned before God and are not capable of true saving faith. Parents prayed fervently that when their children reached "the age of discretion" (the age at which children would be capable of exercising true faith) they would in fact then respond to Christ.

It was understood that salvation was always the result of divine election, and therefore it would be presumptuous for Christian parents to assume that their children would be saved. Salvation was always a result of the will of God, not the will of humans. Again, a notation from the diary of Isaac Watts in 1688, when he was fourteen, indicates the result of this perspective in the mind of a child; he wrote, "Fell under considerable conviction of sins and was taught to trust in Christ, I hope."[3]

The positive aspect of this approach to childhood salvation was that it took seriously the sinful nature of humanity and the radical nature of saving faith. Because biblical faith was perceived as making serious demands on the life of the believer, it was not to be entered into lightly. Parents believed that theirs was the important task of preparing their children for salvation, but it was beyond their understanding of the nature of Christian faith to see faith in the hearts of children. Christian faith could come only after the "age of discretion" when the child could properly understand the true nature of biblical faith.

The negative aspect of this approach is also obvious. In their zeal to protect the integrity of Christianity, they missed the fact that Scripture clearly teaches that children too can be a part of the kingdom. Jesus taught, "Let the little children come to me, and do not hinder them, for the kingdom of heaven belongs to such as these" (Matt. 19:14). Also, Paul's instructions to the believers in Ephesus to "bring them up in the training and instruction of the Lord" (Eph. 6:4) indicates that, to some extent at least, a child is capable of faith. Therefore, while these revivalists are to be commended for their concern in taking the demands of the Gospel and the sovereignty of God seriously, they must be faulted for their lack of confidence in a child's capacity to have saving faith.

Horace Bushnell

A second perspective, which was clearly a reaction to the abuses of the revivalists, emanated from the Connecticut pastor Horace Bushnell. In 1846 he wrote a small book entitled *Discourses on Christian Nurture*, in which he argued that children should be brought up as believers from their earliest years, rather than be raised as sinners to be converted at a later date. Because of the theological controversy the book created, Bushnell was prompted to publish it twice more in different forms and under somewhat different titles. In the final edition, published in 1861 and entitled simply *Christian Nurture*, Bushnell summarized his position this way:

> My argument is to establish that the child is to grow up a Christian, and never know himself as being otherwise. In other words, the aim, effort and expectation should be not, as is commonly assumed, that the child is to grow up in sin, to be converted after he comes to a mature age; but that he is to open on the world as one that is spiritually renewed, not remembering the time he went through a technical experience, but seeming rather to have loved what is good from his earliest years.[4]

The key concept in Bushnell's argument is that Christian nurture should, in effect, prevent the necessity of radical conversion. He believed that from their earliest days children should be taught about the love of God and to love God. The heart of his argument is that there is some kind of natural connection between the faith of the parents and the child. Lacking in modern terminology, Bushnell referred to a "kind of organic unity"[5] that linked the faith of the parent to the child. He did not mean to imply that children are automatically saved if their parents are believers. Rather, he was trying to deal with Paul's teaching in 1 Corinthians 7:14: "The unbelieving husband has been sanctified through his wife, and the unbelieving wife has been sanctified through her believing husband. Otherwise your children would be unclean, but as it is, they are holy" and in Ephesians 6:4: "Bring them up in the training and instruction of the Lord."

To understand Bushnell properly, we must remember that he was trying to encourage Christian parents to nurture their children in a positive way. He was bothered by the practices of the revivalists and believed that children too had an important place in the kingdom.

Bushnell realized that children can come to faith by means other than radical conversion. He argued that the children of believing parents were to be treated differently from children of unbelieving adults. Bushnell taught that if a child was nurtured into salvation, this regeneration was as much a work of the Holy Spirit as was the radical conversion of an adult. But he believed that it was possible to raise children in such a distinctly Christian way that they would never remember a time when they were not believers. Rather than having to turn to Christ later in life, children raised in the context of a Christian home could be Christian from their earliest days.

In the twentieth century this does not seem to be strange teaching. Many believers raise their children in just this way, teaching them simple prayers and telling them of the love of God. Based on the assumption that children will see the faith as a living reality in their parents' lives and that they will continue as Christians when they are older, Christian parents nurture their children in the faith. However, if their children do not continue in the faith, some parents may be inclined to blame themselves.

There is a certain weakness to Bushnell's position. In his effort to correct the wrongs of revivalism, he failed to take human sinfulness seriously enough. He did state that there is a "natural depravity"[6] that affects all people, but he believed that the propensity toward evil could be counteracted by the positive environment of a Christian home. To Bushnell the process of Christian nurture should be so natural that there is almost no sense of the divine in it. It almost appears that regeneration could be taught like good manners or proper culture. There was little of the supernatural in his view of nurture and the resultant childhood salvation he envisioned.[7]

Child Conversion

A more current approach is the theory presented by some children's evangelistic organizations and some evangelical publishers. This perspective holds that all people are lost and in need of salvation, and that salvation comes to one as the result of believing that Christ died for him or her. Each person must make a decision for Christ, and normally a person should be able to remember at what point in time that decision was made.

The biblical background for this approach grows out of the examples in Scripture of conversions to the Christian faith. For example, Paul's experience on the Damascus road is seen to be at least somewhat normative for all conversion experiences. At one point Paul was not a believer, and at another point he was. This concept of a crisis experience during conversion is considered a proper model for all conversion. Also, Jesus' terminology used with Nicodemus, "You must be born again," implies that just as physical birth is a specific event, so must spiritual birth be a specific event.

The strength of this perspective is the strong concern for seeing especially children won to Christ. It recognizes the fact that all people, including children, are in need of salvation and makes a specific attempt to reach them with the Gospel. The evangelistic desire and concern that children know that they have indeed responded to Christ is important. Also, the fact that children are seen to be of infinite value and worthy of evangelistic outreach is certainly in keeping with the spirit in which Jesus dealt with children.

The weaknesses of this approach are perhaps a bit more subtle, but they need to be considered. This model is built on the assumption that all children are to be converted in the same way that pagan adults were. It does not consider the possibility that the conversions recorded in the book of Acts may not be normative for children. Scripture does not provide any instances when children were converted apart from their entire family. It is clear that in the early church there were instances when entire households were converted (such as the household of Cornelius in Acts 10), but there is no record of children coming to Christ on their own. Arguing from silence does not prove that this did not happen. It only means that there are no clear examples to follow in Scripture.

A second and more significant weakness of the child conversion approach is that it does not allow for the unique situation of the children of believing parents, who in some way must be seen as different from the children of those who do not have faith. While a hard-and-fast case cannot be made regarding the relationship of the faith of the parents to their children, the Bible does provide some insight into this area. In 1 Corinthians 7 Paul indicates that children are in some way affected by the faith of their

> *The nature of conversion for the child who has been raised in a Christian home may be significantly different from the nature of the conversion experience of a pagan adult.*

believing parent. Also, the environmental difference needs to be considered. If children are born into a home where they have been prayed for since well before their birth, and if from their earliest days they have been trained to honor God and to respond to him in faith, it seems that these children would not have to be evangelized in the same way as children from a pagan background would. If the parents are in fact raising their children in the training and instruction of the Lord, it seems strange and unnecessary to invite them to make a response of faith to Christ when this has been the focus of their training.

The nature of conversion for the child who has been raised in a Christian home may be significantly different from the nature of the conversion experience of a pagan adult. Rather than expecting the kind of salvation experience that was evident in the life of the apostle Paul, perhaps the children of believers should be considered to be more like Timothy, to whom Paul wrote, "From infancy you have known the holy Scriptures, which are able to make you wise for salvation through faith in Christ Jesus" (2 Tim. 3:15). Salvation for such children may not be a crisis experience in which a specific decision is made, but rather it may be a process of training by which faith in Christ (on the human level) is the natural result of nurture. For children raised in a Christian home, faith may have always been a normal part of their experience and not the result of a specific decision. Their conversion is a process experience rather than a crisis experience.

John Inchley

A fourth approach has been proposed by John Inchley in his book *Kids and the Kingdom*. Inchley states:

> I cannot help but believe that all children belong to the Lord before the age of accountability. Their inborn sinfulness is covered by the atoning work of Christ, and their acts of wrongdoing, which have not been committed willfully, may also be covered by the atonement, even though this has not yet been appropriated by an act of will. I firmly believe that all children are included in the great atoning sacrifice and belong to Jesus Christ until they deliberately refuse Him.[8]

The heart of Inchley's concern is that children must be seen differently from adults and that their salvation must be understood differently. To a great extent he bases his perspective on Jesus' teaching in Matthew 18–19. Here Jesus treats children as though they do belong to him. Inchley believes that children need not experience a crisis conversion, but that if they are raised properly, according to biblical teaching, they will grow naturally into faith and will be regenerated by the Holy Spirit. Inchley goes on to offer very helpful and practical suggestions for nurturing children effectively.

The strength of his position is that it takes seriously the teachings of Jesus in reference to the relationship of children to the kingdom of God. It encourages us to believe that the kingdom does in fact belong to all children and that Jesus' high view of children needs to be respected. (It does seem significant that while we focus on the church's ministry to children, Jesus spoke of children's ministry to the church.)

Also, Inchley's view provides a solution to the difficult theological (and emotional) problem of children who die before birth (as in abortions), at birth, or in infancy before they are capable of exercising saving faith. Salvation prior to an age of accountability is an important antidote to the dilemma of original sin and total depravity. It makes the grace of God, rather than the sinfulness of humankind, preeminent.

The difficulty of this view, however, is with the age of accountability. Inchley will not attach a specific age to it. Rather, the age of accountability is considered that time when children willfully reject the grace of God on their behalf. However, this concept is not specifically taught in Scripture. There is the account of the children under the age of twenty not being held responsible by God for the rebellion of Israel after they were led out of Egypt (Num. 14:29). But there is also the case of the children of the people of Jericho who were slaughtered along with their parents because of the sins of the people (Josh. 6:21). Therefore, it could be argued that the age of accountability is applicable only to the children of God's people, and not to all children. Age of accountability is a derived concept resulting from theological considerations. It is not always wrong to hold to a derived or implied doctrine; the doctrine of the Trinity is also a derived doctrine. But while the idea of the age of accountability relieves the emotional strain regarding the fate of infants, it is not rooted clearly in biblical teaching.

A second problem with Inchley's view is closely connected with the first. The primary biblical basis for his position is Jesus' teaching in Matthew 18–19. It is clear that in verses 1–5 of chapter 18, Jesus is speaking in reference to children as an example of humility in the kingdom. But from verse 6 on, a strong case can be made that the term "little ones who believe in me" refers not to children, but rather to Jesus' disciples. Our Lord's concern was that his followers not be led astray by the false teachers of Israel. Also, in chapter 19 Jesus states that the kingdom "belongs to such as these" (v. 14). It is too much to draw from these sayings that all children therefore are members of the kingdom until they choose to reject Christ. The most we can conclude is that the kingdom belongs to people with humility and simple trust similar to those of a child. Therefore, while this view does make sense from a purely theological perspective, it is difficult to substantiate it on a biblical basis.

Jesus certainly was very open to children. He valued them and he used them as models for what a person of the kingdom should be like. But to say that all children belong to Christ seems unwarranted.

Ronald Goldman

A final approach to the problem of child evangelization grows out of a developmental perspective. Based on the work of the genetic epistemologist Jean Piaget, refined by Ronald Goldman,[9] this view focuses on the cognitive and moral development of children and argues that the natural developmental capabilities of children must be considered. The developmental pattern of cognition indicates that a child is not capable of conceptual thinking until about the age of eleven or twelve. Since religious thinking requires conceptualization, it is considered improper to expect children to understand the theological concepts necessary for salvation till they are developmentally capable.

The task of educational ministry to children is to provide Christian content for their cognitive structures (that is, their categories of thinking), which will later be incorporated into their conceptual framework.

Goldman believed that theology and religious concerns are adult business (in the sense that they are framed and discussed in adult terms) and are not really designed for the minds of children or, more accurately, that the minds of children are not designed for them. Such concepts as the holiness of God, the sinfulness of humankind, the requirements of divine justice, and the substitutionary death of Christ are all beyond the understanding of children. Therefore, it is best to wait until the child is capable of understanding these ideas before expecting a true conversion.

Goldman makes an honest attempt to integrate the findings of psychological research with theological considerations. Rather than choosing to ignore the data of developmental psychology, he attempts to deal properly with its findings. The fact of the matter is that people do develop cognitively and morally and that some types of thinking are developmentally beyond the range of a child. Therefore we should not expect too much from the young child, especially in the realm of conceptualization.

But while there is much to be said regarding the developmental capabilities of children and the implications of these capabilities to Christian education, can we conclude that it is impossible for children to be true Christians? The issue revolves around the question of what God requires for salvation. To what extent is the understanding of propositional truth necessary for salvation? The statements of Scripture always focus on *faith* (as cognitive, affective, and volitional) as the essential ingredient for salvation. While there must be some kind of rational basis to one's faith, faith in the biblical sense is not tied solely to theological considerations as much as it is to the person and work of the Lord Jesus Christ. The two foundational requirements of the Gospel are the renunciation of sin and trust in Christ. Certainly there is a developmental aspect to these requirements in that as people grow, the implications of these requirements will become more profound to them. But even a young child is capable of some degree of repentance and faith.

Most writers who are concerned with the developmental questions do not take such an extreme position. Most developmentalists with theological concerns believe that children indeed can be saved but that their understanding of the meaning and the requirements of their salvation will go through a developmental process as the child matures cognitively.

TOWARD A THEOLOGY OF CHILD EVANGELIZATION

There are a variety of approaches to the issue of evangelizing children. Each has certain strengths, but also certain limitations. When we take the various biblical, theological, and developmental aspects of this issue and integrate them into a coherent system, it is easy to do injustice to one or more of these related concerns. But there are some general guidelines that are helpful for developing a theology and practice of evangelizing children—guidelines that are compatible with the biblical, theological, and developmental issues related to this concern.

First, *all people, including children, are sinful and in need of redemption.* The sin of Adam has been passed on to the entire race, so that all have been found guilty before God. This point is clear in Scripture and is the basis for the need of salvation for all people, including children.

When Scripture describes all of humanity as being "under sin" (Rom. 3:9), it includes children. However, in keeping with the grace of God, it does seem appropriate to believe that a child who has died never having had the opportunity to exercise faith will be with the Lord, due to the atoning work of Christ. When David's son by Bathsheba died in infancy, David believed that the child had gone to be with God (2 Sam. 12:22–23). Both God's justice and mercy must be considered in relation to this issue.

Second, *salvation is by faith in the person of the Lord Jesus Christ.* Saving faith focuses on the person of the Lord

Jesus Christ (as opposed to only his death on our behalf) and is expressed by obedience. Therefore, salvation does not come by praying a simple prayer asking for God's forgiveness. It is gained by placing our faith in Jesus for both the forgiveness of our sins and the direction of our lives.

Third, *children are characterized by a natural inclination toward belief.* Within the nature of a child is a propensity for belief (credulity), which our Lord described as of great value, and which allows children to accept readily what is taught them.

Fourth, *children are capable of childlike faith in the Lord Jesus Christ.* This guideline is a conflation of the previous two. Our concept of the nature of saving faith need not be reduced simply because we are dealing with children.

> *If our children are growing in their faith, it is not critical that the exact moment of their salvation be identified. It is important that they continue to grow in their walk with the Lord.*

While it is certainly true that children cannot comprehend the full implications of their decisions, they can at their own level choose to place their trust in Christ as both Lord and Savior. If children were not capable of saving faith, it would be pointless to try to train them in the way of the Lord (Prov. 22:6). But because credulity is in the nature of the child, it makes sense to lead them to faith in Christ.

Fifth, *the task of nurture is to give shape and content to credulity so that it may be directed to Christ.* One of the great mercies of God is that he has designed children to believe the Gospel readily. As a result, it is not difficult to lead children to Christ. What is more difficult is to help them understand the implication of faith in the biblical sense. The danger in evangelizing children is that we are tempted to reduce the message to a false gospel that does not result in saving faith.

The great joy of working with children is that they quite naturally believe what is taught them. Because of this, the task of nurture is not onerous, but delightful. The task must be taken seriously, but faith (in the natural sense) is already present in the child. It need only be directed to the Lord Jesus Christ. When a child reaches adolescence, natural faith becomes more enmeshed in its own constructs, and the task becomes more difficult. But with children, nurture is simply providing content and direction to their God-given credulity.

It is wrong to perceive the natural credulity of a child as saving faith. Obviously their capacity to believe is expressed in many different ways. Belief in Santa Claus, the Easter bunny, and the tooth fairy are all examples of natural faith. When we nurture a child into Christian faith, we direct the natural tendency to believe to belief in the Lord Jesus Christ.

Sixth, *only the Father knows when a person is truly saved.* As Christians in process, we may make many decisions regarding our faith in Christ, but only God knows when salvation actually takes place. During the process of nurture, children are apt to make a variety of decisions in relation to their faith, especially as they grow in their understanding of the nature of Christianity. We may not always know at what point the child was in fact regenerated, but we do not have to know.

Sometimes believers with misguided zeal insist that people must be able to point to a specific time when they made a commitment to Christ. However, if children have been raised from their earliest days to follow the Lord, they may not be able to say specifically when regeneration took place. Their parents may not be able to point to a single decision either, because the children have made many decisions in reference to their Christian faith. In reality only God knows for sure when true faith has been exercised.

This point is especially significant when the developmental implications are considered. Children of three or four years of age may make some kind of commitment to Christ, which may or may not be a true salvation experience. If, as they grow, their commitment to Christ continues to grow also, then that decision may have been the time of their conversion. But it also may be that they had no real understanding at that time and that their decision was preparatory for their actual conversion at a later age. We cannot say with certainty either way.

But if nurture is an ongoing process in the life of our children, we do not have to say when regeneration took place. Rather, we must continue to be obedient to our responsibility of nurturing children in the faith. We must remember that our task is nurture, and God's task is regeneration. If our children are growing in their faith, it is not critical that the exact moment of their salvation be identified. It is important that they continue to grow in their walk with the Lord.

Seventh, *children of believers are in some way different from children of unbelievers*. This does not mean that they are automatically saved as a result of their parent's faith; but it does mean that the environment of a Christian home and the prayers of the parents and others on behalf of the child are strong, effective factors in spiritual nurture. Children who have been the objects of prayer since before birth and who experience the presence of God in their own home are not the same as children with no spiritual heritage whatsoever. Although the full implications and meaning of 1 Corinthians 7:14 are not readily understandable, this text does show some kind of relationship between the faith of the parent and the spiritual life of the child. Because of this, some churches baptize their infants and others dedicate them to the Lord. Both practices are based on the concept that because these children have been born to believing parents they will from their earliest days, by God's mercy, be uniquely set apart as children who belong to the Lord.

This guideline should affect those people who work with children in the church. Rather than focusing on evangelizing these children, it is more appropriate to treat them as the children of believers and to complement the nurture that is taking place in their homes. Helping them explore the Christian faith will be more important than attempting to lead them to another decision. Nurture rather than evangelism should be the focus of the ministry to the children of believing parents.

From the earliest days of the church, ministry to children has been a vital concern. This concern has been carried over into the twentieth century, and rightly so. But unfortunately, at times the practice of Christian educators today, especially in relation to children, has not been as carefully grounded as it might have been. As Christian education continues to come of age within evangelicalism, it is imperative that practitioners be guided by the principles of Scripture and sound theology.

Notes

1. For a more complete study of this topic, see Dietrich Bonhoeffer, *The Cost of Discipleship* (New York: Macmillan, 1949); Juan Carlos Ortiz, *The Disciple* (Carol Stream, Ill.: Creation House, 1975); Walter Chantry, *Today's Gospel, Authentic vs. Synthetic* (Carlisle, Pa.: Banner of Truth Trust, 1970); John F. MacArthur, Jr., *The Gospel According to Jesus,* rev. ed. (Grand Rapids: Zondervan, 1994).

2. E. Paxton Hood, *Isaac Watts: His Life and Writings, His Home and Friends* (London: Religious Tract Society, 1875), 7.

3. Ibid., 342.

4. Horace Bushnell, *Christian Nurture* (Grand Rapids: Baker, 1979), 10.

5. Ibid., 342.

6. Ibid., 22.

7. A blending of the natural with the supernatural is a constant phenomenon in Bushnell's theology and is not unique to this issue. It is generally considered that understanding the relationship of the natural to the supernatural in Bushnell's thought is the key to unlocking his entire theological system.

8. John Inchley, *Kids and the Kingdom* (Wheaton, Ill.: Tyndale House, 1976), 33.

9. Ronald Goldman, *Religious Thinking From Childhood to Adolescence* (New York: Seabury, 1964). More recent attempts to replicate Goldman's studies by John Peatling and later by Ruth Beechick have not been convincing.

Names

Name Index

Subjects

Scriptures

Teaching for Spiritual Growth